JOHN
WESLEY'S
THEOLOGY
TODAY

JOHN WESLEY'S THEOLOGY TODAY

COLIN W. WILLIAMS

ABINGDON PRESS NASHVILLE

JOHN WESLEY'S THEOLOGY TODAY

Preface

AN ARTICLE IN *Life* magazine some years ago concluded with the statement, "Methodism is long on organization and short on theology." If this is a just judgment of contemporary Methodism, it means that she has departed from her earliest tradition, for Methodism represented in her origins a revival of theology as well as a revival of life, and the former was inseparable from the latter.

Contemporary Methodism is showing signs of renewed theological examination and of a concern to re-examine her original theological tradition, especially in view of the new relations with other traditions brought about by the rapid rise of the ecumenical movement. As a recent communication from the Board of Missions of the American Methodist Church put it:

> The failure of Methodism adequately to make its witness, theologically and spiritually, to the ecumenical movement is a matter of growing concern to Methodists on both sides of the Atlantic.[1]

The ecumenical commitment represented by membership in the World Council of Churches, the International Missionary Council, and regional and local ecumenical bodies, has drawn Methodism into dialogue with other traditions with whom she has found a real unity in Christ, but from whom she is still divided in matters of faith and order. Increasingly it is being recognized that Methodism is in duty bound to investigate the meaning of this ecumenical commitment for her existence as a church, and also to investigate her own tradition to see whether God has given her something to share with the churches.

[1] From an October 1, 1957, letter from the Division of World Missions of The Methodist Church to participants in a theological study group with members on both sides of the Atlantic.

This work seeks to undertake the second part of this investigation by analyzing the Methodist tradition at the point of its origin.

The significance of the modern ecumenical movement roots in the rediscovered awareness of the importance of unity to the life and mission of the Church. The movement back to unity, therefore, represents both an act of obedience to Christ the Head of the Church and an act of repentance for the continuing sin of our division. But our dilemma is that we have repented without a clear awareness of what our repentance involves. Not being fully aware of where our sin lies, we are unable to make the full turn that repentance implies—the full turn from disunity to unity.

The present ecumenical situation reflects this dilemma. Recognizing Christ in one another we have joined together in the mutual covenant of the World Council of Churches, but so far we have been unable to move on from engagement to marriage. We are required to seek to do away with the obstacles to our marriage that lie in our divided traditions, but we are also required to search those traditions to discover any dowries that can be brought to the life of the one family.

In the conversation that must take place in this situation there is a necessary "no" that participants must give to the demand that we should surrender our allegiance to our own tradition. It is in that tradition that God has called us, and it is only as we make our witness from within our tradition that a real ecumenical dialogue can take place, in which others may find the meaning of their repentance by hearing the word that God would speak to them through us.

However, there must also be a "yes" to the demand that we should hold our allegiance to our tradition in question. Our commitment to the ecumenical movement means that we must be prepared to hear God's word of judgment on our divided tradition, and also that we must be ready to receive the riches that lie beyond our boundaries.

This work seeks to contribute to the understanding of the tradition of Methodism in the light of the ecumenical dialogue. It asks whether Methodism has any distinctive witness in her tradition which is needed by the whole Church, and it asks whether this tradition has any light to throw on the vital issues which at present divide the churches.

There is a serious procedural difficulty. There is a danger that by simply going back to investigate the Methodist tradition, Methodists may become so attached to it that they will be determined to preserve it at all costs and so will become less open to hear the word that God is speaking to us through the other churches. This is perhaps the greatest danger that is confronting the ecumenical movement today. The encounter with other churches has forced the participants back to an examination of the roots of their own tradition and has led churches of a common tradition to draw together on a world-wide scale. The result has been the rise of the world confessional church bodies, such as the World Methodist Council and the Lutheran World Federation. This is necessary to the extent that it is only from a full understanding of our own church life that we can engage creatively in the wooing that leads to a happy union. But it also gives rise to the danger that these churches may find that it is much easier to remain within the bosom of their familiar church family than to venture forth into the wider family that marriage brings.

Great as this danger is, however, we must still recognize that it is only as we speak from our full family traditions that the true richness of the ecumenical dialogue can result. At this point the Methodists have some homework to do. Methodists have witnessed that in various parts of the world the representatives of other traditions were able to present a clearly defined position, while they were unable to give a clear answer when asked for the Methodist position on doctrines such as the ministry. If Methodism is to make her contribution to the ecumenical dialectic, she must first grapple seriously with her own traditional viewpoint.

It may be objected that since Methodism has not been static in the two hundred years since her rise, the attempt here made to establish Methodism's basic position from the theology of her founder is historical obscurantism. The fact remains, however, that the authoritative documents of present-day Methodism still make the theology of John Wesley the official standard of Methodist doctrine.

In British Methodism this Wesleyan basis is quite explicit. Each year every Methodist minister must renew his vows to "believe and preach our doctrines," as contained in forty-four sermons of Wesley and his *Explanatory Notes upon the New Testament*. In these sermons and notes Wesley affirms what he takes to be the catholic theological stream as represented by the creeds, the "Articles of Religion" of the Church of England, and the *Book of Common Prayer*. Yet he also affirms his belief that certain doctrines in this tradition, in particular the doctrine of sanctification, have received insufficient emphasis and clarification. He thus believed that God has given Methodism a responsibility to serve the Church catholic by bringing these emphases into their right place in the total orbit of the catholic faith. In British Methodism the Church is still committed to Wesley's general position.

In American Methodism the legal position is not quite as explicit. Wesley's sermons, for example, are no longer part of the official doctrine. Nevertheless the doctrinal standards are still largely drawn from Wesley. Not only are "Wesley's Twenty-five Articles" (his shortened form of the thirty-nine "Articles of Religion" of the Church of England) and his "General Rules" [2] given as "unalterable" standards of doctrine,[3] but the answers given by every candidate for admission into full connection give strong expression to Wesley's characteristic convictions concerning the doctrine of sanctification.[4]

It is not only a question of Methodism's legal position, however. It also seems reasonable to assume that the message she was given at the time God raised her up has peculiar significance when we ask whether Methodism has been entrusted with a particular word God would have us say to the Church. This is

[2] *Doctrines and Discipline of The Methodist Church*, 1956, ¶¶ 91-98.
[3] *Ibid.*, ¶ 9. Among the five "Restrictive Rules" are the following:
"1. The General Conference shall not revoke, alter, or change our Articles of Religion, or establish any new standards or rules of doctrine contrary to our present existing and established standards of doctrine."
"4. The General Conference shall not revoke or change the General Rules of the United Societies."
[4] *Ibid.*, ¶ 1924. The order for "Admission of Candidates to Membership in an

not to say that subsequent developments in Methodism have no significance, or that Methodism is bound at all points to the eighteenth century views of Wesley. In fact, the significance of the ecumenical encounter is understood only when we see that it is not simply a meeting of different traditions but is also a real growing together of these traditions through increasing interchurch contact. Many of the hard edges of theological differences have disappeared already, and it would be disloyalty to this ecumenical growth to try to erect Wesley's theology into an unbending Methodist orthodoxy as though nothing had happened to theology since that time.

For this reason the analysis of Wesley's theology given here is not an "objective" statement of his position. An attempt is made to relate his viewpoint to the ecumenical commitment of Methodism in the light of the theological developments that have taken place since his time. In stating the distinctive elements in Wesley's theology, an effort is made to show their relevance to the contemporary situation, and there has been no hesitation in expressing a personal view as to how these doctrines must be reformulated in the light of this situation. On such crucial present-day issues as the doctrine of the Church and the ministry, an opinion is given as to where Methodism is bound to be loyal to her history and tradition, and as to where she should be ready to accept changes.

It is clear that what is said here can serve only as one Methodist's contribution: first, to his own denomination as it undertakes clarification of its own position, and second, to other participants in the ecumenical encounter as they seek to hear what God would say to them from another tradition with whom they have made an ecumenical covenant.

The substance of this work was presented as part of a dissertation at Drew University. To Prof. G. Calvert Barker of Queens College, Melbourne, who first taught me theology and was re-

Annual Conference" under "Admission into Full Connection" directs that all candidates be asked, "in accordance with the . . . historic usages of our communion," such questions as: "Are you going on to perfection?" "Do you expect to be made perfect in love in this life?" "Have you studied the doctrines of The Methodist Church?" and "Will you preach and maintain them?"

sponsible for my visit to Drew, I am deeply indebted. It would be ungrateful to fail to mention the great help I received, as an Australian strange to so many American ways from three members of the Drew faculty. To Edwin Lewis, Carl Michalson, and Stanley Hopper my debt is great. One other American has given me more. To Phyllis, my wife, my debt is greater.

COLIN W. WILLIAMS

Contents

I THE CATHOLIC SPIRIT: DOCTRINE AND OPINION

ⓓ Before we proceed to discuss Wesley's theology, it is necessary that we enter into an area of popular misunderstanding. We still hear it said that John Wesley was not really concerned with theology. We hear one of his favorite scripture texts, "Is thine heart right, as my heart is with thy heart? . . . If it be, give me thine hand," [1] used to infer that Wesley was interested in sincerity rather than doctrine. We hear his oft-repeated "The distinguishing marks of a Methodist are not his opinions of any sort. . . . We think and let think" [2] used as though Wesley was indifferent to all doctrinal differences.

Here we must pause to review Wesley's real position, for our attitude to ecumenical discussion is largely determined by our view at this point. If we minimize doctrinal differences, we will be impatient with the way Faith and Order Commission discussions proceed in the World Council of Churches and with those who insist on thorough examination of doctrinal differences as a precondition of actual church union. Regarding pragmatic considerations as primary, we will look upon the attempt to chart a thorough theological basis for union as a snare and a delusion. But if we believe that there are vital theological concerns involved, which are essential to the very being of the Church, we

---

[1] *The Standard Sermons of John Wesley*, II, 129; *The Letters of John Wesley*, II, 8-9, 86-87.
[2] *The Works of John Wesley, A.M.*, VIII, 340, "The Character of a Methodist."

will engage in the ecumenical encounter with a determination that nothing shall compromise the truth which we believe to be essential to the Church's life.

That Wesley was concerned for the unity of the Church there can be no doubt.

Would to God that all party names and unscriptural phrases and forms which have divided the Christian world were forgot, and that we might all agree to sit down together, as humble, loving disciples, at the feet of our common Master, to hear His word, to imbibe His Spirit, and to transcribe His life on our own! [3]

Wesley believed that the spirit of unity is intended by Christ to be of the very essence of the Church. As he comments on Matt. 5:47:

And if ye salute your friends only—Our Lord probably glances at those prejudices, which different sects had against each other, and intimates, that he would not have his followers imbibe that narrow spirit. Would to God this had been more attended to among the unhappy divisions and subdivisions, into which the Church has been crumbled! And that we might at least advance so far, as cordially to embrace our brethren in Christ, of whatever party or denomination they are! [4]

Not only is disunity injurious to the spirit of the churches, harming the lives of the members by introducing discord and bitterness, it is also injurious to the mission of the Church. For Wesley the mission and unity of the Church must be considered together. As he wrote to Henry Vann in June, 1763:

I desire to have a league offensive and defensive with every soldier of Christ. We have not only one faith, one hope, one Lord, but are directly engaged in one warfare. We are carrying the war into the devil's own quarters, who therefore summons all his hosts to war. Come, then, ye that love Him, to the help of the Lord, to the help of the Lord against the mighty! [5]

[3] John Wesley, *Explanatory Notes upon the New Testament*, p. 8.
[4] *Ibid.*, p. 35.
[5] *Letters*, IV, 215-18. The importance of the spirit of unity for the mission of

14

Here was the reason why Wesley was concerned to see behind the differences to our "given unity." This was why he tried to display the catholic spirit through which unity could emerge and differences fall away. Unity is essential to the mission of the Church. At first sight it may appear that in his eagerness to create this unity Wesley was willing to hide his eyes from the depth and importance of theological differences.

I do not mean, "Be of my opinion." You need not: I do not expect or desire it. . . . Keep you your opinion; I mine; and that as steadily as ever. You need not even endeavour to come over to me, or bring me over to you. I do not desire you to dispute those points, or to hear or speak one word concerning them. Let all opinions alone on one side and the other: only "give me thine hand." [6]

This sounds like the statements of some of the early protagonists of the "Life and Work" movement, who, under the slogan "Doctrine divides, service unites," sought to develop organs of co-operation in which differences of doctrine should be excluded from discussion; only to find that even co-operation on common social problems raised important theological questions which forced them back to a consideration of their differences.[7]

It becomes apparent that Wesley is not of that camp when we notice that he draws a distinction between doctrine and opinion. That such a distinction is hard to maintain is becoming increasingly apparent. Still the necessity to speak of some doctrines as central and as minimal bases for Christian co-operation is recognized (implicitly or explicitly) as the only basis on which ecumenical relations can proceed.

---

the Church is indicated by an entry in the Journal where Wesley is seeking to discover the reason why the awakening had been "almost entirely stayed in Scotland, and in great measure in New England." He confesses that he can make no certain judgment, but says that one reason may be that "many of them were bigots, immoderately attached either to their own opinions or mode of worship. Mr. Edwards himself was not clear of this. But the Scotch bigots were beyond all others, placing Arminianism (so called) on a level with Deism, and the Church of England with that of Rome." (*The Journal of John Wesley*, IV, 123.)
[6] *Sermons*, II, 139.
[7] *A History of the Ecumenical Movement*, p. 547 ff.

We turn then to the way in which Wesley distinguishes between doctrine and opinion.[8] We see the distinction begin to emerge in a passage from his sermon on Whitefield's death.

Let us keep close to the grand scriptural doctrines which he every-where delivered. There are many doctrines of a less essential nature, with regard to which even the sincere children of God (such is the present weakness of human understanding) are and have been divided for many ages. In these we may think and let think; we may "agree to disagree." But, meantime, let us hold fast the essentials of "the faith which was once delivered unto the saints"; and which this champion of God so strongly insisted on, at all times, and in all places! [9]

A review of Wesley's writings indicates that the essential doctrines on which he insisted included original sin,[10] the deity of Christ,[11] the atonement,[12] justification by faith alone,[13] the

[8] F. Hildebrandt, *Christianity According to the Wesleys*, pp. 10-11, writes: "He draws a clear distinction between doctrine and opinion which is fundamental to his thought: 'You have admirably expressed', he writes to a friend, 'What I mean by an opinion contra-distinguished from an essential doctrine. Whatever is "compatible with a love to Christ and a work of grace", I term an opinion, . . . (but) right opinions are a slender part of religion, if any part of it at all.' . . . In taking this for granted, Wesley proves himself a true son of the eighteenth century; but it never leads him to overlook or neglect, even for one moment, what the New Testament means by 'sound doctrine'. Three of our travelling preachers have eagerly desired to go to America; but I could not approve of it by any means, because I am not satisfied that they throughly like either our discipline or our doctrine. I think they differ from our judgement in one or both.' "

[9] *Sermons*, II, 522.

[10] *Works*, IX, 429. "A denial of original sin contradicts the main design of the gospel, which is to humble vain man, and to ascribe to God's free grace, . . . the whole of his salvation. Nor, indeed, can we let this doctrine go without giving up, at the same time, the greatest part, if not all, of the essential articles of the Christian faith. If we give up this, we cannot defend either justification by the merits of Christ, or the renewal of our natures by his Spirit."

[11] *Ibid.*, VIII, 340. "We believe Christ to be the eternal, supreme God; and herein we are distinguished from the Socinians and Arians. But as to all opinions which do not strike at the root of Christianity, we think and let think."

[12] *Letters*, VI, 297-98. "Indeed, nothing in the Christian system is of greater consequence than the doctrine of Atonement. It is properly the distinguishing point between Deism and Christianity. 'The Scriptural scheme of morality,' said Lord Huntingdon, 'is what every one must admire; but the doctrine of Atonement I cannot comprehend.' Here, then, we divide. Give up the Atonement, and the Deists are agreed with us."

[13] *Sermons*, II, 226-27. "If any doctrines within the whole compass of Christianity may be properly termed 'fundamental,' they are doubtless these two,—the doctrine of justification, and that of new birth."

16

work of the Holy Spirit,[14] and the Trinity.[15]

It is important to notice, however, that Wesley refuses to list a definite number of "fundamental" articles. He seemed to believe that doctrines which may be called opinions in certain circumstances may become fundamentals in others. For example, he believed that those who are divided on major points of doctrine which are basic in the nurture of believers could nevertheless unite in witnessing to the world concerning their common faith in Christ.

In his sermon on Whitefield's death he allows that the opinions of Whitefield and his Calvinist followers differed from his on such matters as predestination and "imputed righteousness." But these, he claimed do not preclude co-operation in witness to Christ. In his sermon on "The Catholic Spirit," he goes even

P. 425. "'THE LORD OUR RIGHTEOUSNESS'; a truth this, which enters deep into the nature of Christianity, and, in a manner, supports the whole frame of it. Of this undoubtedly, may be affirmed, what Luther affirms of a truth closely connected with it; it is *articulus stantis vel cadentis ecclesiae*: the Christian Church stands or falls with it. It is certainly the pillar and ground of that faith, of which alone cometh salvation; of that catholic or universal faith which is found in all the children of God, and which 'unless a man keep whole and undefiled, without doubt he shall perish everlastingly.'"

[14] *Letters*, VII, 231 (to his nephew Samuel, who had turned Roman Catholic). "My dear Sammy, your first point is to repent and believe the Gospel. Know yourself a poor, guilty, helpless sinner! Then know Jesus Christ and Him crucified! Let the Spirit of God bear witness with your spirit that you are a child of God, and let the love of God be shed abroad in your heart by the Holy Ghost, which is given unto you; and then, if you have no better work, I will talk with you of transubstantiation or purgatory."

Works, VIII, 341. A Methodist is not "distinguished by laying the whole stress of religion on any single part of it. If you say, 'Yes, he is; for he thinks "we are saved by faith alone:"' I answer, You do not understand the terms. By salvation he means holiness of heart and life. . . . Is this placing a part of religion for the whole? . . .

"'Who is a Methodist, according to your own account?' I answer: A Methodist is one who has, 'the love of God shed abroad in his heart by the Holy Ghost given unto him;' one who 'loves the Lord his God with all his heart, and with all his soul, and with all his mind, and with all his strength.'"

[15] *Works*, VI, 200. "There are ten thousand mistakes which may consist with real religion; with regard to which every candid, considerate man will think and let think. But there are some truths more important than others. It seems there are some which are of deep importance. I do not term them *fundamental* truths; because that is an ambiguous word: And hence there have been so many warm disputes about the number of *fundamentals*. But surely there are some which it nearly concerns us to know, as having a close connexion with vital religion. And doubtless we may rank among these that contained in the words above cited: 'There are three that bear record in heaven, the Father, the Word, and the Holy Ghost: And these three are one.'"

17

further, listing his differences from Presbyterians, Independents, Baptists, and Quakers, and claiming that even these differences should not preclude those who know Christ as God and Saviour, and who are seeking to do his will together, from joining in common witness.

> I ask not, therefore, of him with whom I would unite in love, Are you of my church, of my congregation? Do you receive the same form of church government, and allow the same church officers, with me? Do you join in the same form of prayer wherein I worship God? I inquire not, Do you receive the supper of the Lord in the same posture and manner that I do? nor whether, in the administration of baptism, you agree with me in admitting sureties [godparents] for the baptized; in the manner of administering it; or the age of those to whom it should be administered. Nay, I ask not of you (as clear as I am in my own mind), whether you allow baptism and the Lord's Supper at all. Let all these things stand by: we will talk of them, if need be, at a more convenient season; my only question is this, "Is thine heart right, as my heart is with thy heart?" [16]

Wesley's great concern was for unity in witness. But this did not mean that he considered the points of difference of no importance. Instead, he believed that when the task moved from witness to the world to nurture of the faithful, some of these differences were of very great importance. He was quite certain that the Quakers were seriously wrong in their rejection of the sacraments,[17] the Baptists wrong in their view of baptism,[18] and the Independents faulty in their church order.[19] He was certainly convinced that the Calvinist doctrine of double predestination was a serious barrier to the nurture of the faithful.

Q. 74. What is the direct antidote to Methodism, the doctrine of heart-holiness?

A. Calvinism: All the devices of Satan, for these fifty years, have done far less toward stopping this work of God, than that single doctrine. It strikes at the root of salvation from sin, previous to glory, putting the matter on quite another issue.

---

[16] *Sermons*, II, 135-36.
[17] *Letters*, II, 125, and see Chapter IX below on the Lord's Supper.
[18] See the section on Baptism in Chapter VII.
[19] See Chapter IX on the Church and the Appendix.

Q. 75. But wherein lie the charms of this doctrine? What makes men swallow it so greedily?

A. It seems to magnify Christ; although in reality it supposes him to have died in vain. For the absolutely elect must have been saved without him; and the non-elect cannot be saved by him.[20]

Nevertheless Wesley believed that he was obliged to seek unity in witness to the world with those whom he believed to be in serious error, yet in whose lives Christ was manifest. For this he can hardly be accused of "speculative latitudinarianism."

A Catholic spirit is not *speculative* latitudinarianism. It is not an indifference to all opinions: this is the spawn of hell, not the offspring of heaven. This unsettledness of thought, this being "driven to and fro, and tossed about with every wind of doctrine," is a great curse, not a blessing; an irreconcilable enemy, not a friend, to true catholicism. A man of a truly catholic spirit has not now his religion to seek. He is fixed as the sun in his judgment concerning the main branches of Christian doctrine. It is true, he is always ready to hear and weigh whatsoever can be offered against his principles; but as this does not show any wavering in his own mind, so neither does it occasion any. . . . Observe this, you who know not what spirit ye are of: who call yourselves men of a catholic spirit, only because you are of a muddy understanding. . . . Go, first, and learn the first elements of the gospel of Christ, and then you shall learn to be of a truly catholic spirit.[21]

His recognition of the call to seek for common witness with those he believed to be in serious error did not mean that Wesley was prepared to surrender any of these truths for pragmatic considerations of unity. A catholic spirit is no more "practical latitudinarianism" than it is speculative latitudinarianism."

It is not indifference as to public worship, or as to the outward manner of performing it. This, likewise, would not be a blessing, but a curse. . . . He is clearly convinced, that this manner of worshiping God is both scriptural and rational. . . .

He is fixed in his congregation as well as his principles. He is united to one, not only in spirit, but by all the outward ties of Christian fellowship. There he partakes of all the ordinances of God [22]

[20] *Works*, VIII, 336.
[21] *Sermons*, II, 142-43.
[22] *Ibid.*, 144.

19

Because of these differences of faith and order Wesley believed that it would be necessary for believers to stay in separate congregations so long as the differences remained unresolved. But he was convinced that they could unite across their differences in proclaiming the central elements of the gospel to the world.[23] It is not clear whether Wesley envisaged further steps toward organic union—that was a step he did not have to face, for his appeal for unity in witness went unheeded. However, it does seem that he conceived of societies within the one church, in which unresolved differences important to the nurture of Christians could be held together in the larger unity of common worship and witness.[24]

One more point needs to be made. Wesley did not require for entrance into his society, a clear knowledge of doctrine; nor did he believe that a clear knowledge was essential to salvation.

There is no other religious society under heaven which requires nothing of men in order to [secure] their admission into it but a desire to save their souls. Look all around you; you cannot be admitted into the Church, or society, of the Presbyterians, Anabaptists, Quakers, or any others, unless you hold the same opinions with them, and adhere to the same mode of worship.

The Methodists alone do not insist on your holding this or that opinion; but they think and let think. Neither do they impose any particular mode of worship; but you may continue to worship in your former manner, be what it may. Now, I do not know any religious society, either ancient or modern, wherein such liberty of conscience is now allowed, or has been allowed, since the age of the Apostles. Here is our glorying; and a glorying peculiar to us. What society shares it with us?[25]

Once admitted to the societies, however, great care was taken to teach the people true doctrine, and while a clear knowledge was not demanded of the layman, it was required of those called to preach. "No person shall be allowed to preach or exhort among our people," Wesley wrote, "whose life is not holy and

---

[23] *Ibid.*, II, 523-24; *Letters* IV, 237.
[24] This is discussed further in Chapter IX on the doctrine of the Church.
[25] *Journal*, VII, 389.

unblameable, nor any who asserts anything contrary to the gospel which we have received." [26]

Approaches to Union

Visser 't Hooft delineates "three main approaches to the ecumenical problem, three different ways of reconstituting the unity of the Church." [27] He calls them the Erasmian, the Church-centered and the Pietist approaches. The first sought union "on the basis of common agreement concerning a few necessary and fundamental points of doctrine" such as those contained in the Apostles' Creed, insisting on great freedom in all other non-essential points. The second, concerned with God's total design in calling his people, believed that unity must be sought, not on the level of the lowest common denominator, but on the level "in which the Christian faith is taught in its wholeness and fullness." The third, believing that life is more important than doctrine and form, and that "all Christians who are truly saved belong together, whatever their Church allegiance," sought to bring together those who shared the one experience of Christ in common witness and mission.

Visser 't Hooft argues that the first tradition, the Erasmian has outlived its usefulness, but that the two others are still very relevant for us. The Erasmian idea has, in part, already been accepted by the churches participating in the World Council of Churches, who are linked together by the common acceptance of a fundamental basis which is accepted as having a certain power to unite. But it is now clear that this minimum basis is not sufficient to produce full unity, and that this can never be reached by a process of reduction. The ecumenical movement has now moved into a period of confrontation of total traditions, and the Erasmian ideal, having performed its partial task, has now had its day.

The second viewpoint has now moved into prominence, for we have learned that we must recognize "the great objective fact that the Church of Christ *exists* and that our task is to participate in the manifestation of its holiness and unity." Similarly,

[26] *Letters*, IV, 3.
[27] *The Ecumenical Review*, Vol. VII, No. 4, July, 1955, 309-20.

the Pietist tradition still has an important bearing upon the situation.

It has rightly proclaimed that the Church exists for the kingdom of God and that it is therefore to preach the gospel in season and out of season to all men in all parts of the world. . . . The Church-centered approach by itself can easily lead to a stale clericalism. . . . The Church needs to be reminded again and again that it exists to serve. . . .

Similarly the Pietist approach needs the correction of the Church-centered tradition. With its concentration on the undoubtedly Biblical call to evangelism, it can easily forget that other Biblical concept of the Church as the visible manifestation of God's work in history.[28]

It is easy to see that Wesley would have accepted the Erasmian viewpoint in so far as on this basis churches could come together for mutual witness. But, as we have seen, he, too, rejected the idea of unity by reduction. He was prepared to reach out the hand of faith to those who accepted the common Lord, but he rejected that speculative and practical latitudinarianism which declared that differences in remaining matters of doctrine and order were matters of indifference.

Clearly, too, he had a great deal in common with the Pietist tradition, with his strong emphasis upon the fact that the Church exists for mission, and in his impatience with that stale clericalism which insisted that unity in mission must wait on agreement in the total area of faith and order.

Wesley was far from being, however, a simple Pietist. As we have seen, he was concerned with the wider manifestation of the Church's unity, and we shall have occasion to see further, that while Wesley never forgot that the Church exists first of all to serve and to witness, he also knew that this witness becomes inadequate whenever it is forgotten that the Church herself, in the total range of her faith and order—in ministry, teaching, sacraments, liturgy, corporate life—is of vital importance in the growth of believers into the fulness of the life of the kingdom of God.

[28] Ibid.

2 AUTHORITY AND EXPERIENCE

ᴆ   Conflicting views as to the nature of religious authority have become evident in the ecumenical encounter. It is not that any of the traditions gives exclusive emphasis to a single form of authority. It is a question as to which element in the constellation of authority becomes dominant. It can be said that in the "Catholic" framework, the *tradition* of the Church—given not only in Scriptures but also in the continuing tradition, such as the doctrinal decisions of the Councils, and the creedal and liturgical forms that have emerged in the context of worship— is the final authority in matters of faith and order. In "Classical Protestantism" it is the living *word of God* as recorded in the Scripture that is the final authority, while in "Free Church Protestantism" the tendency is to shift the ultimate seat of authority to the living voice of the *Holy Spirit* spoken to true believers.

At first sight Wesley would seem to fit neatly into the "Classical Protestant" mold. That Wesley continually subjected tradition and experience to the "written Word of God" even a casual reading of his works will reveal. In the "Character of a Methodist" he wrote:

> We believe, indeed, that "all Scripture is given by the inspiration of God"; and herein we are distinguished from Jews, Turks, and Infidels. We believe the written word of God to be the only and

23

JOHN WESLEY'S THEOLOGY TODAY

sufficient rule both of Christian faith and practice; and herein we are
fundamentally distinguished from those of the Romish Church.[1]

This, of course, is not the whole story. Wesley was far from
being a conservative proof-texter, creating doctrine by pasting
together texts from various parts of Scripture. Here his own
practice speaks for itself.

> I want to know one thing—the way to heaven; how to land safe
> on that happy shore. God Himself has condescended to teach the
> way; for this very end He came from heaven. He hath written it down
> in a book. O give me that book! At any price, give me the book of
> God! I have it: here is knowledge enough for me. Let me be *homo
> unius libri*. Here then I am, far from the busy ways of men. I sit down
> alone: only God is here. In His presence I open, I read His book;
> for this end, to find the way to heaven. Is there a doubt concerning
> the meaning of what I read? Does anything appear dark or intricate?
> I lift up my heart to the Father of Lights: "Lord, is it not Thy word,
> 'If any man lack wisdom, let him ask of God'? Thou 'givest liberally,
> and upbraidest not.' Thou hast said, 'If any be willing to do Thy
> will, he shall know.' I am willing to do, let me know, Thy will."
> I then search after and consider parallel passages of Scripture, "com-
> paring spiritual things with spiritual." I meditate thereon with all
> the attention and earnestness of which my mind is capable. If any
> doubt still remains, I consult those who are experienced in the things
> of God; and then the writings whereby, being dead, they yet speak.
> And what I thus learn, that I teach.[2]

The phrase *homo unius libri* was a favorite one with Wesley.[3]
This did not mean, of course, that he rejected all other writings as of no value. Apart from his strong belief in the value of
study in subjects such as logic, in order to develop the faculty
of thought, and in the fields of medicine, history, and literature,
in order to become a more effective servant of God through
better health, better understanding of the human situation, and

[1] *Works*, VIII, 340.
[2] *Sermons*, L, 31-32.
[3] See e.g., *Letters*, IV, 299 (1765). "In June 1730, I began to be *homo unius libri*, to study (comparatively) no book but the Bible." *Works*, XI, 373 (1777). "This (Christian perfection) is the very point at which I aimed all along from the year 1730, when I began to be *homo unius libri*, 'a man of one book,' re-garding none, comparatively, but the Bible."

better powers of expression,[4] Wesley stressed also the importance of reading the works of the saints of the Church down through the centuries in order to share in the insights God gave them into his (God's) revelation. His "Christian Library" was prepared to bring the riches of the Church's storehouse to his people, and if this library with its amazing variety of authors from many Christian traditions was a business failure, Wesley's determination to proceed with it is further evidence of his estimate of its importance. Wesley's was the truly ecumenical mind, constantly seeking to listen to the insights God has given to all his children concerning his revelation. All such reading may be seen as comparative exegesis, for the final authority is the Scripture; but as it is seen in that light, it has great importance.

In the 1770 Minutes Wesley said to his preachers:

> Read the most useful books, and that regularly and constantly. . . .
> "But I read only the Bible." Then you ought to teach others to read only the Bible, and by parity of reason, to hear, only the Bible: but if so, you need preach no more. Just so said George Bell. And what is the fruit? Why, now he neither reads the Bible nor anything else. This is rank enthusiasm. If you need no book but the Bible, you are got above St. Paul. He wanted others too. "Bring me the books," says he, "but especially the parchments," those wrote on parchment. "But I have no taste for reading." Contract a taste for it by use, or return to your trade.[5]

By homo unius libri Wesley means a reliance upon the way of salvation given in the Scriptures. His point is that the final authority in matters of religion is the Bible, and all other writings must be judged in the light of this once-for-all revelation.

> The Scriptures are the touchstone whereby Christians examine all, real or supposed, revelations. In all cases they appeal "to the law and testimony" to try every spirit thereby.[6]

Wesley then must be placed with the Reformers in his principle of sola scriptura, in the sense that Scripture is the final

---

[4] James R. Joy, "Wesley, Man of a Thousand Books and a Book," Religion in Life, VIII (Winter, 1939), 71-84.
[5] Sermons, I, 30-31.
[6] Letters, III, 117.

authority in matters of faith and practice; [7] not in the sense that tradition and experience have no value, but in the sense that these further sources of insight must be congruous with the revelation recorded in Scripture.

It is clear, too, that Wesley based his principle of *sola scriptura* on a type of verbal inspiration theory.

The Inspiration of Scripture

If there be any mistakes in the Bible, there may as well be a thousand. [8]

The language of His messengers, also, is exact in the highest degree: for the words which were given them accurately answered the impression made upon their minds; and hence Luther says, "Divinity is nothing but a grammar of the language of the Holy Ghost." [9]

It is true that Wesley was open to textual criticism and was quite sure there are corruptions in the received text. [10] It is true that he recognized that the Apostles did not write simply by passive dictation, but used their memories, accepted traditions, not necessarily accurate, and quoted Scripture without exactness. [11] It is true that, with the Reformers, he insisted on the *testimonium Spiritus Sancti internum*—the need for the Spirit to illumine the heart of the reader so that he may receive the truth of Scripture. [12] It is also true that he taught that understanding comes not by mechanical proof texting but by the careful setting of texts in the context of the whole story of Scripture. [13]

Through the use of these limitations to his verbal view, we could undoubtedly go far to bring Wesey's doctrine into line

[7] *Works*, VII, 198. "The faith of the Protestants, in general, embraces only those truths, as necessary to salvation, which are clearly revealed in the oracles of God. Whatever is plainly declared in the Old and New Testament is the object of their faith. They believe neither more nor less than what is manifestly contained in, and provable by, the Holy Scriptures. . . . The written word is the whole and sole rule of their faith, as well as practice. They believe whatsoever God has declared, and profess to do whatsoever he hath commanded. This is the proper faith of Protestants: By this they will abide, and no other."
[8] *Journal*, VI, 117; also *Journal*, V, 523.
[9] *Notes*, 9.
[10] *Ibid.*, 6.
[11] *Ibid.*, 814, on Heb. 2:7; 15 on Matt. 1:1; 19 on Matt. 2:6.
[12] *Ibid.*, 794, on II Tim. 3:16.
[13] *Works*, X, 482.

with modern biblical scholarship. Yet it must be said that when we turn to his argument for the divine authority of the Scripture, we come to a point in his view of authority that cannot be sustained.

The Bible, he argues, is written either by God, or by good men or angels, or bad men or devils. The second is impossible, for good men or angels would not say "Thus saith the Lord" if it were their own invention. Neither could it be written by bad men or devils, for they would not so consistently condemn themselves and consign their souls to hell. The conclusion is clear— God wrote it! [14]

It must be admitted that this is scarcely good exegesis. His interpretation of "Thus saith the Lord" is a mechanical view which fails to do justice to the dynamic of the divine-human encounter. That the prophets believed God had given them a word to speak is clear; that they declared that God dictated the words is false. Wesley has oversimplified the alternatives.

Admitting, however, that his *theory* of inspiration is inadequate, it is still true that his *use* of the Scriptures as the authority for doctrine does not depend upon his theory. His biblical interpretation was brought into relation with tradition, reason, and experience in such a way that he was relieved of the dangers of a static and mechanical literalism.

The Method of Biblical Interpretation

William Arnett [15] draws together Wesley's rules of biblical interpretation in a useful form.

1. The literal sense is emphasized, "unless it implies an absurdity," [16] and "if it be not contrary to some other texts; but in that case the obscure text is to be interpreted by those that speak more plainly." [17]

2. It is important to interpret a text in its total context.

3. Scripture must be compared with Scripture, and therefore a thorough knowledge of the whole is necessary for an interpreta-

[14] Works, XI, 478-79.
[15] John Wesley—Man of One Book, Ph.D. thesis (Madison, N.J.: Drew University, 1954), 98 ff.
[16] Works, VI, 395.
[17] Letters, III, 129.

tion of a part, "seeing scripture interprets scripture; one part fixing the sense of another." [18]

4. Wesley was always anxious that, where possible, Scripture should be confirmed by experience.[19]

5. Reason is to be employed to understand what the Scriptures declare, and how this truth is to be declared to men.[20]

6. The resultant exposition should be "plain truth for plain people," free "from all nice and philosophical speculations; from all perplexed and intricate reasonings." [21]

Tradition

This list of Arnett's does not give a full account of Wesley's biblical interpretation. We have seen already the importance that Wesley gave to tradition in checking his own interpretation against the great interpreters of the Church. In a letter to William Dodd he wrote:

In your last paragraph you say, "You set aside all authority, ancient and modern." Sir, who told you so? I never did; it never entered my

[18] *Works*, X, 482. We see here one important reason for Wesley's strong emphasis on listening to other witnesses. One man cannot be a master of the whole of Scripture, and it is necessary to share in the wide fellowship of exegesis.

[19] *Journal*, I, 471-72.

[20] *Works*, VI, 354-55.

[21] *Sermons*, I, 30. For this practical use of the Scriptures, Wesley gives guidance which still is of great value.

"First, set apart some time, if possible, every morning and evening to read the Scriptures.

Second, read a chapter out of the Old and one out of the New Testament, if possible. If that cannot be done, read one chapter or part of one.

Third, read the Scripture, with the single purpose of knowing the whole will of God, and with a fixed determination to do that will.

Fourth, in order to know the will of God, there should be a constant eye to the analogy of faith; the connection and harmony there is between those grand fundamental doctrines—Original Sin, Justification by Faith, the New Birth, Inward and Outward Holiness.

Fifth, serious and earnest prayer should be made before approaching the oracles of God, seeing that Scripture can only be understood through the same Spirit whereby it was given. Prayer should be offered at the close in order that what is read may be written upon the heart.

Sixth, there should be periods of self-examination during the reading of the Scripture, with both heart and life being scrutinized. And whatever light is given 'should be used to the uttermost, and that immediately. Let there be no delay. Whatever you resolve, begin to execute the first moment you can. So shall you find this word to be indeed the power of God unto present, and eternal salvation.' " Quoted in Arnett, op. cit., 115-16 from Wesley's *Explanatory Notes Upon the Old Testament*.

thoughts. Who it was gave you that rule I know not; but my father gave it me thirty years ago (I mean concerning reverence to the ancient church and our own), and I have endeavored to walk by it to this day. But I try every doctrine by the Bible. This is the word by which we are judged in that day.[22]

The principle of *sola scriptura* did not necessitate the abandonment of the real authority of the continuing tradition of the Church. The Ante-Nicene Fathers Wesley believed to have particular value because of their proximity to Christ and the Apostles and because of the undivided nature of the Church in their time. He even went so far as to say "I regard no authority but those of the Ante-Nicene Fathers; nor any of them in opposition to the Scripture." [23] This statement, however, must be re-regarded as a relative judgment, as he clearly set great store on the continuing tradition of the Church after the Ante-Nicene period, regarding highly not only the authority of the standards of his own church—particularly in the Prayer Book and the Homilies—but also placing great value on the writings of a wide range of Christians throughout the centuries—a fact to which his *Christian Library* attests.

So far we have been speaking of the importance of tradition as being vital for the discovery of the right interpretation of Scripture, which is the final authority. But there is a further important question here. Does the principle of *sola scriptura* imply the exclusion from the worship and order of the church of all that is not sanctioned directly in Scripture? Or can the order and worship which evolved in the life of the church, and while not being sanctioned directly in Scripture, is not contrary to it, be considered as authoritative? At this point we see a Catholic tendency in Wesley. For while he did not consider that such forms which are without direct Scripture mandate are of absolute authority, he believed that such important traditional forms as the three-fold order of the ministry and the liturgy of the church have very great authority and should not be altered lightly.[24]

[22] *Letters*, III, 172.
[23] *Letters*, VII, 106.
[24] This is discussed further in the chapter on the Church.

Reason

It is a sign of Wesley's fear that the principle of *sola scriptura* may be misinterpreted in such a way as to open up the faith to all the vagaries of unchecked and enthusiastic private exegesis, that he placed a strong emphasis not only upon the place of tradition in the structure of authority, but also upon the place of reason.

It is a fundamental principle with us (the Methodists) that to renounce reason is to renounce religion, that religion and reason go hand in hand, and that all irrational religion is false religion.[25]

In his "Earnest Appeal to Men of Reason and Religion," Wesley says that to decry reason, as the Mystics do, is utterly unscriptural, and that he joins "men of reason" in "desiring a religion founded on reason, and every way agreeable thereto." [26] Often he appeals to scripture and reason,[27] or to scripture, reason, and experience.[28]

It is important, however, to see the role that he gives to reason. In his sermon on "The Case of Reason Considered," he says that we must "acknowledge that it is utterly incapable of giving either faith, or hope, or love; and, consequently, of producing either real virtue, or substantial happiness." These are a gift from God. But reason is of essential service "both in laying the foundation of true religion, under the guidance of the Spirit of God, and in raising the superstructure." [29]

From this it might appear that Wesley agrees with the view of Thomas that while the supernatural virtues of faith, hope, and love, and such doctrines as the Incarnation, the Atonement, and the Trinity, come from revelation, reason is capable of erecting a "natural theology," which then rises into a harmonious structure with "revealed theology." But a further investigation shows a vital difference. Wesley, for example, makes no use of arguments for the existence of God and draws his ethics entirely

---

[25] *Letters*, V, 364. See also *Notes*, 630 on I Cor. 14:20. "Knowing religion was not designed to destroy any of our natural faculties, but to exalt and improve them, our reason in particular."
[26] *Works*, VIII, 11-12.
[27] *Sermons*, II, 98.
[28] *Works*, X, 511.
[29] *Works*, VI, 360.

from revelation. The reason is that Wesley believed that in the matter of our relation to God, reason has no pre-established principles which would enable it to develop a "natural theology."

Your reasoning justly, not only on this, but on any subject whatsoever, pre-supposes true judgments already formed, whereon to ground your argumentation. . . . And seeing our ideas are not innate, but must all originally come from our senses, it is certainly necessary that you have senses capable of discerning objects of this kind: Not those only which are called natural senses, which in this respect profit nothing, as being altogether incapable of discerning objects of a spiritual kind; but spiritual senses, exercised to discern spiritual good and evil. It is necessary that you have *the hearing ear*, and the *seeing eye*, emphatically so called; that you have a new class of senses opened in your soul, not depending on organs of flesh and blood. . . .

The ideas of faith differ *toto genere* from those of external sensation. . . . What a gulf is here! By what art will reason get over the immense chasm? This cannot be, till the Almighty come in to your succor, and give you that faith you have hitherto despised. Then upborne, as it were, on eagles' wings, you shall soar away into the regions of eternity; and your enlightened reason shall explore even "the deep things of God"; God himself "revealing them to you by his Spirit." [30]

It is true that Wesley agrees that the existence of the creatures implies the existence of God. But he insists that this knowledge has no real content, and that it leaves unanswered the only important question: "What kind of God?" [31] Reason cannot take the veil away and disclose this unknown God. "O my friend how will you get one step further, unless God reveal himself to your soul?"

Wesley further shows his belief as to the existential irrelevance of natural theology in his sermon on "Original Sin."

We had, by nature, no knowledge of God, no acquaintance with Him. It is true, as soon as we came to the use of reason, we learned "the invisible things of God, even His eternal power and Godhead, from the things that are made." From the things that are seen we inferred the existence of an eternal, powerful Being, that is not seen.

[30] *Works*, VIII, 13.
[31] *Ibid.*, 197-98.

But still, although we acknowledged His being, we had no acquaintance with Him. As we know there is an Emperor in China, whom yet we do not know; so we knew there was a King of all the earth, yet we knew Him not. Indeed we could not by any of our natural faculties. By none of these could we attain the knowledge of God. We could no more perceive Him by our natural understanding, than we could see Him with our eyes. For "no one knoweth the Father but the Son, and he to whom the Son willeth to reveal Him." [32]

The existential irrelevance of the natural knowledge of God is further emphasized by Wesley through a hypothetical example.

Were two infants . . . to be brought up from the womb without being instructed in any religion, there is little room to doubt but (unless the grace of God interposed) . . . they would have no religion at all: they would have no more knowledge of God than the beasts of the field, than the wild ass's colt. Such is natural religion, abstracted from traditional, and from the influences of God's Spirit.[33]

The importance of reason is not that it provides another source of revelation, but that it is a logical faculty enabling us to order the evidence of revelation; and that, with tradition, it provides us with the necessary weapons for guarding against the dangers of the unbridled interpretation of Scripture.

Experience

Finally we must consider the place given to personal experience in the structure of authority. There can be no doubt that Wesley placed great stress on experience and was concerned lest the acceptance of the authority of Scripture and tradition should lead to a formal religion that short-circuited the living relationship with God to which they bear witness.

I am not afraid that the people called Methodists should ever cease to exist, either in Europe or America. But I am afraid, lest they should only exist as a dead sect, having the form of religion without the

[32] *Sermons*, II, 216.
[33] *Ibid.*, 216-17.

power. And this undoubtedly will be the case, unless they hold fast both the doctrine, spirit and discipline with which they first set out.[34]

Because of this fear of formalism there is in Wesley's writing a constant stress on experience. "The theory of religion," he wrote concerning a friend, "he certainly has. May God give him the living experience of it." [35] The acceptance of the authority of Scripture and of the right tradition is never adequate until it is seen that their authority is conferred on them by the Spirit. It is the Spirit who uses them to bring believers into faith relationship with Christ to whom all authority on earth and in heaven is given. Their authority, then, lies in the fact that they are the given instruments for bringing us to a true and living faith relationship with Christ. Consequently they are authority for me only when they bring me to the living experience of which they speak.

We must be careful, however, that we do not draw the wrong conclusion concerning the place of experience in the structure of authority. It is true that only by the inward witness of the Spirit can we understand the meaning of true faith in Christ, but the Spirit brings this understanding to us through the Church's witness to Christ. Experience therefore is the appropriation of authority, not the source of authority.

Rattenbury errs when he writes concerning the "conversion" experiences of Charles and John Wesley in May 1738:

All that the Wesleys said of permanent value to the human race came out of their evangelical experience. All their distinctive doctrine was discovered in that realm of the Spirit—which had been supernaturally revealed to them in May 1738. . . .

There was, of course, much in their teaching that did not come out of their experience, but that is the commonplace and, to some extent, misleading part of it.[36]

Rattenbury then lists three doctrines which he considers to be the great contribution of the Wesleys: universal love, the

[34] Luke Tyerman, *The Life and Times of the Reverend John Wesley* (New York: Harper and Brothers, 1870), III, 519.
[35] *Letters*, VII, 47.
[36] J. E. Rattenbury, *Wesley's Legacy to the World* (London: Epworth Press, 1938) 83.

witness of the Spirit, perfect love. He then proceeds with the statement:

What really killed Calvinism in England was the Wesleys' personal discovery of God's amazing love. John Wesley preached his famous sermon on Free Grace on April 29, to which Charles Wesley's hymn on "Universal Redemption" was appended. Both hymn and sermon gave great offence to Whitefield.[37]

Rattenbury misses the irony of the last sentence, for Whitefield had shared the evangelical experience of the Wesleys, and it is clear that it failed to lead him to the same doctrine. We can scarcely expect personal experience to decide the question as to whether God's saving grace is free to all, or whether some are elected to receive it. This is a mystery of revelation which drives us back to exegesis not to self-analysis.

Workman seeks to overcome the weakness of the view represented by Rattenbury by widening the canon of experience.

The conjunction of belief in the authority of an organic Church with the insistence upon the value and reality of individual experience as the final test, gives to Methodism its special position in the Catholic Church. We have the root idea of the Independent joined to the root idea of the Anglican, a primary insistence upon the value of the subjective joined to a constant maintenance of the objective authority of the Church.[38]

The appeal to individual experience is ever checked and balanced by the appeal to collective experience.[39]

This too must be rejected, for in Wesley experience is not the test of truth, but truth the test of experience. Wesley feared any approach to doctrine and worship which overlooked the necessity for personal experience, but he equally feared any reliance upon experience which left the question of truth to the vagaries of individual or collective feeling. He knew the danger of the Christian faith being torn from its historical moorings by being subjected to the vagaries and limitations of human ex-

[37] Ibid., 94.
[38] H. B. Workman, The Place of Methodism in the Catholic Church (London: Epworth Press, 1921), 30.
[39] Ibid., 46.

perience, and so he insisted upon the priority of the Word. Speaking in his *Journal* of the "Life of Mr. Marsay," he wrote:

He was a man of uncommon understanding, and greatly devoted to God. But he was a consummate enthusiast. Not the Word of God, but his own imaginations, were the sole rule of his words and actions.[40]

Wesley knew that

There is an irreconcilable variability in the operation of the Holy Spirit on the souls of men, more especially as to the manner of justification. Many find Him rushing upon them like a torrent, while they experience the o'erwhelming power of saving grace. This has been the experience of many; perhaps of more in this late visitation than in any other age since the time of the Apostles. But in others he works in a different way:

He deigns His influence to infuse,
Sweet, refreshing, as the silent dews. . . .
Let Him take His own way: He is wiser than you.[41]

Because of this variability, no experience can be made normative, but all experience must be submitted to the touchstone of Scripture. Commenting on the Quakers, Wesley objects that they make Scripture "a secondary rule, subordinate to the Spirit." He answers that

The Scriptures are the touchstone whereby Christians examine all, real or supposed, revelations. . . . For though the Spirit is our principal leader, yet He is not our rule at all; the Scriptures are the rule whereby He leads us into all truth.[42]

Wesley also knew the danger of delivering believers to the vagaries of their own feeling; and thus while he stressed the importance of "heart religion," he also stressed the importance of continually attuning our lives upward to the promises of the gospel, rather than inwards to a dependence upon feeling.

That some consciousness of our being in favour with God is joined

[40] *Journal*, VI, 202.
[41] *Letters*, VII, 298.
[42] *Letters*, II, 117.

35

with the Christian faith I cannot doubt; but it is not the essence of it. A consciousness of pardon cannot be the condition of pardon.[48]

Faith may subsist for a time with very little joy, especially if there was little sorrow before. It is very possible to mistake joy for faith, and then certainly we shall trust in joy instead of Christ. The promises are the most strengthening and comforting truths in all the oracles of God; particularly (to believers in Christ) the promises of full sanctification. They are designed for this very thing, to strengthen the weak and to comfort the feeble-minded.[44]

It is undoubtedly our privilege to "rejoice evermore," with a calm, still, heartfelt joy. Nevertheless this is seldom long at one stay. Many circumstances may cause it to ebb and flow. This, therefore, is not the essence of religion, which is no other than humble, gentle, patient love. I do not know whether all these are not included in that one word resignation. For the highest lesson our Lord (as man) learned on earth was to say, "Not as I will, but as Thou wilt." [45]

This does not mean that Wesley deprecated feeling. Far from it. " 'Righteousness, and peace, and joy in the Holy Ghost.' These must be felt or they have no being." [46] He knew, however, the ebb and flow of feelings, and therefore the necessity for directing the attention of believers away from their subjective state to the promises of the gospel. In this way he sought to keep them ever open to receive the new gifts God has in store for all who believe.

Hildebrandt has the following statement of Wesley in answer to a question as to how to keep Methodism alive after his death:

Preach our doctrine, inculcate experience, urge practice, enforce discipline. If you preach doctrine only, the people will be antinomians; if you preach experience only they will become enthusiasts; if you preach practice only they will become pharisees; and if you preach all of these and do not enforce discipline, Methodism will be like a highly cultivated garden without a fence, exposed to the ravages of the wild boar of the forest.[47]

[48] Letters, VII, 61.
[44] Ibid., 64.
[45] Ibid., 120. See also Letters, VIII, 190: "You are not to judge by your own feelings, but by the Word of God."
[46] Journal, V, 426.
[47] Hildebrandt, Christianity According to the Wesleys, p. 12. Used by per-

Here in a succinct statement we have the balanced concern of Wesley. For him true religion consists in the living relationship to God, made alive in us by the Holy Spirit who comes to us through the witness to the revelation in Jesus Christ, recorded in Scripture, proclaimed in preaching, and practiced in the fellowship of the Church. Authority is living and dynamic—the Spirit speaks to us through the Scripture which he uses as his final authority; but to give us a vital awareness of the revelation there recorded, he calls to witness the believers through whom he has spoken to the Church in time past, and the believers in whom his promises are being realized now. And while the Spirit works in a variety of ways, the promises of God are changeless, and therefore there is a "common salvation" offered to all, which it is the task of theology and preaching to describe. "Wesley was suspicious," Lee rightly says, "of peculiar experiences. Willing to allow for individual variations, he yet insisted on 'common salvation.' " [48]

In summary, we may say that Wesley takes his stand with the Classical Protestant view of authority in exalting the Scriptures as the final authority in matters of faith and practice. He is also at one with Luther and Calvin in relating the authority of Scripture to experience by the living witness of the Holy Spirit, who brings the truth of the gospel to the heart of the believer through the record of Scripture.[49] It is also true that Wesley shares a good deal of the Catholic view in the vital place he gives to tradition—particularly the tradition of the early undivided Church and the historic forms of church order and worship. It is true again, that without allowing it to rise to a position of primacy in matters of doctrine, he also shares in the Free Church insistence on experience. But all this does not mean that Methodism can serve as a bridge church in the ecumenical encounter, showing a way to the reconciliation of the divergent views! Rather it means that the Methodist tradition is marked by an openness which should bring with it a readiness to listen

---

mission of Epworth Press, London. He adds: "I have not been able to verify this quotation which has the authentic ring of Wesley, and appears under an early picture of Wesley in Nicolson Square Church, Edinburgh."

[48] U. Lee, John Wesley and Modern Religion, Cokesbury Press, 1936, p. 139.
[49] F. Hildebrandt, From Luther to Wesley, op. cit., pp. 25-32.

to the differing witness of the various traditions, as we seek in the present ecumenical encounter to grapple anew with this thorny question of authority.

We mentioned earlier that the problem of authority is the more difficult because none of the church traditions gives exclusive emphasis to a single form of authority. It is rather a question of the relative importance given to the various elements in the constellation of authority. But the problem is even further complicated by the fact that the relative emphasis varies according to the doctrine under consideration. When we are considering the more "objective" doctrines such as the nature of God, Scripture is the final authority, and tradition is of value only in the explication of the "once-for-all" revelation recorded in Scripture. But when we are considering doctrines such as the Church and the ministry, Scripture itself suggests that tradition has a greater importance, because we are there concerned with the emerging life of the people of God under the guidance of the Holy Spirit. It is for that reason that agreement on the more "objective" doctrines has proved much easier to reach, while our greatest differences lie in the latter realm.

As we proceed to deal with Wesley's outline of the "common salvation" offered by Jesus Christ, provided for in the Church, and received in the experience of the Christian life, we will observe the varying place he gives to the different elements of the total structure of authority.

We see then that the ecumenical problem of authority is highly complex. It requires not only a discussion on the abstract level that has so far concerned us, but also a continuing dialogue through the wide range of particular doctrines from the contexts of the separated traditions.

3 THE ORDER OF SALVATION: PREVENIENT GRACE

For Wesley, theology has its true context in the preaching and fellowship of the Church. His theological concern is to lead man along the road of salvation, carefully charting the way that he should take and holding out before him the grace that will enable him to walk that way. As he proceeds, he pauses only long enough to give such background information as is strictly necessary. For example, Wesley does not single out the doctrine of the Atonement for separate treatment; it is unfolded in the context of its living relevance to justification and the new birth. He does not separate the doctrine of the Church for theological treatment; he handles the issues as they arise in connection with the life and discipline of the people committed to his care.

For the purposes of placing his theology in the midst of the problems of ecumenical discussion, however, it will be necessary to separate such doctrines for special treatment. This is not foreign to Wesley, for when a controversy on a specific issue arose, as on the doctrine of original sin, he was ready to isolate it in this manner. Nevertheless it is important to remember that such doctrines only gain their proper significance when they are woven into the context of the pilgrim way.

The Order of Salvation

Sometimes Wesley gives his outline of the order of salvation in a short summary, as in his famous:

Our main doctrines, which include all the rest, are three,—that of repentance, of faith, and of holiness. The first of these we account, as it were, the porch of religion; the next, the door; the third, religion itself.[1]

Sometimes he outlines it in detail, as in his sermon, "On Working Out Your Own Salvation."

Salvation begins with what is usually termed (and very properly) *preventing grace*; including the first wish to please God, the first dawn of light concerning his will, and the first slight transient conviction of having sinned against him. All these imply some tendency towards life; some degree of salvation; the beginning of deliverance from a blind, unfeeling heart, quite insensible of God and the things of God. Salvation is carried on by *convincing grace*, usually in Scripture termed *repentance*; which brings a larger measure of self-knowledge, and a farther deliverance from the heart of stone. Afterwards we experience the proper Christian salvation; whereby, "through grace," we are "saved by faith;" consisting of those two grand branches, justification and sanctification. By justification we are saved from the guilt of sin, and restored to the favour of God; by sanctification we are saved from the power and root of sin, and restored to the image of God. All experience, as well as Scripture, show this salvation to be both instantaneous and gradual. It begins the moment we are justified, in the holy, humble, gentle, patient love of God and man. It gradually increases from that moment, as "a grain of mustard-seed, which, at first, is the least of all seeds," but afterwards puts forth large branches, and becomes a great tree; till, in another instant, the heart is cleansed from all sin, and filled with pure love to God and man. But even that love increases more and more, till we "grow up in all things into Him that is our Head;" till we all attain "the measure of the stature of the fulness of Christ." [2]

To be true to Wesley, therefore, we must present his theology through the order of salvation (*ordo salutis*), pausing only where necessary to explicate essential theological questions as they arise from the existential concern of the pilgrim.

Wesley's definition of salvation is given in the sermon on the text "Ye are saved through faith."

What is salvation? The salvation which is here spoken of is not what is frequently understood by that word, the going to heaven,

---

[1] *Works*, VIII, 472. *Letters*, II, 268.
[2] *Works*, VI, 509.

eternal happiness. It is not the soul's going to paradise, termed by our Lord, "Abraham's bosom." It is not a blessing which lies on the other side of death; or, as we usually speak, in the other world.

Wesley, of course, includes eternal destiny in salvation. So, in speaking on this same text in Sermon I he comments: "Not, *Ye shall be* (though that is also true), but, '*Ye are saved* through faith.' " [3] The point Wesley is after is that salvation is the total work of God, and that we can be in real though not total possession of it now. So he continues:

> The very words of the text itself put this beyond all question: "Ye *are saved*." It is not something at a distance: it is a present thing; a blessing which, through the free mercy of God, ye are now in possession of. Nay, the words may be rendered and that with equal propriety, "Ye *have been saved*": so that the salvation which is here spoken of might be extended to the entire work of God, from the first dawning of grace in the soul, till it is consummated in glory.[4]

Prevenient Grace

The central focus of Wesley's theology is on the saving work of Christ and the human appropriation of that work. As we saw in the last quotation, the saving work of Christ begins with the first dawning of grace in the soul, which Wesley called prevenient grace. This prevenient grace has very great significance in his theology. He insisted on the one hand, that man cannot move himself toward God, being entirely dependent on God's enabling grace. But he also insisted that man is responsible before God for his own salvation, being free to accept God or reject him. Wesley holds these two (man's inability to move himself toward God and his freedom to respond to God) together, without resorting to any form of Pelagianism, by his twin doctrines of original sin and prevenient grace. Because of original sin, the natural man is "dead to God" and unable to move toward God or respond to him. It is through the work of prevenient grace that he is given the power to respond or resist. Prevenient grace creates within us the power to accept faith or to refuse it.

[3] *Sermon*, I, 41.
[4] *Sermon*, II, 445.

It is under his doctrine of prevenient grace that Wesley treats conscience.

Can it be denied that something of this is found in every man born into the world? And does it not appear as soon as the understanding opens, as soon as reason begins to dawn? Does not every one then begin to know that there is a difference between good and evil; how imperfect soever the various circumstances of this sense of good and evil may be? . . .

This faculty seems to be what is usually meant by those who speak of natural conscience; an expression frequently found in some of our best authors, but yet not strictly just. For though in one sense it may be termed natural, because it is found in all men; yet properly speaking, it is not natural, but a supernatural gift of God, above all his natural endowments. No; it is not nature, but the Son of God, that is "the true light, which enlighteneth every man that cometh into the world." So that we may say to every human creature, "He," not nature, "hath showed thee, O man, what is good." And it is his Spirit who giveth thee an inward check, who causeth thee to feel uneasy, when thou walkest in any instance contrary to the light which he hath given thee.[5]

Thus because God is directly at work within even the natural man, man is responsible; not because he is naturally free to do God's will, but because he resists God's grace. This is not to say that this prevenient grace, apparent in the conscience, is enough to enable man to turn to God in faith. Further gifts of grace are necessary to enable man to come to repentance and then to justification. What it means is that God directly intervenes in the lives of men seeking to start them on the road to salvation. This prevenient grace gives us our first opportunity for responding to or resisting his work. This is why Wesley never bothers to use the traditional arguments for the existence of God. These are quite irrelevant, for God makes himself known directly; first, in a preliminary way (through conscience) by prevenient grace, and then in a direct way (through the gospel) by convincing grace. The task, therefore, of theology and preaching is to explain God's immediate relation to man and to urge man to accept the grace by which God seeks to bring us to himself.

[5] *Works*, VII, 187-88. Sermon "On Conscience."

Prevenient grace, then, marks the beginning of God's work of salvation, and this grace is present in all men.

Allowing that all the souls of men are dead in sin by *nature*, this excuses none, seeing there is no man that is in a state of mere nature; there is no man, unless he has quenched the Spirit, that is wholly void of the grace of God. No man living is entirely destitute of what is vulgarly called *natural conscience*. But this is not natural: It is more properly termed, *preventing grace*. . . . Every one, unless he be one of the small number whose conscience is seared as with a hot iron, feels more or less uneasy when he acts contrary to the light of his own conscience. So that no man sins because he has not grace, but because he does not use the grace which he hath.[6]

As it stands, this quotation is hardly satisfactory. It is clear that Wesley is far from believing that the grace given in the conscience is sufficient to bring man into conformity with God's will or to overcome the effects of original sin. How then can he say "no man sins because he has not grace"? This can be understood only when we recognize that Wesley has a double definition of sin, and that he believes that a response to the grace within us brings a further gift of grace.

Wesley's definition of sin, in terms of original sin, is total; under these terms no man can ever cease to be a sinner in this life. But Wesley looks at man not only in this absolute sense but also in terms of his immediate relationship to God. In this sense man can be at the same time a sinner (as measured by absolute standards) and yet sinless (if he consciously uses the grace God is giving him). The peculiarity of Wesley's theology is that he stretches this concept back behind justification where it is central to the Reformers, to man under prevenient grace, as well as forward beyond justification into his doctrine of perfection.

At each stage, however, the concept has a different significance. The man who responds to prevenient grace and seeks to obey his conscience is not thereby justified. But he is ready to receive more grace and to be led on to justifying grace. "Stir up the spark of grace which is now in you, and he will give you

* *Works*, VI, 512.

more grace." [7] It is because God is working even in the natural man to lead him on to salvation that it is true to say that "no man sins because he has not grace."

We should not believe, however, that this use of prevenient grace is meritorious; for it is a response that is possible only by the strength supplied by God's grace, and the way to salvation, of which this is the first step, can be covered only when God strengthens us continually by his grace. "He worketh in you of his own good pleasure, without any merit of yours." [8]

Wesley is one with Calvin in his doctrine of original sin, so that man is seen as having no natural capacity to turn to God.

Q. 23. Wherein may we come to the very edge of Calvinism?
A. In ascribing all good to the free grace of God. (2.) In denying all natural free-will, and all power antecedent to grace. And (3.) In excluding all merit from man; even for what he has or does by the grace of God. [9]

Nevertheless he broke the chain of logical necessity by which the Calvinist doctrine of predestination seems to flow from the doctrine of original sin, by this doctrine of prevenient grace. This view of universal grace—God's grace "free for all, and in all"—undoubtedly gave great impetus to the evangelistic appeal of his message. It also carried important theological consequences which become evident in his formulation of the doctrines of justification and sanctification, but it also brought with it serious difficulties that must be faced.

The grace or love of God, whence cometh our salvation, is FREE IN ALL, and FREE FOR ALL.

First. It is free IN ALL to whom it is given. It does not depend on any power or merit in man; no, not in any degree, neither in whole, nor in part. It does not in anywise depend either on the good works or righteousness of the receiver; not on anything he has done, or anything he is. It does not depend on his endeavours. It does not depend on his good tempers, or good desires, or good purposes and intentions; for all these flow from the free grace of God; they are streams only, not the fountain. They are the fruits of free grace, and

[7] Works, VI, 513.
[8] Ibid., 512.
[9] Works, VIII, 285. Minutes, 1745.

not the root. They are not the cause, but the effects of it. Whatsoever good is in man, or is done by man, God is the author and doer of it. Thus is his grace free in all; that is, no way depending on any power or merit in man; but on God alone, who freely gave us his own Son, and "with him freely giveth us all things." [10]

But even though God's prevenient grace is free in all and for all, how can those who never hear the gospel be said to have a free opportunity of salvation, if it is still true that man can be justified by faith in Christ alone? Wesley is prepared to accept the logic of his own viewpoint. First, it is his belief that Christ works even in those who do not hear the gospel in this life.[11] Second, he believes that those who do not hear the gospel are judged according to their response to this grace by which Christ works within them in a hidden way.[12] Finally, there is the state of Paradise—"the intermediate state between death and resurrection"—in which a full knowledge of Christ is given and the souls of just men are made perfect.[13]

In paradise the souls of good men rest from their labours and are with Christ from death to the resurrection. This bears no resemblance at all to the Popish purgatory, wherein wicked men are supposed to be tormented in purging fire till they are sufficiently purified to have a place in heaven. But we believe (as did the ancient Church) that none suffer after death but those who suffer eternally. We believe that we are to be *here* saved from sin and enabled to love God with all our heart.[14]

For Wesley this constitutes no break with the doctrine of justification by faith alone. Those who, not having heard the gospel, yet have responded to the prevenient work of Christ in their souls,[15] are, like the patriarchs, justified by faith in anticipation of the Christ who will at last be revealed to them. For those who do hear the gospel, of course, faith in the direct sense is necessary. Nor is there any escape from our responsi-

[10] *Works*, VII, 373-74.
[11] *Ibid.*, 188.
[12] *Works*, VI, 206 and *Letters*, II, 118.
[13] *Letters*, VI, 214.
[14] *Letters*, VII, 168.
[15] To keep it completely Christocentric Wesley insists that prevenient grace is available by virtue of the Atonement; *Works*, VIII, 277-78.

bility for preaching the gospel to all, for it gives the inestimable privilege of present salvation from sin, and that is a gift which God would have all men share.

That Wesley's viewpoint hardly solves all problems is obvious. But it can be argued that within the serious limits of our knowledge, he has given a clear exposition of the scope of God's grace, and in such a way that God's universal offer of faith is maintained in all its clarity.

While Wesley stays within the Classical Protestant framework in his affirmation that the only source of our justification is the faith which is the gift of God's grace, his emphasis that prevenient grace is "in all and for all," gives to Wesley's doctrine a more Catholic tone than that of the Reformers. More stress is placed on the successive moments involved in God's leading of the natural man to salvation. In each moment man is given the freedom to respond or resist, and thus each moment has its own peculiar and decisive significance. We shall see, for example, how he separated the moments of repentance and justification which the Reformers had coalesced in their doctrine of justification. This brought him to place greater emphasis on the importance of the response of man in terms of works, before as well as after justification, while still insisting with the Reformers that these works cannot be judged in terms of merit in the framework of the law, but in terms of faith-dependence in the framework of the personal relationship given by God moment by moment.

This formulation of the faith relation, beginning with prevenient grace, breaking the pattern of logical necessity involved in the traditional doctrine of predestination, and emphasizing the continuing relation of man to God in terms of submission or resistance to grace, may well have real ecumenical significance in speaking to the Catholic fear that the Classical Protestant emphasis on justification by faith alone involves a devaluation of the significance of works in man's saving relation to God, and leads to a relaxation of ethical endeavour.

But before we discuss this reformulation, we must look at Wesley's doctrine of original sin to see that Wesley keeps the initiative in the work of salvation totally with God.

4 ORIGINAL SIN

We have stressed already the fact that Wesley avoids any form of Pelagianism. The whole work of salvation is by God's intervening grace; this being necessary because man suffers from the disease of original sin. This description of our human situation was, for Wesley, a necessary counterpart of the message that we are saved by grace alone.

All who deny this, call it "original sin," or by any other title, are but heathens still, in the fundamental point which differences Heathenism from Christianity. They may, indeed, allow that men have many vices; . . . But here is the *shibboleth:* Is man by nature filled with all manner of evil? Is he void of all good? Is he wholly fallen? Is his soul totally corrupted? Or to come back to the text, is "every imagination of the thoughts of his heart only evil continually"? Allow this, and you are so far a Christian. Deny it, and you are but an Heathen still.[1]

The point that Wesley is after is the same as that made by Kierkegaard in his famous statement that there is great "edification implied in the thought that against God we are always in the wrong." [2] For the Christian who knows of the amazing grace available in Christ, this is a central affirmation of the good news that we have no natural ability to do anything to return

[1] *Sermons*, II, 223.
[2] S. Kierkegaard, *Either—Or* (Princeton: Princeton University Press, 1944), II, 287 ff.

to God. By this awareness we are released from all concern for self-reliance, knowing that we can turn to God in total dependence upon him.

Kierkegaard's statement, like Wesley's doctrine of total depravity, can be understood only when we see that they are here describing man's condition *before* God. They are not denying that fallen man has many good natural gifts or that he can perform many noble deeds; they are only denying that man standing face to face with God has anything to plead. It is before God, not before society, that man is utterly helpless. The meaning of this distinction becomes clear when we see Wesley's claim that the Fall entails the complete loss of the moral image, while the natural image and the political image are retained, albeit in a distorted manner.

The moral image, however, is the image proper. Speaking of Adam in the pre-Fall state as endowed with "original righteousness," Wesley defines this original righteousness in terms of his relation to God. The real image of God in man—that which separates him from the animal world beneath is not so much his capacities as his relation to the Creator.

It was not reason. Set aside that ambiguous term: Exchange it for the plain word, understanding: And who can deny that the brutes have this? We may as well deny that they have sight or hearing.[3]

The real image is that "man is capable of God";[4] that he is made for personal relationship with his Creator. The meaning of the Fall is that man has fallen away from this relationship, so losing his original righteousness and totally distorting the meaning of his existence.

It is true that the image in the broader sense is not totally destroyed.

"And God," the three-one God, "said, Let us make man in our image, after our likeness. So God created man in His own image, in the image of God created He him" (Gen. 1:26, 27):—not barely in his *natural image,* a picture of His own immortality; a spiritual being, endued with understanding, freedom of will, and various affections;

---

[3] *Works,* VI, 244.
[4] *Ibid.*

nor merely in his *political image*, the governor of this lower world, having "dominion over the fishes of the sea, and over all the earth": but chiefly in his *moral image*; which, according to the Apostle, is "righteousness and true holiness." [5]

The loss of the moral image spells total depravity because separation from God and the substitution of self-government in place of acceptance of the Lordship of God means that the good capacities of man are twisted from their true course and used for a wrong purpose.[6] We are still able to use our capacities for creative social purposes, but actions which are good when judged by objective social or moral standards are religiously corrupt when they issue from a life separated from God. Such works are evil because they "are not done as God hath 'willed and commanded them to be done.'" [7]

The significance of this separation from God is captured in Wesley's affirmation that the "natural man" is "dichotomous" —soul and body—and that when Paul speaks of "spirit, soul, body,"

of the three here mentioned, only the last two are natural constituent parts of man. The first is adventitious, and the supernatural gift of God, to be found in Christians only.[8]

It is the relationship with God which is determinative. Anything which is not of faith is sin, so that even morally good acts, performed by the sinful man, are sinful.

"Man's heart," as Wesley said in his sermon at Oxford on 11 June 1738, "is altogether corrupt and abominable." [9] And from that conviction he never wavered. In his 1733 sermon on "The Circumcision of the Heart" he asserted that the natural man is dead to God and

---

[5] *Sermons*, II, 227-28.
[6] *Notes*, 540, Rom. 6:6. "Our old man—Coeval with our being, and as old as the Fall; our evil nature; a strong and beautiful expression for that entire depravity and corruption which by nature spreads itself over the whole man, leaving no part uninfected."
[7] *Works*, VIII, 283.
[8] *Notes*, 763, I Thess. 5:23. This is of great importance in Wesley's doctrine of the Witness of the Spirit. God does not witness to our feelings or natural capacities, but creates a supernatural power of discernment. It is literally true that God creates his own "point of contact."
[9] *Sermons*, I, 38.

that in our best estate we are, of ourselves, all sin and vanity; that confusion, and ignorance, and error reign over our understanding; that unreasonable, earthly, sensual, devilish passions usurp authority over our will; in a word, that there is no whole part in our soul; that all the foundations of our nature are out of course.[10]

Man turned away from God is turned in upon himself. Instead of living in joyful obedience to God, he is now himself the proud guide of his own actions. Original sin is rebellion against God resulting in pride and self-idolatry.

Man was created looking directly to God, as his last end; but, falling into sin, he fell off from God, and turned into himself. Now, this infers a total apostasy and universal corruption in man; for where the last end is changed, there can be no real goodness. And this is the case of all men in their natural state: They seek not God, but themselves. Hence though many fair shreds of morality are among them, yet "there is none that doeth good, no, not one." For though some of them "run well," they are still off the way; they never aim at the right mark. Whithersoever they move, they cannot move beyond the circle of self. They seek themselves, they act for themselves; their natural, civil, and religious actions, from whatever spring they come, do all run into, and meet in, this dead sea.[11]

Here Wesley's analysis of man's plight parallels the thought of Luther with his cor incurvatum in se, the vicious circle of inward idolatry in which man is caught as the result of turning away from God to seek his satisfaction in himself and finite things. The result is that man finds himself in a position where his sensual appetites claim him captive and "drag him to and fro, in spite of his boasted reason." [12]

While therefore his natural abilities are not lost, they are twisted. Wesley sees man, in Pauline fashion, as a total man. Man related to God is "spiritual"; man turned away from God is "fleshly," and his whole nature is twisted by the turning away of his life from God. In his discussion of Gal. 5, Wesley notes that:

[10] Ibid., 268.
[11] Works, IX, 456.
[12] Sermons, II, 219.

some of the works here mentioned are wrought principally, if not entirely, in the mind; and yet they are called "works of the flesh." Hence it is clear, the Apostle does not by "the flesh" mean the body, or sensual appetites and inclinations only, but the corruption of human nature, as it spreads through all the powers of the soul, as well as all the members of the body.[13]

This state of separation from God is now the situation into which all are born as the result of Adam's Fall, so that all inherit this twisted nature. So Wesley speaks of

the loathsome leprosy of sin, which he brought with him from his mother's womb, which overspreads his whole soul, and totally corrupts every power and faculty thereof. He sees more and more of the evil tempers which spring from that evil root: the pride and haughtiness of spirit, the constant bias to think of himself more highly than he ought to think; the vanity, the thirst after the esteem or honour that cometh from men; the hatred or envy, the jealousy or revenge, the anger, malice, or bitterness; the inbred enmity both against God and man, which appears in ten thousand shapes; the love of the world, the self-will, the foolish and hurtful desires, which cleave to his inmost soul.[14]

Man separated from God is now subject to guilt and corruption, unable to do anything to stand before the purity of his Creator. Moreover, while he still has something of the light of reason and some capacity for social life, his relations with his neighbor and the world of nature are twisted throughout. Finally, there now stands over his life—a life that was meant for unbroken fellowship with his Creator—the sentence of "death, spiritual and temporal." The conclusion is clear. All men stand under the condemnation of God; of himself man can do nothing to bring himself back into right relationship with God.

So far Wesley's thought parallels closely the thought of Luther and Calvin. Some would suggest that Wesley would differ from them in the large place he gives to experience as a proof for the doctrine. But this is to misunderstand him. It is true that in his long tract on original sin, he gives a lengthy analysis of all sorts and conditions of men from many ages and races, to sug-

[13] *Notes*, 697, Gal. 5:21.
[14] *Sermons*, I, 323.

gest the truth of the Biblical account. But that there is no attempt to prove the doctrine by this analysis is indicated by his statement:

This account of the present state of man is confirmed by daily experience. It is true, the natural man discerns it not: and this is not to be wondered at. So long as a man born blind continues so, he is scarce sensible of his want: much less, could we suppose a place where all were born without sight, would they be sensible of the want of it. In like manner, so long as men remain in their natural blindness of understanding, they are not sensible of their spiritual wants, and of this in particular. But as soon as God opens the eyes of their understanding, they see the state they were in before; they are then deeply convinced, that "every man living," themselves especially, are, by nature, "altogether vanity"; that is, folly and ignorance, sin and wickedness.[15]

Original sin, then, is a truth of revelation known only to "grace-healed eyes." So in speaking of heathenism Wesley says:

as none of them were apprised of the fall of man, so none of them knew of his total corruption. They knew not that all men were empty of all good, and filled with all manner of evil. They were wholly ignorant of the entire depravation of the whole human nature, of every man born into the world, in every faculty of his soul. . . . This, therefore, is the first grand distinguishing point between Heathenism and Christianity.[16]

Original Sin and God's Justice

So far, then, Wesley is at one with the other main Reformers, but a question now arises on which his distinctive position begins to emerge. If all men are subject to damnation because of inherited sin, what does this do with God's justice?

To this question Calvin answers:

I say with Augustine, that the Lord created those who, he certainly foreknew, would fall into destruction, and that this was so because He actually willed it; but of His will it belongs not to us to demand the reason, which we are incapable of comprehending; nor is it reasonable that the Divine Will should be made the subject of controversy

[15] *Sermons*, II, 215.
[16] *Ibid.*, 222.

with us, which, whenever it is discussed, is only another name for the highest rule of justice.[17]

Calvin here scores an important point. To take issue with God's will on the grounds of justice is impossible, for justice is not an abstract principle but must be measured by God's will. The only question is whether Calvin has interpreted correctly the will of God given in revelation. It is here that Wesley takes issue. The doctrine of predestination, he asserts, makes

Revelation contradict itself. For it is grounded on such an interpretation of some texts (more or fewer it matters not) as flatly contradicts all the other texts, and indeed the whole scope and tenor of Scripture.[18]

If you ask, "Why then are not all men saved?" the whole law and the testimony answer, First, Not because of any decree of God; not because it is his pleasure they should die; for, "As I live, saith the Lord God," "I have no pleasure in the death of him that dieth." (Ezek. xviii:3, 32.) Whatever be the cause of their perishing, it cannot be his will, if the oracles of God are true; for they declare, "He is not willing that any should perish, but that all should come to repentance;" 2 Peter iii:9;) "He willeth that all men should be saved." And they, Secondly, declare what is the cause why all men are not saved, namely, that they will not be saved: So our Lord expressly, "Ye will not come unto me that ye may have life." (John v:40.) "The power of the Lord is present to heal" them, but they will not be healed.[19]

It was this conclusion which the Calvinists feared, for if the cause of a man being saved or not saved could be laid to free will, what would become of doctrines of total depravity and salvation by grace through faith alone? George Whitefield expressed this fear in a letter written to Wesley from Georgia:

For Jesus Christ's sake, consider how you dishonour God by denying election. You plainly make man's salvation depend not on God's free grace, but on man's free will. Dear, dear sir, give yourself to reading. Study the covenant of grace. Down with your carnal reasoning. Be a little child; and then, instead of pawning your salvation, as you

[17] *Institutes*, III, 13, 15.
[18] *Works*, VII, 379-80.
[19] *Ibid.*, 381.

have done in a late hymn-book, if the doctrine of *universal redemption* be not true, instead of talking of *sinless perfection*, as you have done in the preface to that hymn-book, and instead of making man's salvation to depend upon his own *free will*, as you have in this sermon, you will compose a hymn in praise of sovereign, distinguishing love; you will caution believers against striving to work a perfection out of their own hearts, and will print another sermon the reverse of this, and entitle it "Free Grace *Indeed*"—free because not free to all; but free, because God may withold or give it to whom and when he pleases.[20]

Whitefield had missed Wesley's distinctive position. Wesley was able to hold the doctrines of total depravity and salvation by grace with a doctrine of God's unlimited offer of salvation to all because of his doctrine of prevenient grace. By this grace God enables the deaf to hear, the blind to see, the paralyzed to walk. By the hearing and seeing made possible by prevenient grace, man is given the freedom to accept or reject the redeeming grace which enables him to walk in the way of salvation. He can submit to the Spirit or resist the Spirit.

The knowledge that this grace is free for all and sufficient for all allows the call to "go preach" to take on its full wonder and our response to God's offered grace to take on its full awe. Here we see the distinctive way in which Wesley combines what Gordon Rupp calls a "pessimism of nature" with an "optimism of grace," [21] and we shall see how this theme runs its ascending curve through Wesley's theology into his doctrine of perfection and on to the final fulfillment in glory. The basis for it is laid here in the juxtaposition of the doctrine of prevenient grace with the doctrine of original sin. In the very midst of his tract on Original Sin, when answering how it is possible at the one time to speak of God's unlimited love and of all men being condemned because of original sin, he replies:

This is noways inconsistent with either the justice or goodness of God, provided all may recover through the Second Adam, whatever they lost through the first; nay, and recover with unspeakable gain.[22]

[20] Tyerman, *Life and Times, op. cit.,* I, 324.
[21] G. Rupp, *Principalities and Powers* (London: Epworth Press, 1952), pp. 77 ff. Used by permission.
[22] *Works,* IX, 332.

Carter is right in saying that "of supreme importance, therefore is the fact that Wesley's doctrine of sin was never presented in isolation; always the love of God in Christ stood over against the sin of man." [23] First, through Christ all that has been lost through the Fall can be regained.

Here is a remedy for all our disease, all the corruption of our nature. For God hath also, through the intercession of his Son, given us his holy Spirit, to renew us both "in knowledge," in his natural image;—opening the eyes of our understanding, and enlightening us with all such knowledge as is requisite to our pleasing God;—and also in his moral image, namely, "righteousness and true holiness." [24]

But not only can that which is lost through the Fall be regained, there is even great gain through the Fall.

Where then is the man that presumes to blame God for not preventing Adam's sin. Should we not rather bless him from the ground of the heart, for therein laying the grand scheme of man's redemption, and making way for that glorious manifestation of his wisdom, justice, and mercy . . . by bestowing on all who would receive it an infinitely greater happiness than they could possibly have attained if Adam had not fallen. [25]

Is This Doctrine of Original Sin Relevant Today?

Accepting the fact that we can no longer interpret the Adam story in a literal fashion by speaking with Wesley of a historical state of "original righteousness" and of a Fall by our progenitor which brought the whole race into the inheritance of a diseased nature, the question arises as to whether this historic doctrine still has relevance.

This is not the place to launch into a discussion of the various modern attempts to reinterpret the meaning of our separation from God. All that can be done is to register the conviction that the existential account Wesley gives of the natural man is con-

---

[23] H. Carter, The Methodist Heritage (Nashville, New York: Abingdon-Cokesbury Press, 1951), p. 167.
[24] Works, VI, 223.
[25] Ibid., 240. The whole sermon "God's Love to Fallen Man," with his listing of the benefits that are ours as a result of the Fall, if we accept in faith the remedy for our disease, is deeply reminiscent of Irenaeus.

sistent with a reinterpretation of the Adam story as a myth so that

1. original righteousness is a picture of the destiny for which we are intended rather than the historical state from which we fell.

2. the flaming sword is the symbol of the mystery of our personal and social inheritance, so that we are forced to speak of man being "born in sin" and of "sin as inevitable"; and yet,

3. in the light of prevenient grace we can speak of every man being his own Adam, so that we become aware of our separation from God as incurring guilt, because of the possibility of the repair of that relationship constantly offered by God.

We must take care not to underplay the second point by stressing the truth that every man is his own Adam to the point where the fallenness of the race for which the symbol of the First Adam stands is lost. It is only in the light of God's offer of a restored relationship (through prevenient grace) that every man becomes his own Adam.

Further, the symbol of Adam describes not just an event which occurs to us, say at the first dawning of infant responsibility. It is the symbol of a continuing moment-by-moment relationship to the God who in his grace constantly is approaching us and seeking to draw us back to himself. We live "in Adam" until by faith we allow ourselves to be lifted out of our fallen state by the "Second Adam."

This is the existential picture of our human plight with which Wesley presents us, so that its restatement in terms of modern Biblical understanding leaves his essential position untouched.

5 THE ORDER OF SALVATION: REPENTANCE AND JUSTIFICATION

⏺ The work of salvation, we have seen, begins with the operation of prevenient grace. In his 1739 sermon on "The Spirit of Bondage and Adoption," in terms often strikingly similar to Kierkegaard's description of the three stages—aesthetic, ethical, and religious [1]—Wesley describes man in three situations: "first, the state of a 'natural man;' secondly, that of one who is 'under the law;' and, thirdly, of one who is 'under grace.' " [2]

The *natural man* is a man not yet aware of the working of God's grace within him. He is in what

the Scripture represents as a state of sleep . . . , utterly ignorant of God, knowing nothing concerning Him as he ought to know. . . Because he is fast asleep, he is, in some sense, at rest. Because he is blind, he is also secure. . . . He sees not that he stands on the edge of the pit; therefore he *fears* it not. . . .

From the same ignorance of himself and God, there may sometimes arise, in the natural man, a kind of *joy*, in congratulating himself upon his own wisdom and goodness; and what the world calls joy he may often possess. He may have pleasure in various kinds; either in gratifying the desires of the flesh, or the desire of the eye, or the pride of life; particularly if he has large possessions. . . .

It is not surprising, if one in such circumstances as these, dosed

---

[1] See S. Kierkegaard, *Stages on Life's Way* (Princeton: Princeton University Press, 1940).
[2] *Sermons*, I, 181.

57

with the opiates of flattery and sin, should imagine, among his other waking dreams, that he walks in great *liberty*. . . .

For all this time he is a servant of sin. He commits sin, more or less, day by day. Yet he is not troubled: he "is in no bondage," as some speak; he feels no condemnation. . . .

Such is the state of every *natural man*; whether he be a gross, scandalous transgressor, or a more reputable and decent sinner, having the form, though not the power, of godliness.[3]

But God does not leave man in this natural state. By the working of his prevenient grace in the conscience, he seeks to bring him under the judgment of the law so that he may become aware of his fallen condition. For this reason the preaching of the law is the normal means God has ordained for the awakening of the sinner. It is a mistake, Wesley asserts, to imagine that we should normally begin with

preaching the gospel, . . . speaking of nothing but the sufferings and merits of Christ. . . . It does not answer the very first end of the law, namely, the convincing men of sin; the awakening those who are still asleep on the brink of hell. There may have been here and there an exempt case. One in a thousand may have been awakened by the gospel: but . . . the ordinary method of God is, to convict sinners by the law, and that only. The gospel is not the means which God hath ordained, or which our Lord Himself used, for this end. . . . "They that be whole," as our Lord Himself observes, "need not a physician, but they that are sick." It is absurd, therefore, to offer a physician to them that are whole, or that at least imagine themselves so to be. You are first to convince them that they are sick; otherwise they will not thank you for your labour. It is equally absurd to offer Christ to them whose heart is whole, having never yet been broken.[4]

It is necessary to remember, however, that Wesley in obeying his injunction, took great care to weave the law and the gospel together so that as its first work in convincing of sin was accomplished, the law could lead on to its second work as the schoolmaster "to bring him unto life, unto Christ, that he may live."[5]

---

[3] *Ibid.*, 181-85.
[4] *Sermons*, II, 61. See also *Notes*, 791, on II Tim. 2:15.
[5] *Ibid.*, 53. Notice in his thirteen discourses on the Sermon on the Mount in his Standard Sermons, the wonderful way in which law and gospel are woven together.

First, however, God by his prevenient grace brings man to a recognition of his fallen state, and so to repentance. In line with his emphasis on man's complete dependence on the continuing work of grace, Wesley stresses that the bringing of sinners to repentance is solely the work of the Holy Spirit.

The first use of it [the law], without question, is, to convince the world of sin. This is, indeed the peculiar work of the Holy Ghost; who can work it without any means at all, or by whatever means it pleaseth Him. . . . But it is the ordinary method of the Spirit of God to convict sinners by the law. . . . By this is the sinner discovered to himself. All his fig-leaves are torn away, and he sees that he is "wretched, and poor, and miserable, and blind, and naked." The law flashes conviction on every side. He feels himself a mere sinner. He has nothing to pay. His "mouth is stopped," and he stands "guilty before God." [6]

Here we reach the first positive step on the road to salvation —repentance, the porch of religion, leading to the door (justification) through which the house of religion (sanctification) is entered.[7] Repentance, or conviction of sin, Wesley describes as always previous to faith,[8] and it is in his description of this repentance and its fruits, as normally a necessary condition of faith, that Wesley shows a distinct variation from the other main Reformers, Luther and Calvin, and provides us with one of the most difficult problems of his theology.

Lindstrom is right in saying that after 1738 repentance and its fruits are steadily given increased attention and are more and more stressed as a necessary precondition of faith.[9] Article XIII of the XXXIX Articles, "Of Good Works Before Justification," with its statement that all works before justification are evil in the sight of God, increasingly left Wesley dissatisfied, and finally in 1784, when preparing a revised edition of the Articles for America, he omitted it entirely.[10]

[6] Simon, John Wesley, the Master Builder, 294-97.
[7] Letters, II, 268.
[8] Ibid.
[9] H. Lindstrom, Wesley and Sanctification (London: Epworth Press), pp. 93-94.
[10] John S. Simon, John Wesley and the Methodist Societies (London: Epworth Press, 1923), p. 259.

In the Minutes of 1745 in speaking of works before justification the question is asked:

Q. 7. Have we duly considered the case of Cornelius? Was not he in the favour of God, when "his prayers and alms came up for a memorial before God;" that is, before he believed in Christ?
A. It does seem that he was, in some degree. But we speak not of those who have not heard the gospel.
Q. 8. But were those works of his "splendid sins?"
A. No; nor were they done without the grace of Christ.[11]

Here we see that the reason for Wesley's dissatisfaction with the traditional Protestant statement of man's condition before justification lies in his emphasis upon Christ working by prevenient grace in the life even of those who have not heard the gospel. It should be noticed, too, that the test of whether such works done before justification are good is not the test of objective moral standards, but the test of inward response to the prevenient grace of God. This is clear from the question that immediately follows.[12]

Q. 9. How then can we maintain, that all works done before we have a sense of the pardoning love of God are sin, and, as such, an abomination to Him?
A. The works of him who has heard the gospel, and does not believe, are not done as God hath "willed and commanded them to be done." And yet we know not how to say that they are an abomination to the Lord in him who feareth God, and, from that principle, does the best he can.[13]

Because of his emphasis on the way God works in the natural man to produce a "bad conscience" and a desire to please him, increasingly Wesley began to stress repentance and works meet for repentance as the precondition of justifying faith. He believed that the way in which justification by faith alone was being interpreted was encouraging people to underestimate the importance of responding to God's grace through a sincere sor-

[11] Works, VIII, 283. See also Notes, 432 on Acts 10:4.
[12] Notice that the reason those who respond to prevenient grace can be accepted by God is that this grace carries with it the virtue of the Atonement. Works, VIII, 277-78.
[13] Ibid., 283.

row for sin and a desire for amendment and so was resulting in antinomianism. Just as constantly Wesley sought to prevent any Pelagian interpretation of his emphasis by stressing that this repentance and its fruits are a work of God's intervening grace, and that man is judged not on the moral basis of performance but on the religious basis of inward response to God. But the struggle against antinomianism led to severe tension in his teaching, which becomes clear in his 1765 sermon on "The Scripture Way of Salvation."

God does undoubtedly command us both to repent, and to bring forth fruits meet for repentance; which if we willingly neglect, we cannot reasonably expect to be justified at all: therefore both repentance, and fruits meet for repentance, are, in some sense, necessary to justification. But they are not necessary in the *same sense* with faith, nor in the *same degree*. Not in the *same degree*; for those fruits are only necessary *conditionally*; if there be time and opportunity for them. Otherwise a man may be justified without them, as was the *thief* upon the cross . . . ; but he cannot be justified without faith; this is impossible. . . . Repentance and its fruits are only *remotely* necessary; necessary in order to faith; whereas faith is *immediately* and *directly* necessary to justification.[14]

The Problem of 1770

The final distinction reveals a real tension in his doctrine of justification by faith alone. Five years later the tension seems to reach a breaking point, for the bombshell of the "1770 Minutes" seems to throw us right back into the realm of justification by faith and works. These Minutes are of such crucial importance that I must quote the relevant section in full.

We said in 1744, "We have leaned too much toward Calvinism." Wherein?

(1.) With regard to man's faithfulness. Our Lord himself taught us to use the expression: therefore we ought never to be ashamed of it. We ought steadily to assert upon his authority, that if man is not "faithful in the unrighteous mammon, God will not give him the true riches."

(2.) With regard to "working for life," which our Lord expressly

[14] *Sermons*, II, 451-52.

commands us to do. "Labour," ἐργάζεσθε, literally "Work, for the meat that endureth to everlasting life." And in fact, every believer, till he comes to glory, works for as well as from life.

(3.) We have received it as a maxim, that "a man is to do nothing in order to justification." Nothing can be more false. Whoever desires to find favour with God, should "cease from evil, and learn to do well." Whoever repents, should "do works meet for repentance." And if this is not in order to find favour, what does he do them for? Once more review the whole affair: (1.) Who of us is now accepted of God? He that now believes in Christ with a loving, obedient heart. (2.) But who among those that never heard of Christ? He that, according to the light he has, "feareth God and worketh righteousness."

(3.) Is this the same with "he that is sincere?" Nearly, if not quite.

(4.) Is not this salvation by works? Not by merit of works, but by works as a condition.

(5.) What have we been disputing about for these thirty years? I am afraid about words. . . .

(6.) As to merit itself, of which we have been so dreadfully afraid. We are rewarded according to our works, yea because of our works. How does this differ from, "for the sake of our works?" And how differs this from secundum merita operum? which is no more than, "as our works deserve." Can you split this hair? I doubt I cannot.

(7.) The grand objection to one of the preceding propositions is drawn from matter of fact. God does in fact justify those, who, by their own confession, neither "feared God" nor "wrought righteousness." Is this an exception to the general rule?

It is a doubt whether God makes any exception at all. But how are we sure that the person in question never did fear God and work righteousness? His own thinking so is no proof. For we know how all that are convinced of sin undervalue themselves in every respect.

(8.) Does not talking . . . of a justified or sanctified state, tend to mislead men; almost naturally leading them to trust what was done in one moment? Whereas we are every moment pleasing or displeasing to God, according to our works; according to the whole of our present inward tempers and outward behaviour.[15]

These Minutes threw the Calvinists of the Countess of Huntingdon's connection into a fury, for they immediately interpreted them as a reversion to papal doctrine and an abandonment of

[15] Works, VIII, 337-38.

the Reformation article of justification by faith alone.[16] That they have not been alone in interpreting them in this way is revealed by the fact that Roman Catholic writers have welcomed the Minutes as a rejection of the solafidean character of Protestantism. Father Burridge, for example, in his tract on Methodism, makes a great point of the "Catholic" tendencies in Wesley and claims that the "leaven of frankly Papist doctrine steadily purged out the antinomianism of Wesley's societies, yet was not fully operative till put into the vigorous and concrete form of the Minutes of 1770." [17]

That Wesley himself rejected any such interpretation of them is seen from the sermon he preached on Whitefield's death a few months later[18] and from the declaration of the following Conference of 1771.[19]

Whereas the doctrinal points in the Minutes of a Conference, held in London, August 7, 1770, have been understood to favour Justification by Works: now the Rev. John Wesley, and others assembled in Conference, do declare, that we have had no such meaning; and that we abhor the doctrine of Justification by Works as a most perilous and abominable doctrine; and as the said Minutes are not sufficiently guarded in the way they are expressed, we hereby solemnly declare, in the sight of God, that we have no trust or confidence but in the alone merits of our Lord and Saviour Jesus Christ, for Justification or Salvation either in life, death or the day of judgment; and though no one is a real Christian believer, (and consequently cannot be saved) who doth not good works, where there is time and opportunity, yet our works have no part in meriting, or purchasing our salvation from first to last, either in whole or in part. [20]

[16] Simon, John Wesley, the Master Builder, 294-57.
[17] Rev. A. Burridge S. J., Methodism, Catholic Truth Society, London, p. 12. Lee, in his John Wesley and Modern Religion, op. cit., pp. 161-73, claims that Wesley gradually repudiated the Reformers' "by faith alone" in favor of "by faith with conditions." As we shall see, this is a misunderstanding, for repentance is a form of faith and its fruits are works of grace.
[18] Sermons, II, 522 ff. (Sermons, LIII, III, 2-5).
[19] Tyerman, Life and Times, III, C, and facsimile in Journal, V, 427.
[20] It was generally accepted that Wesley had expressed himself badly in the 1770 Minutes. So, for example, Fletcher in a letter to Wesley speaks of his attempt to heal the breach that they occasioned with Lady Huntingdon. "I wrote among the rest, and showed the absurdity of inferring from these Minutes that you had renounced the Protestant doctrine and the Atonement. I defended

We cannot dismiss this whole matter, however, as a simple misunderstanding due to poor wording. We must note first that a good deal of the conflict disappears when we see that Wesley gives a narrower definition to justification than do Luther and Calvin. The latter include two movements in justifying faith: (1) repentance (2) trust in Christ. Wesley limits it to the latter moment of conscious acceptance of Christ, accompanied by a sense of forgiveness. In the terms of the earlier Reformers, then, repentance works are not works done *before* faith but works of faith.

That Wesley also recognized that repentance is "a species of faith" prior to justification, is shown by his 1744 Minutes. There he affirmed that repentance

and works meet for repentance, go before this faith. Without doubt; if by repentance you mean conviction of sin; and by works meet for repentance, obeying God as far as we can, forgiving our brother, leaving off from evil, doing good, and using his ordinances, according to the power we have received.[21]

After describing faith "in general" and pointing out that repentance is "a low species of faith," the Conference expressed the conviction that "justifying faith is a supernatural sense or sight of God in Christ reconciling the world unto himself."

The problem connected with the separation of these two moments of faith, and the limitation of justifying faith to the second moment of conscious acceptance of the grace of Christ bringing with it a sense of forgiveness, is illustrated in Wesley's own life. Wesley declared in his Journal that prior to May 24, 1738, he had not been a Christian. He was not denying that prior to that date there had been real evidence of the work of

---

your sentiments, by explaining them, as I have heard you do, and only blamed the unguarded and not sufficiently explicit manner in which they were worded." Simon, *John Wesley, the Master Builder*, p. 288. But that both Wesley and Fletcher believed that there were important issues at stake in the 1770 Minutes and that a danger in the Protestant doctrine, as interpreted by the Calvinists of the day, had to be guarded against, is clearly indicated by the fact that Fletcher's "Vindication" of the 1770 Minutes was published by Wesley immediately following the 1771 Conference, and that by 1775 this had grown into Fletcher's famous Five Checks to Antinomianism.

[21] *Works*, VIII, 275-76.

God's grace in his life, and on his part a real desire to do God's will. But in terms of his own limitation of justification to the second moment of conscious reliance upon Christ accompanied by a sense of forgiveness, he concluded that prior to Aldersgate St. he was not a Christian.

It is noticeable, however, that years later, he added to this declaration that he had not been a Christian until then, the footnote: "I am not sure of this." [22] He had come to see that while, previous to 1738, he had received the "faith of a servant," he had not received the "faith of a son." [23] In this distinction Wesley provides us with the solution to the difficulty. Justification has two movements: (1) Preliminary faith, which includes the free response to God's prevenient grace and a desire to please him but is still only the "faith of a servant." (2) Justifying faith proper, which is a sure trust and confidence in Christ bringing a conviction of forgiveness, this being "the faith of a son." Such a distinction is valuable, drawing attention to the way the law is used to prepare the way for the gospel and pointing up the truth that God is seeking to lead us to an assurance of our forgiveness and of our adoption as sons.

Second, we are now in a position to see that Wesley's stress on works is far from a capitulation to the Roman Catholic view that "faith is formed by love" and that the believer must make such good use of the grace given to him as to be able to merit his justification. Rather we have here:

(1) Repentance faith—the faith of a servant, before justification, in which God works in the heart producing a sense of sin and need. Here man is not a purely passive agent, waiting for the revivifying power of justifying faith. God, through his prevenient grace produces in him a desire to amend his ways and turn to him (God). Where there is opportunity then, the works meet for repentance will precede justifying faith. Sometimes, as in the case of the thief on the cross, there is no opportunity, but normally God leads man to turn to him for further grace through waiting actively on him in obedience to his ordinances.

[22] Journal, I, 423.
[23] Ibid. And see Works, VII, 199 in the sermon "On Faith" for his working out of this distinction.

These works, therefore, the fruit of this repentance faith, are *remotely* necessary to justification; that is, God demands the free response of repentance faith as the condition of his continuing work in us. But there is no question here of reaching desired standards; it is only a question of responding to God as a sign of our readiness to receive his further gifts.

(2) *Justifying faith*—the faith of a son. Our readiness for justification is not measured by our repentance works but by our readiness to allow Christ to work within us. It requires in fact, an awareness that we are saved by faith alone, not by these works, before we can receive the faith that justifies. As Wesley put it in "An Earnest Appeal to Men of Reason and Religion,"

[Faith] "is the gift of God." No man is able to work it in himself. It is a work of omnipotence. It requires no less power thus to quicken a dead soul, than to raise a body that lies in the grave. It is a new creation. . . .

It is the free gift of God, which he bestows, not on those who are worthy of his favour, not on such as are previously holy, and so fit to be crowned with all the blessings of his goodness; but on the ungodly and unholy; on those who till that hour were fit only for everlasting destruction; those in whom there was no good thing, and whose only plea was, "God be merciful to me, a sinner!" No merit, no goodness in man precedes the forgiving love of God. His pardoning mercy supposes nothing in us but a sense of mere sin and misery; and to all who see, and feel, and own their wants, and their utter inability to remove them, God freely gives faith, for the sake of Him in whom he is always "well pleased." [24]

His increasing emphasis on fruits meet for repentance did nothing to alter his doctrine of justification by faith alone, for these works are the fruit of repentance faith and the gift of God's grace, and far from making us fit in any moral sense to receive justifying faith, they are simply the sign of our readiness to allow God to continue his work within us.

Transformation Without Merit

In line with his insistence that faith necessarily involves a readiness to allow God to work within since it is a personal reli-

[24] *Works*, VIII, 5-6.

ance upon Christ as over against "a bare assent," Wesley stresses the fact that transformation of the believer must necessarily follow.

Only beware thou do not deceive thy own soul, with regard to the nature of this faith. It is not, as some have fondly conceived, a bare assent to the truth of the Bible, of the articles of our Creed, or of all that is contained in the Old and New Testament. The devils believe this, as well as I or thou! And yet they are devils still. But it is, over and above this, a sure trust in the mercy of God, through Christ Jesus. It is a confidence in a pardoning God. It is a divine evidence or conviction that "God was in Christ, reconciling the world to Himself, not imputing to them their" former "trespasses"; and in particular, that the Son of God hath loved me, and given Himself for me; and that I, even I, am now reconciled to God by the blood of the cross.[25]

It is in the context of this insistence that faith is a personal reliance upon Christ and involves the opening of our lives to his work within us that we must see Wesley's reconciliation of the views of Paul and James on justification. In the Minutes of the 1744 Conference Wesley wrote:

Q. 14. St. Paul says, Abraham was not justified by works; St. James, he was justified by works. Do they not contradict each other?
A. No.: (1) Because they do not speak of the same justification. St. Paul speaks of that justification which was when Abraham was seventy-five years old, above twenty years before Isaac was born; St. James, of that justification which was when he offered up Isaac on the altar. (2) Because they do not speak of the same works; St. Paul speaking of works that precede faith; St. James, of works that spring from it.[26]

Hildebrandt wonders whether Wesley, by this explanation, would qualify to receive the doctor's beret which Luther offered to any who could harmonize these statements of Paul and James.[27] In this simple form it can hardly be said that he does. It may seem, in fact, that Wesley is crossing over to the Roman Catholic view that there are two justifications—the first, by faith

[25] Sermons, I, 159-60.
[26] Works, VIII, 277.
[27] Hildebrandt, Christianity According to the Wesleys, op. cit., p. 40.

67

alone, but the second and final justification coming only when this faith is formed by love in such a way that at last, by the proper use of God's grace, the believer is able to merit his salvation by the works that follow faith. But Luther's point is that we must not speak of faith formed by love. We are justified by faith alone. It is true that faith forms love—that out of our faith relationship to Christ works of love flow, but it is not these works that bring us final justification. In fact, judged by the rigors of the law, we still would fall. At the end, as now, we are justified by faith alone.

How close Wesley came to the Roman Catholic view is seen in the fact that he did have a doctrine of "double justification." In his sermon, "On The Wedding Garment," [28] he speaks of sanctification being a condition of the *final* (not the present) justification. This is in line with his interpretation of the text, "Without holiness no man shall see the Lord." Yet he is careful to avoid turning this holiness into a moral achievement requiring purgatory for the completion of the process by which final justification is merited. Holiness comes not by achievement, but through the door of faith in accordance with our readiness to receive the promises. This holiness can be given at any time after justification, but in most it is given at the moment before death.[29] In this way Wesley makes it quite clear that holiness is a gift, not an achievement. Lindstrom is right in saying that "sanctity is regarded as a condition of final salvation, but not as a merit on the strength of which final salvation or justification is accorded to man." [30]

The works, therefore, of which Wesley speaks are the fruits of living faith, for faith is a personal relationship to the living Christ, and where Christ is, transformation must follow. This does not put us back into a legal relationship whereby we are required to reach the full level of moral transformation, as the condition of final justification. If we continue to live in this relationship of justification (and this is a moment-by-moment relationship, not a once-for-all event which then makes us

---

[28] Works, VII, 316.
[29] This question is given full treatment in Chapter X on Perfection.
[30] Lindstrom, *op. cit.*, p. 210.

independent of Christ [31]), Christ will give us this holiness. Some transformation *must* take place in believers.[32] for the very reason that belief is personal relationship to Christ. But if we continue in faith in Christ, even though our faith remains imperfect, Christ will give us that holiness, which is the condition of final justification, "a moment before death."

Third, Wesley, while staying entirely within the Protestant scheme of salvation by faith through grace alone, recognized that the real danger of this doctrine is what Bonhoeffer called "cheap grace." [33] We will not enter here into the question of whether Wesley was right in seeing antinomian tendencies in Luther. I believe that this is not what Luther intended,[34] but that he was often taken in this way is clear.[35] Moreover the Calvinists as well as the Moravians of Wesley's day certainly revealed these tendencies. For this reason it was vital that Wesley should stress the fact that faith requires the opening of the believer's life to the work of God. His separation of repentance faith from justifying faith drew clear attention to this, and his emphasis that justification is not a state, but a moment by moment relationship which therefore has a *terminus ad quem* as well as a *terminus a quo* with the process of sanctification coming between, kept attention upon it. In this spelling out of the *necessary* response which attends the faith evoked by grace, Wesley gave an important refinement of justification by faith.

Simul Justus et Peccator

In summary, we can say that the time when the life of justification begins is usually confined by Wesley to the moment in

---

[31] *Sermons*, II, 389, where Wesley insists that grace is not "given all at once; . . . but from moment to moment."

[32] *Sermons*, II, 66. "We are justified without the works of the law, as any previous condition of justification; but they are an immediate fruit of that faith whereby we are justified. So that if good works do not follow our faith, even all inward and outward holiness, it is plain our faith is nothing worth." Wesley flatly rejects the Roman Catholic view of double justification because it confounds sanctification with justification, teaches justification by works, and keeps men in the order of merit. *Letters*, II, 118; *Letters*, V, 270.

[33] D. Bonhoeffer, *The Cost of Discipleship* (New York: Macmillan, 1951), p. 1.

[34] Hildebrandt, *From Luther to Wesley*, op. cit., 14, 76.

[35] And see Kierkegaard's many references to Luther in his *Journal*, giving strong expression to the same danger.

JOHN WESLEY'S THEOLOGY TODAY

which we receive a sense of forgiveness and pardon. The 1744 Minutes related repentance to justification in this way:

Q. 1. What is it to be justified?
A. To be pardoned and received into God's favour; into such a state, that, if we continue therein, we shall finally be saved.
Q. 2. Is faith the condition of justification?
A. Yes; for everyone who believeth not is condemned; and everyone who believes is justified.
Q. 3. But must not repentance, and works meet for repentance, go before this faith?
A. Without doubt; if by repentance you mean conviction of sin; and by works meet for repentance, obeying God as far as we can, forgiving our brother, leaving off from evil, doing good, and using his ordinances, according to the power we have received.[36]

Response to the work of prevenient grace in our lives (repentance faith) normally precedes justifying faith, because Christ is already at work within us, bringing us to an awareness of our separation from him and producing in us a desire to please him. But this is in no sense an earning of our justification, for justification is simply forgiveness.

Least of all does justification imply, that God is deceived in those whom He justifies; that He thinks them to be what, in fact, they are not. . . . The plain scriptural notion of justification is pardon, the forgiveness of sins. . . . Who are they that are justified? . . . The ungodly. . . . It is only sinners that have any any occasion for pardon: it is sin alone which admits of being forgiven. . . . But on what terms, then, is he justified, who is altogether ungodly, and till that time worketh not? On one alone, which is faith. . . . Justifying faith implies, not only a divine evidence or conviction that "God was in Christ, reconciling the world unto Himself," but a sure trust and confidence that Christ died for my sins, that He loved me, and gave Himself for me.[37]

God in justifying us removes us completely from the order of merit, and this is made even clearer by the care with which Wesley uses the historic word "imputation." The Scripture speaks

[36] Works, VIII, 275-76.
[37] Sermons, I, 120-25.

of our sins not being imputed against us,[38] but it does not speak of "imputed righteousness."

I firmly believe "we are accounted righteous before God, justified only for the merit of Christ." But let us have no shifting the terms. "Only through Christ's imputed righteousness" are not the words of the Article, neither the language of our Church.[39]

Do not dispute for that particular phrase "the imputed righteousness of Christ." It is not scriptural; it is not necessary. . . . It has done immense hurt. I have had abundant proof that the frequent use of this unnecessary phrase, instead of "furthering men's progress in vital holiness," has made them satisfied without any holiness at all.[40]

In justification we are forgiven, but we are even more aware of how far we fall short of the righteousness of Christ whom we have accepted as Lord. Consequently our response is to open our lives to his transforming work. If this does not occur, we have fallen into the error of "cheap grace." For while justification is the ground of our salvation and faith the only basis for our acceptance by God, faith opens the door for the continuing work of God within us. Justification leads to sanctification. Justification

is not the being made actually just and righteous. This is sanctification; which is, indeed, in some degree, the immediate fruit of justification, but, nevertheless, is a distinct gift of God, and of a totally different nature. The one implies, what God does for us through His Son; the other, what He works in us by His Spirit. So that, although some rare instances may be found, wherein the term justified or justification is used in so wide a sense as to include sanctification also; yet, in general use, they are sufficiently distinguished from each other, both by St. Paul and the other inspired writers.[41]

Justification is the real basis and beginning of the Christian life. It is an "objective" work in the sense that it arises not from a change in us but from a word cf God to us—"Son, thy sins be forgiven thee." But when the word is heard, something happens in us. For faith is the opening of the life to Christ. It

[38] Ibid., 121.
[39] Letters, III, 249.
[40] Ibid., 372.
[41] Sermons, I, 119.

is new birth. Then sanctification follows because of Christ's presence.

Ecumenical Significance

Wesley preserves the Reformation protest against seeing salvation within the legal order of merit and adding works to faith as a means by which man can rise to the required standard in order to be pronounced just. He insists that we are justified on the sole basis of our faith relation to Christ and that this relation is a gift of God's grace.

Nevertheless he gives the dynamic of the God-man relation its full scope by cutting away the deterministic framework of the logical doctrine of predestination and by showing that at all stages God works within us by his grace to enable us to make a free response to his transforming presence. In this way he provides for a possible resolution of the Catholic suspicion that the doctrine of justification by faith alone leads to antinomianism and to a lack of concern for present ethical and social transformation.

Reference is often made to Wesley's "synergism." [42] This is valid only when it is seen that this is not a semi-Pelagian synergism. There the downward movement of God's grace meets the upward movement of man's natural will so that man is seen as a co-operator in the work of salvation, with his natural ability being so strengthened by grace that he is enabled to rise to the moral level required for salvation. Wesley's view of original sin with his insistence that God's grace must give even the capacity to respond cuts away the first assumption concerning the natural upward movement of man's will. His view that salvation is kept within the realm of religious relationship and is not a matter of moral achievement, but of personal dependence on Christ, removes the second assumption—that man must achieve a required moral level in order to be saved.

His view is synergistic, however, in the sense that God *creates* in man the freedom to receive or resist his grace. Man is *given* responsibility by God's grace. This recognition that man is given

[42] The term means literally "working with."

by grace, freedom to receive or resist the gospel, would seem to have a double significance:

(1) It provides the way for reconciling the Classical Protestant tradition of justification by faith through grace alone, with the well-nigh universal abandonment of the logical framework of double predestination.

(2) It enables an adequate answer to be given to the strong suspicion, particularly among those of the catholic and liberal traditions, that the Classical Protestant view leads to a certain quietism and to a lack of concern for present personal and social transformation.

There is a further suspicion that this latter view has so far dominated ecumenical discussions and was reflected in the Main Theme document for the Evanston Assembly.[43] It may well be that in Wesley's emphasis on the fact that God gives us the freedom to respond to his grace, and in his "optimism of grace", we are given the theological basis for a greater emphasis on transformation, without running into the danger of collapsing the Christian hope into a moralistic concern for human achievement.

Wesley saw clearly that hope is firmly tied to justification and does not have to wait for sanctification. Our hope is in Jesus Christ, not in the transformation of the world or even of ourselves. Consequently our hope is not destroyed by the failure of the kingdom of God to become visible or even by our own failure to make visible progress to the goal of Christlikeness. Nevertheless, Wesley laid great stress on the fact that because our faith relation is with Christ, we live under the promise of present transformation and are able to move forward in creative, ethical endeavor because Christ continually offers his transforming presence to believers, and, through the Church, to the world.

---

[43] See *Evanston Report*, op. cit., 70, for the Assembly's claim that the note of present expectation needs more stress.

6 THE ATONEMENT

ɔ   Albert Outler has listed as one of the "salient theological motifs" of the Methodist heritage

A complex doctrine of Atonement, which emphasizes the Total Event of Jesus Christ as the atoning "act" by which the power of evil is broken and men are reconciled to God. Methodism has embraced both the patristic notions of *lutron* (what Aulen calls "the dramatic theory of the atonement") and the Abelardian notion of Jesus Christ as the exemplar of God's sacrificial love.[1]

Certainly the Atonement is of very great importance for Wesley. It is the source of the divine grace by which man is rescued from the trammels of sin and reconciled to God. In the created order man is under divine condemnation unless he can stand before God as "righteous," but this no man can do for all share the inheritance of original sin. In fact "the not having our own righteousness [is] (the very first point in the religion of Jesus Christ) leaving all pagan religion behind." [2] But God has provided the grace by which we can be restored to his favor through the death of Christ upon the Cross. Even prevenient grace is a benefit deriving from the Atonement, and this grace reaches out beyond those who have a knowledge of Christ's work, to all the children of men.

Wesley quotes the Quaker Barclay with approval on the fol-

---

[1] Albert Outler in an unpublished paper, *The Methodist Contribution to the Ecumenical Discussion of the Church.*

[2] *Sermons*, I, 326.

lowing three points: (1) that all mankind by nature is separated from God and evil in his sight, (2) that God gave his Son to die for every man and that Christ enlightens every man that cometh into the world, and (3) that this benefit of Christ's death extends even to those who are excluded from the direct knowledge of Christ.[3]

It is, however, only through the direct knowledge of the grace available to us in Christ's death, that we can come to justifying faith.

The gospel (that is, good tidings, good news for guilty, helpless sinners), . . . means the whole revelation made to men by Jesus Christ. . . . The substance of all is, "Jesus Christ came into the world to save sinners"; or, "God so loved the world, that He gave His only-begotten Son, to the end we might not perish, but have everlasting life"; or, "He was bruised for our transgressions, He was wounded for our iniquities, the chastisement of our peace was upon Him; and with His stripes we are healed."

Believe this, and the kingdom of God is thine.[4]

Cell is right when he calls the Atonement the "burning focus of faith" for Wesley.[5] For just as Wesley places great stress on the doctrine of original sin in order to make it clear that it is only by God's grace that man can be saved, so he also places his central emphasis on the Atonement to make it clear that it is only at great cost that God has provided the grace by which we can be forgiven. It is because man can do nothing to overcome

---

[3] *Letters*, II, 117-18. "All mankind is fallen and dead, deprived of the sensation of this inward testimony of God, and subject to the power and nature of the devil, while they abide in their natural state. And hence not only their words and deeds, but all their imaginations, are evil perpetually in the sight of God.

"God out of His infinite love hath so loved the world that He gave His only Son, to the end that whosoever believeth in Him might have everlasting life. And He enlighteneth every man that cometh into the world, as He tasteth death for every man.

"The benefit of the death of Christ is not only extended to such as have the distinct knowledge of His death and sufferings, but even unto those who are inevitably excluded from this knowledge. Even these may be partakers of the benefit of His death, though ignorant of the history, if they suffer His grace to take place in their hearts, so as of wicked men to become holy.

"In these points there is no difference between Quakerism and Christianity."

[4] *Sermons*, I, 159.

[5] G. C. Cell, *The Rediscovery of Wesley* (New York: Henry Holt and Co., 1935), p. 297.

his sin and win reconciliation to God that God himself has provided the way of reconciliation by the death of his Son. The Christian is convinced that

the use of all means whatever will never atone for one sin; that it is the blood of Christ alone, whereby any sinner can be reconciled to God; there being no other propitiation for our sins, no other fountain for sin and uncleanness. Every believer in Christ is deeply convinced that there is no merit but in Him.[6]

It is this conviction that stands behind Wesley's claim that

Indeed, nothing in the Christian system is of greater consequence than the doctrine of the Atonement. It is properly the distinguishing point between Deism and Christianity.[7]

Wesley laid no claim to being able to explain how Christ's death is the source of our reconciliation with God.

It is true that I can no more comprehend it than his lordship Lord Huntingdon; perhaps I might say than the angels of God, than the highest created understanding. Our reason is here quickly bewildered. If we attempt to expatiate in this field, we "find no end, in wandering mazes lost." [8]

Nevertheless Wesley believed that while we cannot explain the work of Christ on the Cross, if we take careful account of the witness of the Scriptures, we can discern the benefits that flow from it.[9] It is in the sense of witnesses to the benefits of the

[6] *Sermons*, I, 243-44.
[7] *Letters*, VI, 297-98.
[8] *Ibid.*, 298. It is important to see where Wesley refused to state essential doctrine as well as where he insisted. The fact of the Atonement is essential, but it is wrong to attempt to insist on an orthodox explanation. That is beyond our capacity. It is true that we must speak of the benefits that derive from the Cross, and therefore it is right to say that the Abelardian view is inadequate. But since we are unable to "comprehend" how these benefits are secured by Christ's death, we cannot make a particular attempt to explain the mystery orthodox. "Fundamentalism" is clearly heretical at this point. It is just as serious to insist on doctrines that the Church has not defined (and should not), as it is to deny doctrines that are essential. It is important to see too (see the end of this chapter) that in the doctrines which are essential Wesley distinguishes between the fact and the "manner how." Clearly Wesley's distinctions here have great ecumenical significance.
[9] *Ibid.*, "The only question is (the only question with me; I regard nothing else), What saith the Scripture?"

Cross rather than as explanations of it that we see the value of the "theories of the Atonement."

For a convenient method of assessing the balance of Wesley's view, we will deal with it under the headings of the three typical views of the atonement that have recurred in Christian history: The Moral Influence Theory, The Penal Substitutionary Theory, and The Ransom or Classical Theory.

The Moral Influence Theory

Perhaps, in view of Wesley's emphasis on man's utter inability to raise himself towards God, we would expect little emphasis on the power of the example of Christ's life and death in drawing men into the way of God. But, in fact, we find a considerable concentration upon Christ as the pattern. No fewer than thirteen of his forty-four sermons are devoted to an exposition of the Sermon on the Mount. He is even prepared to say that the Sermon is an exposition of the way of salvation—the road the Christian must follow in order to be saved.

The Son of God, who came from heaven, is here showing us the way to heaven; to the place which He hath prepared for us; the glory He had before the world began. He is teaching us the true way to life everlasting; the royal way which leads to the kingdom; and the only true way—for there is none besides: all other paths lead to destruction. From the character of the Speaker, we are well assured that He hath declared the full and perfect will of God.[10]

Christ is the One who, in his life, teaching, and death, is the Pattern sent by the Father to guide us along the way of salvation; he is the revealer of that true holiness without which no man shall see the Lord.[11] Wesley is even prepared to say that the beatitudes are successive steps in the ladder of ascent to God, and that "real Christianity always begins in poverty of spirit, and goes on in the order here set down, till the 'man of God is made perfect.' "[12] If this is true, how does this ladder of ascent differ from the mystic way of purgation, from ascent to God by purification and growth in inward holiness?

[10] Sermons, I, 316.
[11] Ibid., 319.
[12] Ibid., 321.

Here we are helped by Wesley's controversy with Law, an expounder of the mystic way. Lindstrom gives an excellent account of the differences involved, and in these differences is revealed again the way in which Wesley combined his pessimism of nature with his optimism of grace, so that he is able to keep his emphasis on sanctification entirely within the framework of justification by faith alone.

Lindstrom shows how Law subordinated justification to sanctification in such a way that

the struggle for sanctification is also regarded as a necessary condition of justification. Salvation, that is, depends upon the sincerity and completeness of man's effort to attain it. Until he has striven to the last ounce of his strength he cannot win God's favour. . . . Christ's suffering on the cross is not regarded as a vicarious suffering for mankind. It is only a representational act in the name of mankind which has been credited to man in the sense that his union with Christ is accepted by God. Christ is a sacrifice to make the sacrifices of mankind acceptable to God.[13] For Law Christ's work of atonement does not constitute the only ground of our deliverance from guilt and the favour of God: another factor is man's own mortification. . . . The restoration of God's favour demands not only "so great an atonement of the Son of God," but also so great a "repentance of our own."[14]

Here we see a classic example of the Catholic view of double justification. Here, the initial justification of man on the basis of Christ's atonement is conditional upon man "making good" through following the way of the cross. Faith is "formed by love" and man is finally justified at last, only when he merits it by the imitation of Christ. We have already distinguished Wesley's view from this, and we now find the basis for his insistence that first and final justification are by faith alone in his view of the Atonement. Wesley, in his famous letter to Law, accuses him of totally denying "the Scripture doctrine of Justification,"

---

[13] Lindstrom has the telling quotation from Law: "To have a true idea of Christianity, we must not consider our Blessed Lord as suffering in our stead, but as our Representative, acting in our name, and with such particular merit, as to make our joining with Him acceptable to God. He suffered, and was a Sacrifice, to make our sufferings and sacrifice of ourselves fit to be received by God." *Wesley and Sanctification*, p. 57. Used by permission of Epworth Press.
[14] *Ibid.*, 57-58.

in affirming that "Salvation, which all divines agree includes both justification and sanctification, is nothing else but to be made like Christ." This, Wesley charges, requires no thought of Christ's death "as that which could only avail with God to have mercy on man." [15]

Law, for his part, insists that there is in the Cross no reconciliation of God, no propitiation of his anger, but only a pure display of his changeless love and mercy and a demonstration of the way man must follow in order to be saved. Man, with the help of God's patient love, must reach the level of the sanctified life for which he was destined before he can be saved. By the help of God's grace he must finally merit his own salvation.

Wesley objects, and on two counts:

(1) Law is wrong in saying that there is no anger or wrath in God that has to be reconciled. Wesley insisted that in the Atonement something "objective" took place, which is the only basis for the "subjective" change that can take place in us now. The satisfaction of God's wrath by Christ's death is the only basis for the pardon of our sins. We can have Christ as our Pattern only when first we have accepted him as the Reconciler.

Christianity begins just where heathen morality ends; poverty of spirit, conviction of sin, the renouncing ourselves, the not having our own righteousness (the very first point in the religion of Jesus Christ), leaving all pagan religion behind. . . . Sink under the mighty hand of God, as guilty of death eternal; and cast off, renounce, abhor, all imagination of ever being able to help thyself! Be it all thy hope to be washed in his blood, and renewed by His almighty Spirit, who Himself "bare all our sins in His own body on the tree" ! [16]

Entrance to the way set forth by Christ and leading to the goal of perfection is possible only for those who have first been reconciled to God through reliance on the sacrificial death of Christ.

Wesley believed that because of our sin, God was genuinely angry with us. "I firmly believe that He was angry with all mankind." [17] This anger is firmly fixed to God's justice—to his re-

[15] *Letters*, III, 351-52.
[16] *Sermons*, I, 326-27.
[17] *Letters*, VI, 298.

quirement that all men should serve him in obedience.[18] His
wrath stands irrevocably over the whole race of men, a fact clearly
attested in Scripture. But this irrevocable sentence Christ accepted on our behalf, and by his suffering and death on our behalf, God is reconciled.

It is certain, had God never been angry, He could never have been
reconciled. So that, in affirming this, Mr. Law strikes at the very root
of the Atonement, and finds a very short method of converting Deists.
Although, therefore, I do not term God, as Mr. Law supposes, "a
wrathful Being," which conveys a wrong idea; yet I firmly believe He
was angry with all mankind, and that He was reconciled to them by
the death of His Son. And I know He was angry with me till I believed in the Son of His love; and yet this is no impeachment to His
mercy, that He is just as well as merciful.[19]

Wesley is aware that if we should speak of God's wrath in
too simple a fashion, we would miss the truth that his justice and
mercy are knit together. He knows therefore, that we cannot
speak in simple anthropomorphic terms. Thus in his comment
on Rom. 5:8-10, he writes:

We shall be saved from wrath through him:—That is, from all the
effects of the wrath of God. But is there then wrath in God? Is not
wrath a human passion? and how can this human passion be in God?
We may answer this by another question. Is not love a human passion? And how can this passion be in God? But to answer directly:
wrath in man, and so, love in man, is a human passion. But wrath in
God is not a human passion; nor is love, as it is in God. Therefore
the inspired writers ascribe both the one and the other to God only
in an analogical sense.[20]

God's wrath is the symbol of our relation to him in the order
of creation, where we stand condemned at the bar of justice.
God's mercy is the symbol of the relationship he offers us in the
order of redemption, for there he makes it possible for us to be
taken out of the order of justice into the order of faith. This
transfer is not without great cost. The requirement of the order
of justice must be met; satisfaction for man's rebellion in the

[18] Letters, III, 346.
[19] Lettters, VI, 298.
[20] Notes, 537.

created order of justice must be made; God's wrath must be reconciled. This God does himself by sending his Son to be a propitiation for our sins.[21]

The cross, then, is an objective event in which God provides his Son as a sacrifice to atone for man. It is only by reliance upon Christ as the Atonement that we can be reconciled to God, receiving Christ as the Pattern because he is first the Saviour.

(2) The second count on which Wesley rejects Law's teaching is that Law introduces the idea that we are saved by merit—our merit merging with the merit of Christ our Example. For Wesley it is true that Christ is an example, but *only after we are justified*. It is only after we are under the New Covenant established by Christ as "a sacrifice and victim for the sins of his people," and therefore are living in a faith relationship to Christ as pardoned sinners, that the Pattern of Christ becomes a possibility for us by the work of his Spirit within us.[22]

Wesley makes it abundantly clear in his exposition of the Sermon on the Mount that the beatitudes can be spoken of as a ladder of ascent, only in the sense that they are the way along which Christ leads the justified sinner. So when he expounds the first beatitude, "Blessed are the poor in spirit," he interprets poverty of spirit as a recognition of our total unworthiness, where the Christian "sees himself therefore utterly helpless with regard to atoning for his past sins; utterly unable to make any amends to God, to pay any ransom for his own soul." [23] At the very beginning Wesley shatters the framework of the ladder of merit by denying that humility can be spoken of as a virtue and by distinguishing it entirely from a human work.

Poverty of spirit then, as it implies the first step we take in running the race which is set before us, is a just sense of our inward and outward sins, and of our guilt and helplessness. This some have monstrously styled "the virtue of humility"; thus teaching us to be proud of knowing we deserve damnation! But our Lord's expression is quite

[21] *Sermons*, I, 328.
[22] *Letters*, III, 334-35; and *Notes*, 815: "It is His Atonement, and His Spirit carrying on 'the work of faith with power' in our hearts, that alone can sanctify us."
[23] *Sermons*, I, 324.

of another kind; conveying no idea to the hearer, but that of mere want, of naked sin, of helpless guilt and misery.[24]

Wesley then proceeds to expound the truth of justification by faith, showing that the righteousness of God outlined in Christ's sermon is not a righteousness of human striving, not an upward way of merit, but a gift to the one who relies on Christ alone, and who sees himself accepted by God only on the basis of Christ's atonement for our sins.[25]

Know and feel, that thou wert "shapen in wickedness," and that "in sin did thy mother conceive thee"; and that thou thyself hast been heaping sin upon sin, ever since thou couldest discern good from evil! Sink under the mighty hand of God, as guilty of death eternal; and cast off, renounce, abhor, all imagination of ever being able to help thyself! Be it all thy hope to be washed in His blood, and renewed by His almighty Spirit, who Himself "bare all our sins in His own body on the tree"! So shalt thou witness, "Happy are the poor in spirit: for theirs is the kingdom of heaven." [26]

The way of the Cross is still a way the Christian must follow, for in following the Pattern of Christ he must expect to be conformed to his sufferings.

"Blessed are ye when men shall revile you and persecute you"— shall persecute by reviling you—"and say all manner of evil against you falsely, for My sake." This cannot fail; it is the very badge of our discipleship; it is one of the seals of our calling; it is a sure portion entailed on all the children of God. . . . Rejoice, because by this mark also ye know unto whom ye belong; and "because great is your reward in heaven"—the reward purchased by the blood of the covenant, and freely bestowed in proportion to your sufferings, as well as to your holiness of heart and life.[27]

---

[24] *Ibid.*, 325.

[25] It is important to reiterate that the sanctification that follows can only be spoken of as the basis for our final justification, in the sense that a living faith necessarily means that Christ will bring a real measure of transformation into our lives. If none results, the faith is not genuine. But faith is the only condition of the final justification, for we are variously sanctified according to our understanding and opportunities, and even those who receive entire sanctification are still imperfect in the moral and legal sense and must rely on the Atonement. See Chapter X below on "Christian Perfection."

[26] *Sermons*, I, 326-27.

[27] *Ibid.*, 372-74.

The life of Christ, culminating in the Cross, is then a way we must imitate. This way is a possibility only for those who are justified by faith in the merits of Christ and have received Christ as a Savior. But Wesley's point is that it is then a real possibility, and that the faith relationship established by Christ the Reconciler leads necessarily to a following of Christ the Pattern.

The Moral Influence Theory is then drawn firmly into Wesley's picture of the Christian life. Nevertheless, because justification is the only doorway to the Christian way, the truth expressed in the second traditional theory is of central importance.

The Penal Substitutionary Theory

The central point of the Penal Substitutionary Theory was of great importance for Wesley. Christ is the satisfier of our sin and guilt, the One who died as the sacrifice to satisfy the divine wrath and to provide for our forgiveness by the infinite value of his sacrifice in satisfaction of God's justice. We hear the tones of Anselm as Wesley states the problem man faces.

But what shall he give in exchange for his soul, which is forfeited to the just vengeance of God? "Wherewithal shall he come before the Lord?" How shall he pay Him that he oweth? Were he from this moment to perform the most perfect obedience to every command of God, this would make no amends for a single sin, for any one act of past obedience; seeing he owes God all the service he is able to perform, from this moment to all eternity: could he pay this, it would make no manner of amends for what he ought to have done before. He sees himself therefore utterly helpless with regard to atoning for his past sins; utterly unable to make any amends to God, to pay any ransom for his own soul.[28]

We are in the same legal scheme in the manner in which Christ is seen as paying the price for our sins that we are unable to pay. But then there is an all-important variation, for we are taken outside the order of merit and removed from the covenant of works into the covenant of grace which is established by Christ's death.

[28] *Ibid.*, 324; Also *Ibid.*, 157-58.

The covenant of works, in order to man's *continuance* in the favour of God, in His knowledge and love, in holiness and happiness, required of perfect man a *perfect* and uninterrupted *obedience* to every point of the law of God. Whereas, the covenant of grace, in order to man's *recovery* of the favour and the life of God, requires only *faith*; living faith in Him who, through God, justifies him that obeyed not.

Yet, again: the covenant of works required of Adam, and all his children, to pay the price themselves, in consideration of which they were to receive all the future blessings of God. But in the covenant of grace, seeing we have nothing to pay, God "frankly forgives us all": provided only, that we believe in Him who hath paid the price for us; who hath given Himself a "propitiation for our sins, for the sins of the whole world." [29]

Wesley does not put the penal substitutionary element of his teaching inside a legal framework in which God is made subject to an eternal, unchangeable order of justice.[30] God is free sovereign and relates himself to man under successive covenants. Under the first, the covenant of works, God subjects us to the law of his justice, so that as a result of our separation from him we are revealed as "sold under sin." Under this first covenant, the law is seen as God's instrument for bringing us to a knowledge of our guilt, and God's wrath is seen as his means for bringing us to a recognition of our total need for his mercy, With this revelation of our guilt and our need for God's mercy, the covenant of works has fulfilled its task and points us on to the covenant of grace which God has established by providing his Son as the satisfaction for our guilt and the satisfier of his wrath.[31]

[29] *Ibid.*, 138-39.
[30] The importance of this is that if we see the Atonement in terms of a cosmic natural law that Jesus had to satisfy, we turn this penal substitution into a rational explanation of the Atonement. When we see it in terms of God's free action in placing us under successive covenants, it is then a pictorial rather than a rational explanation—that is, it is an illustration using legal language to give insight into a relationship which rises above the law.
[31] See Wesley's comments in the *Notes:* "My God, my God, why hast thou forsaken me?—Our Lord hereby at once expresses His trust in God, and a most distressing sense of His letting loose the powers of darkness upon Him, withdrawing the comfortable discoveries of His presence, and filling His soul with a terrible sense of the wrath due to the sins which He was bearing." (p. 134) Also the passage in Heb. 2:10-11 on Christ being made perfect through suffering:

If in faith we rely upon the merit of Christ's atonement, we are taken out of the covenant of works and the order of merit into the covenant of grace and the order of faith. The Christian is no longer judged on a legal basis. He can even be called perfect (when he is very imperfect in an absolute or legal sense) when he lives in unbroken conscious dependence upon Christ.[32] The law is still of importance to him, for it shows him the promises God still is willing to fulfill in his life, but it no longer judges him for now he lives in the covenant of grace, in faith in Christ's atonement.[33]

It is in terms of these two covenants that we must understand Wesley's treatment of Christ as the Mediator. Christ is the Son of God who became man in order to mediate the new covenant between God and man, by acting as the representative of the human race in making atonement for the sins of man. It is in treating Christ's work as the Mediator that Wesley finds it necessary to discuss Christ's deity and twofold nature. As the Mediator of the New Covenant and the bringer of the righteousness of God, he must be seen both as God and man.

What is the righteousness of Christ? It is twofold, either His divine or His human righteousness.

I. His divine righteousness belongs to His divine nature, as He is 'O ὤν. He that existeth "overall, God blessed for ever"; the Supreme; the Eternal; "equal with the Father as touching His Godhead, though inferior to the Father as touching His manhood." Now this is His eternal, essential, immutable holiness; His infinite justice, mercy, and truth; in all which, He and the Father are one. . . .

2. The human righteousness of Christ belongs to Him in His human nature; as He is the "Mediator between God and man, the Man Christ Jesus." . . . In the whole course of His life, He did the will of God on earth, as the angels do it in heaven. . . . But His obedience implied more than all this: it implied not only doing, but suffering [not only active, but passive righteousness]; suffering the whole will of God, from the time He came into the world, till "He bore our sins

---

"Even He Himself was perfect as God and as man, before ever He suffered. By His sufferings, in His life and death, He was made a perfect or complete sin-offering." (p. 815)

[32] See Chapter X below on "Christian Perfection."

[33] See Sermons, II, sermons XXIX, XXX, XXXI, partic. XXIX, IV, 4, 54.

in His own body upon the tree"; yea, till having made a full atonement for them, "He bowed His head and gave up the ghost." [34]

Christ is the Mediator, who though he was God, yet became the representative of man, perfectly obeying God on our behalf (active righteousness) and suffering God's due punishment against us (passive righteousness), in order that full atonement might be made for us and that God's mercy for all might be revealed. It is this atonement that is the basis for our forgiveness.

God will not inflict on that sinner what he deserved to suffer, because the Son of His love hath suffered for him. And from the time we are "accepted through the Beloved," "reconciled to God through His blood," He loves, and blesses, and watches over us for good, even as if we had never sinned.[35]

This justification requires no legal fiction. It is not that we are still in the legal order, and that because of our relation to Christ God declares us to be righteous when we are not. When we believe in Christ, we are taken out of the legal order into the order of faith, for Christ is the end of the law.

Not that God . . . thinketh him to be what he is not. But as "He made Christ to be sin for us," that is, treated Him as a sinner, punishing Him for our sins, so He counteth us righteous, from the time we believe in Him: that is, He doth not punish us for our sins.[36]

Here in the doctrine of the Atonement, Wesley lays the ground for his "optimism of grace." Christ on the Cross represents the whole human race; there he is the "general Savior of mankind," the Second Adam constituting a new covenant in which all are offered membership through the gift of faith.

Wesley is here speaking of Christ as the representative, not in the metaphysical sense of being bound together with us by a common substance, nor in the psychological sense of being united with us in some hidden subconscious stream, but in the sense of a covenant established by a sovereign divine act in which Christ satisfies the requirements of the old covenant of law under which we were bound in order to establish a new covenant of

[34] Ibid., II, 426-28.
[35] Sermons, I, 121.
[36] Ibid., 127.

grace into which we may all enter. Wesley sees us all as "dead in sin" in the First Adam,[37] and therefore subject to God's wrath, but as "made alive unto God" by the Second Adam, and therefore subject to his mercy. It is because of the benefits of the new covenant, established by Christ through the atonement, that God works in all men by prevenient grace to prepare them for faith in Christ.

In this state we were, even all mankind, when "God so loved the world, that He gave His only begotten Son, to the end we might not perish, but have everlasting life." In the fullness of time He was made man, another common Head of mankind, a second general Parent and Representative of the whole human race. And as such it was that "He bore our griefs," "the Lord laying upon Him the iniquities of us all." ... He hath redeemed me and all mankind; having thereby "made a full, perfect, and sufficient sacrifice and satisfaction for the sins of the whole world." ...

This, therefore, is the general ground of the whole doctrine of justification. By the sin of the first Adam, who was not only the father, but likewise the representative, of us all, we all fell short of the favour of God; we all became children of wrath; or, as the Apostle expresses it, "judgement came upon all men to condemnation." Even so, by the sacrifice for sin made by the second Adam, as the representative of us all, God is so far reconciled to all the world, that He hath given them a new covenant; the plain condition whereof being once fulfilled, "there is no more condemnation" for us, but "we are justified freely by His grace, through the redemption that is in Jesus Christ." [38]

The Ransom or Classical Theory

The Ransom or Classical theory is given less emphasis in Wesley than the other two traditional viewpoints. The struggle of Christ against the demonic evil powers that enslave us in our individual and corporate existence and his victory over them

---

[37] See the discussion of this in the final section in Chapter IV on "Original Sin." The representative nature of Christ does not depend on the historical character of the "First Adam." The terms describe the situation of man under the two covenants. All men are naturally "in Adam" because "all have sinned," but Christ is the "Second Adam," representing all men, because by his free decision and action God here offered himself to all. See Notes, 374 on John 18:2.

[38] Sermons, I, 118-19.

in the Cross and Resurrection is included in his writings,[39] but its significance is given little attention. It may well be that this is a weakness which has its reflection in his doctrine of sanctification. There the stress is on a conscious individual relationship to Christ, and little emphasis is given to the need for the deepening awareness of our enslavement to these demonic forces and to the need for the repetition of Christ's victory in us, not only as individuals, but in the corporate life of the church and the world.

We must not, however, take this to mean that Wesley limited the work of Christ to the objective satisfaction of our guilt. Though Wesley is inclined to narrow the work of Christ upon the Cross to his (Christ's) priestly work of reconciling us to God, he insists that the risen, ascended Christ performs the offices of "prophet."

"who of God is made unto us wisdom"; who, by His Word and His Spirit, is with us always, "guiding us into all truth";

and of "king,"

yea, and as remaining a King for ever; as giving laws to all whom He has bought with His blood; as restoring those to the image of God, whom He had first reinstated in His favour; as reigning in all believing hearts until He has "subdued all things to Himself,"—until He hath utterly cast out all sin, and brought in everlasting righteousness.[40]

We see then, in Wesley's doctrine of the Atonement, the objective basis for his "optimism of grace." His central emphasis is on Christ the Representative of all men, dying on the Cross to open a new covenant of grace, so that man can be taken out of the legal order of merit and justified and sanctified by faith alone through the new relationship to God mediated by Christ. The grace made available through the Atonement is free for all and works in all as prevenient grace so that all may be brought

[39] *Ibid.*, 95, and *Notes*, 747 on Col. 2:15. For the suggested weakness in his doctrine of sanctification, see below in Chapter X.
[40] *Sermons*, II, 76-77. See also *Letters*, VI, 134: "If we could once bring all our preachers, itinerant and local, uniformly and steadily to insist on those two points, 'Christ dying for us' and 'Christ reigning in us,' we should shake the trembling gates of hell."

to Christ through the faith that justifies. It is also the sole basis of sanctification which is given to all those who put their complete trust in the righteousness of Christ and allow him to work freely in their lives, remaking their lives according to the Pattern he established as man for man.

We have seen a weakness in Wesley's doctrine in that his concentration on Christ's work in reconciling us to God and making available to us pardon, assurance of God's favor and a knowledge of Christ's presence in us, leads to an underemphasis on Christ's struggle against the demonic forces and his resurrection victory over them. We suggested that this leads, in Wesley's doctrine of sanctification, to an over individualistic emphasis on conscious relationship to Christ with an underemphasis on the work of sanctification as bringing us to deeper awareness of the evil forces that grip our corporate life and call for Christ's conquest.

Nevertheless Wesley's view enabled him to concentrate in his presentation of the order of salvation, upon the immediate faith relationship with Christ [41] and upon such elements as conversion, new birth, assurance, and the gifts of the Holy Spirit, and upon these he has an important word to speak.

Footnote: The Person of Christ and the Trinity

The doctrine of Christ's person is treated as a footnote to the chapter on the Atonement, as an expression of the way the doctrine appears in Wesley's writing. The central interest is in what Christ has done and can do for us, and normally Wesley is able to assume the orthodox formulations of the person of Christ, only occasionally being drawn into further statements through controversy.

As we have seen in the exposition of the Atonement, he makes it clear that Christ's work as Mediator presupposes the fact that in Christ it was God who became man, lived in perfect

[41] Wesley's strong emphasis on the corporate nature of the Christian life and upon loving the neighbor, overcame something of the individualistic weakness of his doctrine of sanctification. Because of his "optimism of grace" he was led almost unawares into quite revolutionary social action, but the weakness soon became apparent among his followers. See Maldwyn Edwards, *John Wesley and the Eighteenth Century* (London, The Epworth Press, 1933).

obedience to the Father, and suffered and died for the whole of mankind. From this it is clear that Wesley accepted the dogma of the divine and human natures of Christ. On Christ's deity Wesley believed that it was essential to insist. "My subject led me to speak strongly and explicitly on the Godhead of Christ," he wrote in his *Journal*. "But that I cannot help, for on this I *must* insist as the foundation of all our hope." [42] It is essential to the atonement to believe that "God was in Christ reconciling the world unto himself." [43]

Wesley was prepared, however, to spell out the implications of the doctrine when necessary. Thus in his "Letter to a Roman Catholic," he spelt out his Christology in some detail, arguing for [44]

(1) the eternal generation of the Son. So he speaks of God as "the Father of His only Son, whom He hath begotten from eternity.[45]

(2) unity of substance with the Father. "He is the proper, natural Son of God, God of God, very God of very God." [46]

Typically, however, Wesley moves on quickly to the offices and work of Christ. He is

(3) the Messiah and Savior of the world. "I believe that Jesus of Nazareth was the Saviour of the world, the Messiah so long foretold."

(4) Prophet, Priest, and King.

Being anointed with the Holy Ghost, He was a Prophet, revealing to us the whole will of God; He was a Priest, who gave Himself a sac-

---

[42] *Journal*, V, 253-54. See also *Notes*, 909 on I John 2:22.
[43] *Sermons*, I, 124-25.
[44] *Letters*, III, 8-9.
[45] See also *Notes*, 302 on John 1:1: "He is the Word whom the Father begot or spoke from eternity; by whom the Father speaking maketh all things; who speaketh the Father to us. We have, in the eighteenth verse, both a real description of the Word, and the reason why He is so called. 'He is the only begotten Son of the Father, who is in the bosom of the Father, and hath declared Him.' And the Word was with God—Therefore distinct from God the Father."
[46] See also *Notes*, 302. "The word rendered *with* denotes a perpetual tendency, as it were, of the Son to the Father, in unity of essence." See also *Notes*, 746 on Col. 2:9: "But in Christ *dwelleth all the fulness of the Godhead*; the most full Godhead; not only divine powers, but divine nature (Col. 1:19). *Bodily*—Personally, really, substantially. The very substance of God, if one might so speak, dwells in Christ in the most full sense."

rifice for sin, and still makes intercession for transgressors; He is King, who has all power in heaven and earth, and will reign till he has subdued all things to Himself.[47]

(5) Lord of all and especially our Lord.

He is the Lord of all, having absolute, supreme, universal dominion over all things; but more particularly our Lord, who believe in Him, both by conquest, purchase and voluntary obligation.

This brings him back to the Person of Christ, for in order to make it clear that it was by the absolute initiative of God that salvation was brought to us in Christ, he affirms

(6) the twofold nature of Christ and the Virgin Birth.

He was made man, joining the human nature with the divine in one person; being conceived by the singular operation of the Holy Ghost, and born of the blessed Virgin Mary, who, as well after as before she brought Him forth, continued a pure and unspotted virgin.

Wesley then returns to the work of Christ, in his

(7) sufferings, death, resurrection, and ascension, "where He remains in the midst of the throne of God, in the highest power and glory, as Mediator till the end of the World, as God to all eternity."

Finally he expresses his belief in

(8) the return of Christ, for "in the end He will come down from heaven to judge every man according to His works, both those who shall be then alive and all who have died before that day."

There can be no doubt then that Wesley accepted the orthodox Christological formulations,[48] but always his interest was

[47] Notes, 734 on Phil. 3:8: "Yea, I still account both all these and all things else to be mere loss, compared to the inward, experimental knowledge of Christ, as my Lord, as my Prophet, Priest, and King, as teaching me Wisdom, atoning for my sins, and reigning in my heart."

[48] Notes, 350 on John 10:30. On the text "I and the Father are one," Wesley comments that the "are" "confutes Sabellius, proving the plurality of persons," while the "one" "confutes Arius, proving the unity of nature in God." His acceptance was no mere form. That we must believe, for example, that Jesus is God, was vital to Wesley. He insisted that it is the apostolic witness that in Jesus we do not confront a fallible, time-conditioned, human wisdom, but that here God speaks and acts directly. It is this certainty which gives the only solid basis to our faith and hope. Works, VII, 292 and Works, VI, 425.

in the saving significance of Christ. He showed a constant dislike for metaphysical speculations. To lead people aside into a discussion of doctrinal subtleties could easily produce an argumentative spirit, and whereas a true living knowledge of Christ produces increasing dependence upon him and fosters a spirit of love, speculative arguments concerning his person can result in division and bitterness.[49]

Where the true living knowledge of Christ is actually at stake, however, Wesley was prepared to pursue the accuracies of doctrinal formulation. Tyerman gives the account of an occasion when a Christological controversy did arise in Wesley's societies. In the account we see both Wesley's desire to reduce speculative controversy and his determination to insist on theological accuracy when the saving significance of Christ was at stake.[50]

One of Wesley's preachers, Benson, had read Watts's "Glory of Christ as God-Man," and had become a convert to his doctrine of our Lord's human soul. Coke began to represent Benson as an Arian and charged him with the heresy at the Conference of 1780. Wesley defended Benson, and as a result Benson was acquitted, and Coke offered to ask his pardon. An interesting sidelight on Wesley's defense of Benson is given in his letter to Charles, reporting on the Conference action.

I would not read over Dr. Watts's tract for an hundred pounds. You may read it, and welcome. I will not, dare not move those subtle, metaphysical controversies. Arianism is not in question; it is Eutychianism or Nestorianism. But what are they? What neither I nor

---

[49] In *Letters*, IV, 159, in a letter to one of his preachers, Alexander Coates, Wesley writes: "Practical religion is your point; therefore . . . keep to this: repentance toward God, faith in Christ, holiness of heart and life, a growing in grace and in the knowledge of Christ, the continual need of His atoning blood, a constant confidence in Him, and all these every moment to our life's end." And while Wesley was well aware that the "speculative" elements of doctrine carry practical implications and can have vital influences on life, he sought to keep doctrine constantly directed toward the immediate concerns of a living relationship to Christ, and to keep the speculative elements subsidiary to that purpose. He made his point in the *Notes*, 575 on Rom. 14:19: "Practical divinity tends equally to peace and to edification. Controversial divinity less directly tends to edification, although sometimes, as they of old, we cannot build without it."

[50] Tyerman, *Life and Times*, III, 334.

anyone else understands. But they are what tore the eastern and western churches asunder.[51]

While we may doubt Wesley's judgment as to the cause of the East-West breach, his dislike of metaphysical speculation is clear. Nevertheless he was not afraid to push into it where he judged that soteriological issues were involved. Thus the very next year, on a sermon on John 3:18, he wrote:

Not that I can at all believe the ingenious dream of Dr. Watts concerning "the glorious humanity of Christ," which he supposes to have existed before the world began, and to have been endued with I know not what astonishing powers. Nay, I look upon this to be an exceeding dangerous, yea, mischievous hypothesis; as it quite excludes the force of very many scriptures which have been hitherto thought to prove the Godhead of the Son. And I am afraid it was the grand means of turning that great man aside from the faith once delivered to the saints;—that is, if he was turned aside; if that beautiful soliloquy be genuine which is printed among his Posthumous Works, wherein he so earnestly beseeches the Son of God not to be displeased because he cannot believe him to be co-equal and co-eternal with the Father.[52]

The Trinity

From the foregoing it should be clear that Wesley was also orthodox in his views of the Trinity, but again we see how he sought to keep attention directed towards the Christian life and to prevent it from running off into a speculative concern for right formulation.

In 1775 he prepared a sermon on I John 5:7, and in his introduction we see again his distinction between essential doctrines and opinions, the distinction being based on the relevance of the doctrines to the work of salvation. He allows that "persons may be truly religious, who hold many wrong opinions," and

that there are ten thousand mistakes which may consist with real religion; with regard to which every candid, considerate man will think and let think. But there are some truths more important than others. It seems there are some which are of deep importance. I do not term

[51] *Letters,* VII, 21-22.
[52] *Works,* VI, 273.

them *fundamental* truths; because that is an ambiguous word: And hence there have been so many warm disputes about the number of *fundamentals*. But surely there are some which it nearly concerns us to know, as having a close connexion with vital religion. And doubtless we may rank among these that contained in the words above cited: "There are three that bear record in heaven, the Father, the Word, and the Holy Ghost: And these three are one." [53]

Immediately, however, Wesley continues with his insistence that it is not necessary to hold a particular "explication" of the doctrine of the Trinity.

I insist upon no explication at all; no, not even on the best I ever saw; I mean, that which is given us in the creed commonly ascribed to Athanasius. I am far from saying, he who does not assent to this "shall without doubt perish everlastingly." For the sake of that and another clause, I, for some time, scrupled subscribing to that creed; till I considered, (1.) That these sentences only relate to *wilful*, not involuntary, unbelievers; to those who, having all the means of knowing the truth, nevertheless obstinately reject it: (2.) That they relate only to the *substance* of the doctrine there delivered; not the philosophical *illustrations* of it.[54]

These last two points are important for the question as to the relevance of Wesley's attitude on doctrinal issues to present ecumenical relations. In point (1) we see Wesley's famous insistence that "ten thousand mistakes may consist with real religion," so that a believer may make serious errors in his attempts to formulate essential truths of our relation to God and still be a genuine Christian living in that relationship. Yet this is no argument for doctrinal latitudinarianism, nor should it serve as a cloak under which those who disagree with the central doctrines of the Church can hide while continuing to teach doctrines that destroy the substance of the Church's faith. For Wesley makes it clear that if one who is aware of what he is doing wrongly describes our relationship to God, it is a sign that he is not truly in that faith relationship. Moreover, so far as "Church doctrine" is concerned, since preaching is determined by it, truth

[53] *Works*, VI, 200.
[54] *Ibid.*

is of great importance, for it is through this preaching that men are led into faith relationship with God.[55]

In point (2) he draws the difficult distinction between the "substance" of a doctrine and its "philosophical illustrations," further insisting that we must distinguish between the "fact" of the doctrine and the "manner how" or explanation of it. The *fact* is what God has revealed; the *manner how* he has not revealed.[56] Here Wesley is surely urging an important distinction, for is it not true that the philosophical language used by the Councils was not used to provide a philosophical explanation, but in order to make the facts of revelation clear in terms of the language of the time? To insist on the *fact* that Christ was fully God and fully man, the Council of Chalcedon used philosophical language, but they used it precisely to insist on facts that the current philosophy could neither explain nor contain. Similarly, to speak of God as one substance in three "hypostases" or "personae" is not to *explain* the fact of the Trinity, but to define it in such a way as to repudiate the false teaching of those who would explain it away.

Wesley, in fact, is insisting that we cannot explain the doctrine, nor must we anathematize anyone for failing to do so, or even for failing to grasp the definition of the fact given in the illustrative language of a particular philosophy. While he knew the great value the historic definitions have, he insisted that all that is essential for believers is that they know the "fact" of the doctrine.[57]

The knowledge of the Three-One God is interwoven with all true Christian faith; with all vital religion.

I do not say that every real Christian can say with the Marquis de Renty, "I bear about with me continually an experimental verity, and a plenitude of the presence of the ever-blessed Trinity." I apprehend this is not the experience of "babes," but rather "fathers in Christ."

But I know not how any one can be a Christian believer till he

---

[55] See *Letters*, IV, 3, for Wesley's insistence on right doctrine among his preachers.

[56] *Works*, VI, 204.

[57] "Where is the wisdom of rejecting what is revealed, because we do not understand what is not revealed? of denying the fact which God has unveiled, because we cannot see the *manner*, which is veiled still?" *Works*, VI, 205.

JOHN WESLEY'S THEOLOGY TODAY

"hath," as St. John speaks, "the witness in himself;" till "the Spirit of God witnesses with his spirit, that he is a child of God;" that is, in effect, till God the Holy Ghost witnesses that God the Father has accepted him through the merits of God the Son. And, having this witness, he honours the Son, and the blessed Spirit, "even as he honours the Father."

Not that every Christian believer adverts to this; perhaps, at first, not one in twenty: But if you ask any of them a few questions, you will easily find it is implied in what he believes.

Therefore, I do not see how it is possible for any to have vital religion who denies that these Three are One.[58]

This same attitude is revealed in the *Notes* on the New Testament. In his note on Heb. 9:14 he explains that the whole Trinity is involved in the work of redemption, for

neither is the Second Person alone concerned even in the amazing condescension that was needful to complete it. The Father delivers up the kingdom to the Son; and the Holy Ghost becomes the gift of the Messiah, being, as it were, sent according to His good pleasure.[59]

If Wesley is right here,—and at this point both British and American Methodists are officially tied to his doctrine—Methodism would be forced to undergo serious doctrinal reformulation before it could unite with churches outside the Trinitarian conviction, for this is no academic matter, but a question of the saving message of the gospel. Our redemption can be described only in terms of the work of the Holy Spirit within, bringing us to accept the saving work and presence of Christ, who alone can deliver us entire and perfect into the family of the Father, and all this is the work of the one God.

We should also ask, however, whether Wesley's distinction between the "fact" and the "manner how" may not have deep ecumenical significance. On the basis of this distinction the Creeds may be said to have a different significance from the Confessions. The Creeds are essentially "recital theology" pointing to the facts of revelation in such a way as to identify God in his action for our salvation—in his acts as Father, Son and

[58] *Ibid.*, 205-206.
[59] *Notes*, 835.

Spirit, and in the meaning for history given in these acts. Consequently they are at the heart of the living tradition of the Church and are recited in her worship. The Confessions, on the other hand (such as the Thirty-Nine Articles and the Twenty-Five, the Augsburg Confession, and the Westminster Confession), are the more detailed spelling out of the faith through which the Church has been summoned back from her errors in times of apostasy. They are therefore more polemical and time-conditioned, and do not have the same significance for the living worship of the Church.

This is not to say that the Creeds use no time-conditioned language or that the Confessions do not preserve vital emphases in the gospel! But it is to say that the Creeds point directly in their four articles to God in his acts of salvation and enshrine in simple form the structure of the gospel, while the Confessions struggle with the more detailed implications of the gospel, in terms of the changing struggles in particular historical moments. For that very reason the Confessions have very great eumenical importance, for they express the word which the separated groups believe that God has given them to say to each other out of their different traditions.

The Creeds have a different function, serving to delineate our common tradition. And is it not true that we need not wait for full agreement on the Confessional level? Agreeing on the central "recital" of our faith, we can bring our differing traditions into the common household of faith. That some further preliminary agreements are necessary in the area of our understanding of the Church, ministry, and sacraments is true. These we shall examine later. But is it not true that in the gospel we are called to proclaim to the world, we do not have to wait for unity on many of the Confessional questions, but can join in "reciting" to the world the faith we hold in common.[60]

---

[60] This question is discussed in more detail in chapter IX on "The Doctrine of the Church."

7 THE ORDER OF SALVATION: THE WORK OF THE HOLY SPIRIT IN NEW BIRTH AND ASSURANCE

۰ Wesley's doctrinal orthodoxy, in terms of his adherence to the historic creeds, is once again clear when we come to his doctrine of the Holy Spirit. We need refer to only one passage to indicate an orthodoxy which accepts the creedal formulations, including the Western "filioque" clause.

The Spirit's coming, and being sent by our Lord from the Father, to testify of Him, are personal characters, and plainly distinguish Him from the Father and the Son; and His title as the Spirit of *truth*, together with His proceeding from the Father, can agree to none but a divine person. And that He proceeds from the Son, as well as from the Father, may be fairly argued from His being called "the Spirit of Christ" (1 Peter 1:11), and from His being here said to be sent by Christ from the Father, as well as sent by the Father in His name.[1]

Wesley spends little time in establishing the doctrine. Assuming it, he concentrates on the work of the Holy Spirit. One of his (Holy Spirit's) offices is working "in the world" to bring believers to a conviction of sin—normally through preaching and miracles.[2] But his main office is his work in believers.

The Christocentric nature of his work is made quite clear. His main task is to help us to receive Christ as lord and to re-

[1] *Notes*, 370 on John 15:26.
[2] *Ibid.*, 371 on John 16:8.

98

veal to us the truth concerning Christ.[3] None can believe in Christ, except by the "experimental assurance" given by the Holy Spirit,[4] and this assurance is made available to us as the Spirit illumines our hearts when we read the Scripture and hear the word preached. "But this does not exclude our need of being taught by them who partake of the same anointing," [5] for the Spirit works within us in the context of his fellowship, the Church. His aim, nevertheless, is to work in us inwardly in such a way that we should receive him as a constant guest in our lives.

So far, in following the order of salvation, we have spoken of prevenient grace, and though this too is brought to us by the Spirit, there he works in a hidden way to "convince us of sin." We have spoken also of justification by faith, and it is at this point that the proper work of the Spirit begins as it is here that the believer is born.

Wesley makes a logical, not a temporal, distinction between justification and the new birth.

Though it be allowed, that justification and the new birth are, in point of time, inseparable from each other, yet they are easily distinguished, as being not the same, but things of a widely different nature. Justification implies only a relative, the new birth a real, change. God in justifying us does something for us; in begetting us again, He does the work in us. The former changes our outward relation to God, so that of enemies we become children; by the latter our inmost souls are changed, so that of sinners we become saints. The one restores us to the favour, the other to the image, of God. The one is the taking away the guilt, the other the taking away the power, of sin: so that, although they are joined together in point of time, yet are they of wholly distinct natures.[6]

Wesley is not suggesting that we can be justified without being newborn. In fact, his emphasis in this distinction is that unless the subjective work of new birth accompanies the belief in Christ; the belief is not the living faith that justifies, but a dead speculative faith. The faith of which the Scripture speaks

[3] Ibid., 367 on John 14:26.
[4] Ibid., 622 on I Cor. 12:3.
[5] Ibid., 909 on I John 2:27.
[6] Sermons, I, 299-300.

is not a barely notional or speculative faith. . . . the true, living, Christian faith, which whosoever hath is born of God, is not only assent, an act of understanding; but a disposition, which God hath wrought in his heart; "a sure trust and confidence in God, that, through the merits of Christ, his sins are forgiven, and he reconciled to the favour of God." [7]

Wesley is here making a distinction in terms of "appropriations." The work of justification is appropriated to Christ, the work of sanctification to the Holy Spirit. Justification is seen as reliance upon the "objective" work of Christ; sanctification, which begins with new birth, is seen as reliance upon the "subjective" work of the Spirit.

Justification . . . is not the being made actually just and righteous. This is *sanctification;* which is, indeed, in some degree, the immediate fruit of justification, but, nevertheless, is a distinct gift of God, and of a totally different nature. The one implies, what God does for us through His Son; the other, what He works in us by His Spirit.[8]

This does not mean that the Spirit is not at work in justification. It is the Spirit who brings us to faith reliance upon Christ. Nor does it mean that Christ is not at work in our new birth and sanctification, for he is the source of all grace through the atonement. But Christ has sent the Spirit to work in us, and while justification is the only and continuing basis of the Christian life in that we must always rely upon the merits of Christ, sanctification results from our inward appropriation of Christ's saving work, and this is the work of the Holy Spirit, whom Christ has sent to transform us into his (Christ's) likeness.

This distinction gives to Wesley's theology its distinctive flavor. In the theology of Luther and Cavin the emphasis remains on justification. The fact that the believer is *simul justus et peccator* and that Christ is our "alien righteousness," holds the center of attention in such a way that the transformation of the believer, though real, is secondary. But in Wesley, while justification is the foundation of the Christian life, the center of attention moves to the transforming work of the Spirit in the life of the justified. Here the "optimism of grace" in Wesley's theology becomes even more apparent.

Conversion or New Birth

The proper work of the Holy Spirit begins with new birth for which a synonym is conversion. The word conversion, perhaps, bears more of the connotation of conscious change, and this element has great importance in Wesley's thought. In 1738 the Moravian Bohler convinced Wesley that conversion is an instantaneous experience.[9] Yates is right when he points out that

this aspect of Bohler's theology, however, did not hold Wesley's assent for long. Later he modified his emphasis on conversion "in a moment" in favour of the sounder view that "there is an irreconcilable variability in the operations of the Holy Spirit in the souls of men." [10]

But be it an instantaneous crisis event or a more gradual change, Wesley remained convinced that conversion is always accompanied by the awareness of real change.

The precise manner how it is done, how the Holy Spirit works this in the soul, neither thou nor the wisest of the children of men is able to explain. However . . . we can give a plain scriptural account of the nature of the new birth.[11]

Wesley gives this account by use of the analogy of our natural birth. Just as we have our senses before birth but only come to an awareness of them after birth, so the Christian comes to an awareness of his spiritual senses only when he is born of God. Then

The "eyes of his understanding are opened" . . . and, He who of old "commanded light to shine out of darkness shining on his heart, he sees the light of the glory of God," His glorious love, "in the face of Jesus Christ." His ears being opened, he is now capable of hearing the inward voice of God, saying, "Be of good cheer; thy sins are forgiven thee"; "Go and sin no more." . . . He "feels in his heart," to use the language of our Church, "the mighty working of the Spirit

[9] Journal, I, 454-55.
[10] A. S. Yates, The Doctrine of Assurance (London: Epworth Press, 1952), p. 57. Used by permission.
[11] Sermons, II, 231-32.

of God." . . . And now he may be properly said to live: God having quickened him by His Spirit, he is alive to God through Jesus Christ. . . . God is continually breathing, as it were, upon the soul; and his soul is breathing unto God. Grace is descending into his heart; and prayer and praise ascending to heaven: and by this intercourse between God and man, this fellowship with the Father and the Son, as by a kind of spiritual respiration, the life of God in the soul is sustained; and the child of God grows up, till he comes to the "full measure of the stature of Christ."

From hence it manifestly appears, what is the nature of the new birth. It is the great change which God works in the soul when He brings it into life; when He raises it from the death of sin to the life of righteousness. . . . In a word, it is that change whereby the earthly, sensual, devilish mind is turned into the "mind which was in Christ Jesus." This is the nature of the new birth: "so is everyone that is born of the Spirit." [2]

It is true that this entire change is not wrought all at once. The new birth is a coming into being as babes in Christ so that the new believer still must grow into Christ's likeness. Nevertheless, Wesley believed that it is scarcely possible for the beginning of this new life to occur without the believer being aware of it, and in line with his belief as to the great change new birth brings, Wesley gives strong emphasis to the fact that assurance is normally associated with it.

Assurance—The Witness of the Spirit

In his analysis of the significance of the famous Aldersgate Street "conversion" experience of May 24, 1738, Yates shows that it was not there that Wesley initially resolved to lead a holy life; it was not there that he first dedicated his total existence to the service of God; it was not there that he received his compassion to save souls; it was not there that he underwent his theological revolution. All these vital elements of his life were gained before that date.

Our view is that 24th May 1738, was the first occasion on which John Wesley gained an assurance of personal salvation centered in

[12] *Ibid.*, 233-34.

a crucified Christ. His Aldersgate experience was the foundation on which John Wesley's doctrine of Assurance or Witness of the Spirit, was based.[13]

It should be noted, however, that Wesley was seeking for such an assurance long before. In 1725 in a letter to his mother he commented on the statement of Jeremy Taylor: "a true penitent must all the days of his life pray for pardon and never think the work completed till he dies. Whether God has forgiven us or no we know not, therefore still be sorrowful for ever having sinned."

Surely these graces are not of so little force, as that we can't perceive whether we have them or no; and if we dwell in Christ, and Christ in us, which He will not do till we are regenerate, certainly we must be sensible of it.[14]

A month later he wrote again to his mother:

That we can never be so certain of the pardon of our sins as to be assured that they will never rise up against us, I firmly believe . . . But I am persuaded we may know if we are now in a state of salvation, since this is expressly promised in the Holy Scriptures to our sincere endeavors, and we are surely able to judge of our own sincerity.[15]

We see also in his 1733 sermon on "The Circumcision of the Heart" a strong emphasis on the doctrine of assurance,[16] and in January 1738 he recorded in his Journal:

The faith I want is "a sure trust and confidence in God, that, through the merits of Christ, my sins are forgiven, and I reconciled to the favour of God." . . . I want that faith which none can have without knowing that he hath it (though many may imagine they have it, who have it not). . . . He is freed from doubt, "having the love of God shed abroad in his heart, through the Holy Ghost which is given unto him"; which "Spirit itself beareth witness with his spirit, that he is a child of God." [17]

[13] Yates, op. cit., 7-11. Used by permission of Epworth Press.
[14] Letters, I, 19-20.
[15] Ibid., 22.
[16] Sermons, I, 271.
[17] Journal, I, 424.

It would seem then that Wesley knew and accepted the scripture teaching long before Aldersgate Street, and yet, when early in May 1738 Peter Bohler began to speak to him of assurance, he spoke of it as a "new doctrine." [18] The foregoing makes it clear that in one sense it was not new. Yet it was new in the sense that up till then, Wesley was being weaned from the belief that a condition of assurance was a consciousness of being a worthy servant of God. We see this failure to correlate assurance with justification by faith in the 1725 letter to his mother, saying that "it is expressly promised in Holy Scriptures to our sincere endeavors, and we are surely able to judge of our own sincerity." However, by January 1738, as the quotation from his *Journal* reveals, there was a growing awareness that assurance is given to us by the Holy Spirit on the sole basis of our trust in the merits of Christ. Finally, early in May 1738, he was convinced by Bohler's teaching that assurance is an instantaneous awareness wrought in the heart of those who trust in Christ.[19]

It is clear then, that the fully fledged doctrinal conviction preceded the experience by more than two weeks and that Yates overstates his case in saying that the "Aldersgate experience was the foundation on which John Wesley's doctrine of Assurance or Witness of the Spirit was based." [20] Here again, the experience was the confirmation of a doctrine already accepted. In fact the crisis in Wesley's life arose precisely from the fact that the doctrine which he accepted pointed to an experience which he did not have. Experience is a vital category, not as a source for doctrine,[21] but as a test of whether we are living in the promises of which the doctrine speaks.

So Wesley wrote in his sermon on "The Witness of the Spirit":

It is objected, first, "Experience is not sufficient to prove a doctrine which is not founded on Scripture." This is undoubtedly true; and it is an important truth: but it does not affect the present question;

[18] *Ibid.*, 442.
[19] See *Journal*, I, 437-55.
[20] Yates, *op. cit.*, 11.
[21] It should be pointed out that the experience of prophets and Apostles is a source of doctrine, for they were involved in the events of revelation. Our experience, however, is not revelatory, but is judged by the "once-for-all" revelation.

for it has been shown, that this doctrine is founded on Scripture: therefore experience is properly alleged to confirm it.[22]

So Wesley came to see that unless this doctrine was confirmed in his life, he lacked a living sense that he was a true child of God and the certainty that he was justified and called to be God's servant. This is the light in which we must see the importance of Aldersgate Street.

In the evening I went very unwillingly to a society in Aldersgate Street, where one was reading Luther's preface to the *Epistle to the Romans*. About a quarter before nine, while he was describing the change which God works in the heart through faith in Christ, I felt my heart strangely warmed. I felt I did trust in Christ, Christ alone for salvation; and an assurance was given me that He had taken away my sins, even mine, and saved me from the law of sin and death.[23]

Of vital importance is the paragraph that follows. Methodist literature is replete with sentimentalism in discussions of the warmed heart, but how little the word "strangely" that precedes it is correlated with the following paragraph.

It was not long before the enemy suggested, "This cannot be faith; for where is thy joy?" Then was I taught that peace and victory over sin are essential to faith in the Captain of our salvation; but that, as to the transports of joy that usually attend the beginning of it, especially in those who have mourned deeply, God sometimes giveth, sometimes withholdeth them, according to the counsels of His own will.[24]

All too often assurance has been made a matter of emotional feeling, but in Wesley it is a divine conviction God works in the soul, or more accurately, the spirit. In discussing his anthropology we noticed Wesley's belief that the natural—that is, fallen —man is soul and body. The third element in the personality, spirit, is the supernatural image given by grace only to the new born.[25] God gives us at new birth the spirit whereby we are able

[22] *Sermons*, II, 352.
[23] *Journal*, I, 475-76.
[24] *Ibid.*
[25] See Chapter IV above. Also *Works*, VI, 223, and *Notes*, 763 on I Thess. 5:23.

to perceive his Spirit. He gives us the spiritual power of perception which is able to sustain us, even when feelings are low, with the assurance of sins forgiven.

Wesley was inclined in the period immediately following 1738 to make a sense of pardon a necessary part of justifying faith, but he subsequently saw that this too is to make justification dependent upon feeling. Sugden quotes a letter of Wesley to Melville Horne:

When fifty years ago my brother Charles and I, in the simplicity of our hearts, told the good people of England that unless they knew their sins were forgiven, they were under the wrath and curse of God, I marvel, Melville, they did not stone us! The Methodists, I hope, know better now; we preach assurance as we always did, as a common privilege of the children of God; but we do not enforce it, under the pain of damnation, denounced on all who enjoy it not.[26]

A vital point is at stake here, having to do with what Luther meant by the experience of being delivered from experience, that is, the experience of being able to rely on the promises of the gospel even when our feelings are in disarray. Yet here we must walk a dialectical tightrope. There may not be a feeling of being forgiven, but there must be a conviction of the truth of the promise of forgiveness and a reliance upon it. Wesley expresses the tension when he writes:

That some consciousness of our being in favor with God is joined with Christian faith I cannot doubt; but it is not the essence of it. A consciousness of pardon cannot be the condition of pardon.[27]

As Luther rightly tells us, our feelings may say "you are a sinner," but we may reply, "I know I am a sinner, but Christ forgives sinners." [28]

That Wesley was aware that it is just as wrong to make an internal condition (of right feelings or tempers) as it is to make an external condition (of right actions or works) a necessary basis for justification is revealed in his preface to a collection of poems and hymns, where he assails the Mystics:

[26] *Sermons*, I, 82, f.n.
[27] *Letters*, VII, 61.
[28] See also *Sermons*, II, 194 ff. in the sermon on "Satan's Devices."

We apprehend them to lay another foundation. They are careful indeed to pull down our own works; and to prove, that "by the deeds of the law shall no flesh be justified." But why is this? Only "to establish our own righteousness" in the place of our own works. They speak largely and well against expecting to be accepted of God for our virtuous actions; and then teach, that we are to be accepted for our virtuous habits or tempers. Still the ground of our acceptance is placed in ourselves. . . . Neither our own inward nor outward righteousness is the ground of our justification. Holiness of heart, as well as holiness of life, is not the cause, but the effect of it. The sole cause of our acceptance with God (or, that for the sake of which, on the account of which, we are accepted,) is the righteousness and the death of Christ, who fulfilled God's law, and died in our stead. And even the condition of it is not (as they suppose) our holiness either of heart or life; but our faith alone; faith contradistinguished from holiness, as well as from good works. Other foundation therefore can no man lay, without being an adversary to Christ and his gospel, than faith alone; faith, though necessarily producing both, yet not including either good works, or holiness.[29]

This emphasis is of great importance today. If *moralism* has been the greatest threat to the Christian life in times past; if it has turned men away from the theocentric gaze of the gospel and the gospel's liberating trust in Christ's work for us and in us so that men have attempted to earn salvation by their own effort; *psychologism*, with its temptation to turn back in upon ourselves and the consequent spiritual paralysis caused by the awareness of our disordered spirits, would seem to pose the greater threat today.

Wesley, of course, places great stress on the fact that the new relationship necessarily produces both good works and holiness, but he knew that no man by taking thought can add one cubit to his moral stature or remove one kink from his spiritual disorder, and that it is only when our gaze is theological (leading us to trust in Christ alone) that the ethical and spiritual fruits are given. These come by faith in the promises of the gospel. Faith forms love, not vice versa, and holiness of heart and life is not the source of justification but the fruit of it.

[29] *Works*, XIV, 332-333.

Even more is involved here. The great truth of the gospel is that just as justification is reliance upon Christ as our "alien righteousness," so the peace the gospel offers is a peace this world can neither give nor take away because it is an "alien peace"—a peace carried by a Word spoken to us, not a feeling resident in us and subject to psychological disruption.

Wesley with all his emphasis on transformation never makes our faith dependent upon our feeling of transformation. This paradox receives its final expression in his statement that even the "perfect" Christian

> may start, tremble, change colour, or be otherwise disordered in body while the soul is calmly stayed on God and remains in perfect peace. Nay, the mind itself may be deeply distressed, may be exceeding sorrowful, may be perplexed and pressed down by heaviness and anguish, even to agony, while the heart cleaves to God by perfect love and the will is wholly resigned to Him. Was it not so with the Son of God Himself? [30]

A further evidence of the way Wesley related the witness of the Spirit to the message of the gospel, so that no "enthusiasm" should separate the experience from its biblical base and make it subject to human criteria, is seen in his strong insistence that all claims to an immediate knowledge of God must be tested against the Scripture.

We see this in his marked distrust of claims to direct guidance. For while he asserted the direct providential intervention of God in the affairs of life, he believed that this providence is largely veiled and is usually apparent only after the event.[31] On direct guidance he wrote:

> I have declared again and again that I make the Word of God the rule of all my actions, and that I no more follow any secret impulse instead thereof than I follow Mahomet or Confucius.[32]

Believing that God guides us through the regular means of grace and especially through the Scriptures, he blamed the

[30] John Wesley, Christian Perfection (ed. by Thomas Kepler; Cleveland, New York: The World Publishing Co., 1954), pp. 62-63.
[31] Notes, 83, on Matt. 16:24 and Notes., 75, on Matt. 14:10.
[32] Letters, II, 205. And see Letters VII, 263, 319 and Letters, VIII, 154.

Quakers, and people such as Swedenborg and Madame Guyon for setting immediate impressions above the Scriptures.[33]

The same insistence upon a criterion beyond the human and a standard of judgment beyond that of feeling is seen when we turn to his two standard sermons on "The Witness of the Spirit." Preaching on Rom. 8:16, "The Spirit himself beareth witness with our spirit that we are children of God," he begins:

How may vain men, not understanding what they spake, neither whereof they affirmed, have wrested this scripture to the great loss, if not the destruction, of their souls! How many have mistaken the voice of their own imagination for this witness of the Spirit of God, and thence idly presumed they were children of God, while they were doing the works of the devil! These are truly and properly enthusiasts.[34]

He then makes two points essential to a separation of assurance from feeling.[35]

1. The testimony of God's Spirit is antecedent to the testimony of our spirit.

The testimony of the Spirit is an inward impression of the soul, whereby the Spirit of God directly witnesses to my spirit, that I am a child of God; that Jesus Christ hath loved me, and given Himself for me; and that all my sins are blotted out, and I, even I, am reconciled to God.

That this testimony of the Spirit of God must needs, in the very nature of things, be antecedent to the testimony of our own spirit, may appear from this single consideration. We must be holy of heart, and holy in life, before we can be conscious that we are so; before we can have the testimony of our spirit, that we are inwardly and outwardly holy. But we must love God, before we can be holy at all; this being the root of all holiness. Now we cannot love God, till we know He loves us. "We love Him, because He first loved us." And we

---

[33] *Journal*, V, 354-55; *Letters*, V, 342.
[34] *Sermons*, I, 202-203.
[35] I do not mean that feeling is not associated with the experience. As Wesley points out, in many there is joy—as exaltation of feeling—especially at the beginning. The point is that the feelings vary from person to person; and also that in persons who at first have a surge of feeling, it subsides and may be followed by a sense of depression. Therefore Wesley is careful to show that feeling is not the test of assurance. In fact, assurance is able to sustain us in changing moods, and so give "the peace which the world cannot give."

cannot know His pardoning love to us, till His Spirit witnesses it to our spirit. Since, therefore, this testimony of His Spirit must precede the love of God and all holiness, of consequence it must precede our inward consciousness thereof, or the testimony of our spirit concerning them.[36]

To use modern terms, the Christian is aware of being grasped by God's Spirit, an awareness which, of course, may bring about feeling reactions, but is self-authenticating and not explicable in terms of sense experience.[37] But because this experience is self-authenticating and cannot be described clearly to those who have not received it, it is easy to mistake feelings for true assurance.

There are, however, scriptural tests that can be applied to see whether the claim is genuine. So, as his second main point, Wesley affirms that

2. there are "objective" marks (objective in the sense of "given") whereby true assurance can be distinguished from false.

The testimony of our spirit that follows the testimony of God's Spirit can be distinguished from "the presumption of a natural mind," for "the holy Scriptures abound with marks, whereby the one may be distinguished from the other." Such tests are

a) repentance, or conviction of sin.[38]

b) an awareness of "a vast and mighty change; a change 'from darkness to light,' as well as 'from the power of Satan unto God'; as a 'passing from death unto life,' a resurrection from the dead." [39]

c) the fruits of the Spirit, such as the lowliness which is the recognition of our unworthiness in the sight of God, accompanied by "meekness, patience, gentleness, long-suffering." [40]

---

[36] Sermons, I, 208. See also Notes, 548 on Rom. 8:16.
[37] "How the divine testimony is manifested in the heart, I do not take upon me to explain. . . . The manner of the things of God knoweth no one, save the Spirit of God. But the fact we know; namely, that the Spirit of God does give a believer such a testimony of his adoption, that while it is present to the soul, he can no more doubt the reality of his sonship, than he can doubt of the shining of the sun, while he stands in the full blaze of his beams." Sermons, I, 210. See also Ibid., 234, where assurance is distinguished from "any sudden flow of spirits."
[38] Ibid., 212.
[39] Ibid., 213.
[40] Ibid., 214.

d) newness of outward life, for assurance is an assurance of a new relationship to God, and "love rejoices to obey; to do, in every point whatever is acceptable to the beloved. A true lover of God hastens to do His will on earth as it is done in heaven." [41] It is this which enables us to speak of the witness of our spirit as "the answer of a good conscience toward God." By the fruits which He hath wrought in your spirit, you shall know the testimony of the Spirit of God. Hereby you shall know that you are in no delusion, that you have not deceived your own soul.[42]

These then, are the tests for distinguishing true assurance from false. But we must be careful. Unless we remember that priority must be given to the testimony of God's Spirit and that this witness of our spirit is only indirect, we can easily slide back into salvation by works.[43] Assurance is the witness of God's Spirit that we are forgiven (justification) and accepted as children of God (adoption). It is not an assurance that we are worthy.

So Wesley insists that the only way to a conscience thus "void of offence," is not by works,

but by a living faith; that no man is a partaker of Christ, until he can clearly testify, "The life which I now live, I live by faith in the Son of God"; in Him who is now *revealed* in my heart; who "loved me and gave Himself for me." Faith alone is that evidence, that conviction, that demonstration of things invisible, whereby, the eyes of our understanding being opened, and divine light poured in upon them, we "see the wondrous things of God's law."

The reason why Wesley pointed to these scriptural tests for distinguishing true from false assurance lies in his conviction that by the Spirit at work within us a faith relationship to Christ is certain to be followed by those inward and outward changes of which the tests speak.

[41] *Ibid.*, 215.
[42] *Ibid.*, 217.
[43] *Letters*, V, 8. "One of our preachers that was (I mean Hampson) has lately made a discovery that there is no such thing in any believer as a *direct, immediate* testimony of the Spirit that he is a child of God, but the Spirit testifies this *only* by the fruits, and consequently that the witness and the fruits are *all one*. Let me have your deliberate thoughts on this head. It seems to be a point of no small importance. I am afraid lest we should get back again unawares into justification by works."
[44] *Sermons*, I, 227.

Nevertheless it is true that his doctrine, particularly in its early expression, ran real dangers. It could produce either Pharisaism in those who measured their lives against the indirect tests and closed their eyes to their own faults, or despair in those who judged that they could not measure up to the rigor of the tests. This danger was particularly apparent in his early writings, for there Wesley tended to suggest that assurance was necessary to salvation, and that the transformation which accompanied the new birth and with which assurance is associated was of such depth that very little (if any) sin remains. But in his mature period he corrected himself on both of these points.

Assurance—Not Necessary to Salvation

Wesley changed his early opinion that assurance is necessary to salvation. Sugden traces the change from the Minutes of 1744, where it is asserted that there is no faith where there is no assurance, through the admission in 1745 that there may be exempt cases, to the important recognition in his 1747 letter to Charles Wesley:

By justifying faith, I mean that faith which whosoever hath not is under the wrath and curse of God. By a sense of pardon I mean a distinct, explicit assurance that my sins are forgiven. I allow (1) that there is such a thing as explicit assurance; (2) that it is the common privilege of real Christians; (3) that it is the proper Christian faith which purifies the heart and overcomes the world. But I cannot allow that justifying faith is such an assurance, or necessarily connected therewith. Because if justifying faith necessarily implies such an explicit assurance of pardon, then every one who has it not, is under the wrath and curse of God. But this is a supposition contrary to Scripture as well as to experience. . . . Again the assertion that justifying faith is a sense of pardon is contrary to reason, it is flatly absurd. For how can a sense of our having received pardon be the condition of our receiving it? [45]

Wesley is right then, when he writes in 1768:

I believe a consciousness of being in the favour of God (which I do not term plerophory or full assurance, since it is frequently weak-

[45] For Sugden's account see Sermons, I, 200-201. For a fuller treatment of the change see Yates, op. cit., pp. 61-71.

ened, nay perhaps interrupted, by returns of doubt or fear) is the common privilege of Christians fearing God and working righteousness. Yet I do not affirm there are no exemptions to this general rule. Possibly some may be in the favour of God and yet go mourning all the day long. But I believe this is usually owing either to disorder of body or ignorance of the gospel promises.

Therefore I have not for many years thought a consciousness of pardon to be essential to justifying faith.[46]

Here Wesley's estimate of his own life before May 24, 1738 is relevant. In January 1738 he details in his *Journal* his attempts to conform his life to the law of God and concludes that unless all this obedience to the ordinances of God is "ennobled by faith in Christ," they are dung and dross meet only to be purged away by "the fire that never shall be quenched." [47] To this Jackson has a later footnote added by Wesley, "I had even then the faith of a servant though not that of a son." Wesley's further estimate that prior to Aldersgate Street he was " 'a child of wrath,' an heir of hell," has also a later footnote, "I believe not"; and to his remark "I who went to America to convert others, was never myself converted to God," is appended the later comment "I am not sure of this."

Cell denies the authenticity of these emendations,[48] but they are in line with Wesley's distinction in his sermon "On Faith" [49] between the "faith of a servant" and "the faith of a son," and they parallel his modification of his doctrine of assurance.

Nearly fifty years ago, when the Preachers, commonly called Methodists, began to preach that grand scriptural doctrine, salvation by faith, they were not sufficiently apprised of the difference between a servant and a child of God. They did not clearly understand, that even one "who feareth God, and worketh righteousness, is accepted of him." In consequence of this, they were apt to make sad the hearts of those whom God had not made sad. For they frequently asked those who feared God, "Do you know that your sins are forgiven?" And upon their answering "No," immediately replied, "Then

[46] *Letters,* V, 358-59.
[47] *Journal,* I, 423.
[48] Cell, *op. cit.,* 178-80.
[49] *Works,* VII, 195 ff. (Written in 1785).

you are a child of the devil." No; that does not follow. It might have been said, (and it is all that can be said with propriety,) "Hitherto you are only a *servant*, you are not a *child* of God. You have already great reason to praise God that he has called you to his honourable service. Fear not. Continue crying unto him, 'and you shall see greater things than these.' " [50]

This description parallels Wesley's experience, and the emendations in the Journal are of real importance for a right assessment of the doctrine of assurance. For while it is not necessary to salvation, it is an important gift of God which brings great freedom to the believer. It instills a confidence in Christ which leads on to the fulfillment of the further promise of sanctification. In Wesley's own case, before Aldersgate Street he was a servant of God and his work was not without its blessing, but after Aldersgate Street he entered into the freedom of a child of God and was ready to become the instrument of the Methodist reformation.

We can see why Wesley felt this doctrine to be vital to his message. Not only does it emphasize the great work of grace God is willing to perform in the life of the believer, it also opens the life of the recipient to that increasing trust in God through which the further promises of the gospel are fulfilled, and the usual reason why believers do not have this assurance is the ignorance of the gospel promises due to their absence from the message of the preacher.

Continuing Sin in the New Born

The second danger in his early teaching on assurance lay in his belief as to the extent of the transformation that necessarily accompanies the new birth. In his 1744 sermon on "The Marks of the New Birth," Wesley urges that

an immediate and constant fruit of this faith whereby we are born of God, a fruit which can in no wise be separated from it, no, not for an hour, is power over sin,—power over outward sin of every kind; over every evil word and work; ... and over inward sin; for it purifieth the heart from every unholy desire and temper.[51]

[50] *Ibid.*, 199.
[51] *Sermons*, I, 285.

Commenting further on the text from John, "Whosoever is born of God does not commit sin," he rejects the suggestion that John means habitual sin and insists that the new birth brings freedom from all sin. It may well be that this early belief was the occasion of returning periods of doubt as to his own new birth,[52] but gradually he began to see that sin continues in believers. In the next sermon on "The Great Privilege of Those That Are Born of God," he discusses this sin,[53] and later he wrote a sermon under the title "On Sin in Believers," [54] specifically denying that new birth brings complete freedom from sin. This being so, the indirect test of assurance—testing by the fruits of faith—is no absolute test. Nevertheless Wesley continued to insist that great changes *begin* to take place in the life of the believer at new birth, and that therefore the indirect test still has its relative validity. If our life is not moving toward these fruits, we can well doubt the validity of our assurance.

Baptism and the New Birth

J. H. Rigg in his book "The Churchmanship of John Wesley" remarks that

it is remarkable, indeed, how very little is found on the subject of baptism in the fourteen volumes of Wesley's works. He revised and reissued, under his own name, in 1756, the treatise on that subject which his father had published over half a century before, and which teaches "baptismal regeneration" after the mildest type of the doctrine, and much as it had been taught by the Puritan divines of the Church of England. Elsewhere all that Wesley says on the subject, besides two sentences in his *Notes on the New Testament*, . . . is in

[52] See *Journal*, II, 91 (Oct. 14, 1738); *Letters*, I, 264 (Oct. 30, 1738); *Letters*, II, 125 (June 4, 1739). Tyerman connects these doubts with the teaching Wesley at first accepted from the Moravians, that the experience of justification is followed after a short delay by the experience of full assurance—a witness of the Spirit which shuts out all doubt and fear. This is not inconsistent with the association of complete freedom from sin with new birth. In fact it is likely that he then supposed this was the prerequisite of full assurance.

[53] *Sermons*, I, 306 ff.
[54] *Sermons*, II, 360 ff.

two sermons, and his Farther Appeal to Men of Reason and Religion, and amounts altogether to but a few lines.[55]

Henry Carter in his "The Methodist Heritage" also comments that "it cannot be said that an adequate account of Christian Baptism is a part of the heritage bequeathed by Wesley." [56]

These estimates may be justified. However, an examination of the passages on baptism reveals an inescapable tension between the ecclesiastical and the evangelical which runs through Wesley's theology and comes to its height in his doctrine of the Church. And since this tension is of central importance in our examination of the Methodist tradition in the light of present ecumenical tensions, we turn now to an examination of it.

In his 1756 "A Treatise on Baptism," [57] Wesley, following his father, gives the traditional ecclesiastical statement of the doctrine of baptism. Speaking of the benefits of baptism to infants he writes:

> The first of these is, the washing away the guilt of original sin, by the application of the merits of Christ's death. . . . By baptism we are admitted into the Church, and consequently made members of Christ, its Head. . . . By water then, as a means, the water of baptism, we are regenerated or born again. . . .
> Herein a principle of grace is infused, which will not be wholly taken away, unless we quench the Holy Spirit of God by long-continued wickedness.[58]

That this is not simply an inconsistent inclusion of his father's teaching is indicated by the fact that this same teaching is included in Wesley's sermons. These leave no doubt that Wesley saw baptism as in some sense a "new birth," and the ordinary

[55] James H. Rigg, The Churchmanship of John Wesley, Wesleyan Methodist Book Room, 1886, 42. Rigg is wrong in saying that the references are limited to two sermons. See the index in N. Lawson, Notes on Wesley's Forty-Four Sermons, Epworth Press, London, 1952. He is wrong also in saying that there are only two sentences on the subject in the Notes, as we shall see. But his basic point—that Wesley gives little direct treatment to the subject—still stands.

[56] H. Carter, op. cit., p. 159.

[57] Works, X, 188-201.

[58] Ibid., 190-92. .

means whereby God begins his work of regeneration in us. As a proof of this we quote:

(1) From *Standard Sermon* III where he speaks of that inward universal change, that "birth from above,"

figured out by baptism, which is the beginning of that total renovation, that sanctification of spirit, soul, and body.[59]

(2) From *Standard Sermon* XIV, where he writes

What is implied in the being a son or a child of God, or having the Spirit of adoption? That these privileges, by the free mercy of God, are ordinarily annexed to baptism (which is thence termed by our Lord in a preceding verse, the being "born of water and of the Spirit").[60]

(3) In the *Notes*, on John 3:5.

Except a man be born of water and the Spirit—Except he experience that great inward change by the Spirit, and be baptized (wherever baptism can be had), as the outward sign and means of it.[61]

(4) In the *Notes*, on Acts 22:16.

Be baptized, and wash away thy sins—Baptism, administered to real penitents, is both a means and seal of pardon. Nor did God ordinarily in the primitive Church bestow this on any, unless through this means.[62]

There can be no doubt that Wesley believed that God ordinarily uses baptism as the means by which he (God) enters the life of the believer to bring new life. It is true that he did not believe that it was the exclusive means. As he wrote to Gilbert Boyce in 1750,

You think the mode of baptism is "necessary to salvation." I deny that even baptism itself is so; if it were, every Quaker must be damned, which I can in no wise believe.

I hold nothing to be (strictly speaking) necessary to salvation but the mind which was in Christ.[63]

[59] *Sermons,* I, 71-72.
[60] *Ibid.,* 283.
[61] *Notes,* 311.
[62] *Ibid.,* 487.
[63] *Letters,* III, 36.

The freedom and sovereignty of God, which mean that we cannot limit his operation to the means which he has ordained as the normal channels of his coming to us, were of great importance to Wesley. As we have seen, this enabled him to seek unity in mission with those he believed to be wrong on vital points of faith and practice, but in whose lives the presence of Christ was manifest. This in itself is an important ecumenical viewpoint. It makes theological sense of our present dilemma in that we have recognized Christ's presence in each other while still believing that we cannot recognize each other as in full-sense churches. If we were to take seriously Christ's sovereignty in this way, we would be seeking more urgently for present unity in mission while still recognizing the importance for seeking increasing unity in doctrine.

The latter Wesley recognized. For while he believed that we are forced to take account of God's sovereignty and freedom, he also believed that God's normal way is to work through established means, and that the Christian is expected to observe them. So he wrote to William Law in 1756.

Vain philosophy! The plain meaning of the expression, "Except a man be born of water," is neither more nor less than this, "Except ye be baptized." And the plain reason why he ought to be thus born of water is because God hath appointed it. He hath appointed it as an outward and visible sign of an inward and spiritual grace; which grace is "a death unto sin and a new birth unto righteousness." [64]

Wesley believed that baptism is normally the beginning of the Christian's new life. He believed also that it normally takes place in infancy, as infant baptism is in line with New Testament thought. Not only did he believe that the New Testament word "household" includes infants, but he also found it difficult to believe "that the Jews, who were so long accustomed to circumcise their children would not now devote them to God by baptism." [65]

[64] Letters, IV, 357.
[65] Notes, 459 on Acts 16:15. See his further arguments for infant baptism in the "treatise in Baptism," W., X., 193-201.

As to the mode of baptism, Wesley argued that while immersion was the "ancient manner of baptizing," sprinkling and pouring are recognized in Heb. 10:22.[66] In fact, if immersion symbolizes "dying and rising with Christ," sprinkling symbolizes the outpouring of the Holy Spirit at Pentecost.[67]

Baptism, then, is a means by which God begins his work of regeneration in our heart. But since God does not work irresistibly, but through his presence gives us that freedom by which we are able to receive or resist the further gifts of his grace, there is a necessary tension in the doctrine of the new birth.

The question is not, what you was made in baptism (do not evade); but, what are you now? . . . I allow you was "circumcised with the circumcision of Christ" (as St. Paul emphatically terms baptism); but does the spirit of Christ and of glory now rest upon you? Else, "your circumcision is become uncircumcision." [68]

Baptism is the God-given sign which declares the fact that it is God who begins the work of regeneration in our lives, but God's purpose is to bring us to conscious acceptance of the new birth, therefore "if we do not experience this, our baptism has not answered the end of its institution." [69] For that reason, to those who have not responded, Wesley can say:

Lean no more on the staff of that broken reed, that ye were born again in baptism. Who denies that you were then made children of God, and heirs of the kingdom of heaven? But, notwithstanding this, ye are now children of the devil. Therefore, ye must be born again.[70]

We see, then, that Wesley speaks of the new birth in two senses: First, in the preparatory sense that God enters the "dead" life of the unregenerate, bringing the grace without which it is impossible to know God or to receive him, and second, in the sense of fulfillment, in which the believer comes to conscious acceptance of Christ.

[66] *Ibid.*, 746 on Col. 2:12.
[67] *Notes*, 22-23 on Matt. 3:6.
[68] *Sermons*, I, 295.
[69] *Notes*, 746 on Col. 2:12.
[70] *Sermons*, I, 296.

It is in the latter sense of fulfillment that Wesley can say "Baptism is not the new birth; they are not one and the same thing." [71] He shows that neither the Dissenters (Presbyterians) nor the Church of England claims that they are identical and follows this by the distinction that whereas infants "who are baptized in their infancy are at the same time born again," in adults baptism only brings the new birth when there is also a conscious response bringing with it a new life of holiness.[72] This difficult passage can be understood only in the light of this distinction between the preparatory and fulfilled senses of the term.

Since the latter (fulfilled) sense is the purpose of the former (preparatory) sense, Wesley associates assurance with the new birth that comes with conscious acceptance of Christ. But, as a result, the tension in his doctrine of baptism and the new birth falls away in his doctrine of assurance. Instead of relating it with Luther to the "I am baptized" as well as to the present witness of the Holy Spirit, Wesley relates it only to the latter. This I believe is a weakness in his statement of the doctrine. The "objective" and "subjective," which normally he keeps in creative tension, here fall apart and the emphasis falls too much on the side of the "subjective."

Rigg argues that these two sides of Wesley's teaching on baptism are in contradiction to each other, and that gradually the traditional ecclesiastical (objective) side was overcome by the evangelical (subjective) side. Thus by 1784 when Wesley prepared "The Sunday Service of the Methodists, with other Occasional Services," he was ready to omit some of the references to baptismal regeneration and to reduce the Article on Baptism along the same lines. Rigg concludes that this "proves, at all events, that Wesley had in 1784 concluded not to insist on the doctrine of baptismal regeneration in any sense." [73] Lindstrom, on the other hand, argues that Wesley kept the tension to the end and in no way abandoned the teaching of his Standard Ser-

[71] Ibid., II, 237.
[72] Ibid., 237-39.
[73] Rigg, op. cit., pp. 45-46.

mons on Baptism.[74] I believe that from the evidence already given we can see that there is no need to accept Rigg's view. The fact that Wesley stressed the need for coming to a conscious acceptance of the work of regeneration which God begins in infant baptism is sufficient reason for his reduction (but not elimination) of the references to baptismal regeneration. There is no evidence to suggest that he ever abandoned his belief that God has appointed means of grace through which he normally enters our life, and that these ordinances are to be accepted not only because Christ commanded them, but also because they give us visible assurance of his presence and serve as a sign of the initiative he takes in the realm of redemption.[75]

This teaching and the tension between the objective and subjective are maintained by Wesley in his teaching concerning the holiness of the Church. There is an essential sense in which the holiness is "given"—that is, in which it consists of Christ's given presence in the Church through Word and Sacraments. Yet again, this is only one, albeit the prior side of the holiness of the Church, for unless there is the response of the members bringing forth holiness of life, the Church is not truly the Church.[76]

So here in his teaching on baptism, we see again that creative tension between the Catholic and Protestant views of the Church and the Sacraments which is of great importance in the present ecumenical struggle. It must be admitted, however, that while Wesley kept both sides of the tension, he did not spell it out with sufficient force, with the result that there has been great confusion on the subject in Methodism since his death. Apparently understanding only the second emphasis in Wesley, American Methodism has since reduced the service of Baptism to the point where it is little more than a dedication, and in British Methodism, while far more of the structure of the service has been kept, all references to regeneration were excluded in 1882.

An insistent emphasis in Wesley is that the purpose of baptism is to lead us to conscious new birth which the previous regenerating work of God has made possible. As we have seen, however,

[74] Lindstrom, op. cit., pp. 106-109.
[75] See Sermons, I, 238-60 in the sermon on "The Means of Grace."
[76] See below in Chapter IX on "The Doctrine of the Church."

he kept the word assurance for the conscious presence of Christ in our lives through the witness of the Spirit that we are pardoned, adopted as God's children and heirs of the promises of salvation. This emphasis is vital. Nevertheless we miss in Wesley's doctrine of assurance something of Luther's vigorous "I am baptized"; something of the reliance upon the promises of the gospel, objectively symbolized by baptism, which is able to sustain us in the midst of the assaults of our emotional enemies.

Yates, after coming to the conclusion that the main features of Wesley's doctrine of assurance still stand the test of biblical analysis, nevertheless concludes that

Wesley did not attach enough importance to the objective and historical aspects of assurance in the New Testament. We are not saying that he did not treat adequately in his teaching generally, the historical facts of the Gospel; but that he did not sufficiently relate his doctrine of assurance to these in the course of his exposition. . . . We would supplement further the biblical data of Wesley's doctrine by pointing out that Paul not only teaches the inner witness of the Spirit, but rests this subjective assurance on a broad basis of fact in the Person and work of Christ: "I know Him whom I have believed." [77]

It is this objective side of the Word—the promise of the Gospel made to me in baptism—that is involved in Luther's "I am baptized," and it is to keep this objective assurance in tension with the necessity for a living reliance upon the Word that Luther speaks of the repentance of believers as a daily return to baptism. Wesley, however, points more strongly than Luther to the necessary transformation of life which is the result of the new relation to Christ initiated by baptism. In this way he avoids the danger of the "I am baptized" being turned into "cheap grace"; which overlooks the transformation that necessarily flows from the living faith relation with Christ which baptism effects and to which it points.

Limits to Assurance

To understand the full significance of Wesley's doctrine of assurance, we must notice that at one essential point he broke

---

[77] Yates, op. cit., p. 136. Used by permission of Epworth Press.

away from both the earlier Catholic and Reformation traditions. Whereas they thought of assurance as the assurance of salvation, and for that reason were very careful to guard against presumption, Wesley rejected the doctrine of predestination which lay behind their assumption, and therefore insisted that assurance relates not to final salvation, but to present salvation from which it is possible to fall. As he wrote to his brother Samuel:

The gospel promises to you and me, and our children, and all that are afar off, even as many of those as the Lord our God shall call as are not disobedient to the heavenly vision, 'the witness of God's Spirit with their spirit that they are the children of God'; that they are now at this hour all accepted in the Beloved: but it witnesses not that they shall be. It is an assurance of present salvation only; therefore not necessarily perpetual, neither irreversible.[78]

Wesley cut the knot of present hesitation and future presumption by his teaching that we can have the assurance of present salvation, while waiting in hope for our final salvation. He recognized the danger of presumption in the belief "Once saved, always saved," claiming that the doctrine or unconditional perseverance "leads the way by easy steps, first to presumption, and then to black despair." [79] It was this danger that led men like Pope Gregory I to deny that there could be any certain assurance. In rejecting the demand of one of the court ladies-in-waiting who wrote asking him how she could gain assurance, Gregory wrote: "Holy Church mingles hope and fear for her faithful children." [80] Because assurance was associated with the certainty of final salvation, due to the doctrine of predestination, this hesitation was inevitable. But Wesley removed the presumption by cutting away the doctrine of double predestination and so freed the scripture doctrine of assurance from its long night of neglect.

Wesley also reintroduced the scriptural distinction between

[78] *Letters*, I, 308.
[79] *Letters*, VIII, 159.
[80] J. S. Whale, *The Protestant Tradition* (Cambridge University Press), p. 85.

the "assurance of faith" and the "assurance of hope." In a letter to Dr. Lavington in 1751, Wesley pointed out that "the full assurance of faith does not imply the full assurance of perseverance: this bears another name, being styled by St. Paul 'the full assurance of hope.' " [81] He continues to show that the claim to a full assurance of faith implies not a full conviction of future perseverance, but a conviction of present pardon.

This distinction Wesley based firmly on Scripture.[82] He proclaimed the freeing message that the assurance of faith can be the common inheritance of all believers. Nor is the absence of a full assurance of hope a source of depressing fear, for we know that he is faithful and that he who has begun a good work in us will continue it. It is true that we may fall, but it is also true that we need not. The God who by his grace has given us the assurance of our adoption has resources sufficient to keep us in his grace. We can take to ourselves then

the hope of salvation. The lowest degree of this hope is a confidence that God will work the whole work of faith in us; the highest is a full assurance of future glory, added to the experimental knowledge of pardoning love.[83]

Wesley believed that to some God does give the full assurance that they will endure to the end, a conviction "given immediately by the power of the Holy Ghost." [84] Yet it is not common, and it is not a necessary gift. The assurance of which he speaks as the gift available to all believers is the "assurance of faith," which is the present conviction wrought in our lives by the Holy Spirit that we are pardoned and adopted as children of God.

Wesley's message carried power, because he knew that God's grace is free for all, and that "all may be saved and come to a knowledge of the truth." Breaking free from the limiting bonds of the doctrine of double predestination, Wesley offered to all

[81] Letters, III, 305.
[82] Notes, 722 on Eph. 6:17; Notes, 825 on Heb. 6:11; See Yates, op. cit., pp. 126-32.
[83] Notes, 722 on Eph. 6:17.
[84] Notes, 825 on Heb. 6:11.

the new birth, and with it, the witness of God's Spirit to our spirit that we are the children of God and joint heirs with Christ.

Ecumenical Significance

Wesley wrote:

It more nearly concerns the Methodists, so called, clearly to understand, explain, and defend this doctrine [of assurance]; because it is one grand part of the testimony which God has given them to bear to all mankind. It is by His peculiar blessing upon them in searching the Scriptures, confirmed by the experience of His children, that the great evangelical truth has been recovered, which had been for many years well nigh lost and forgotten.[85]

I have tried not only to state Wesley's doctrine, but also to discuss the way in which it can be restated to avoid the misunderstandings that have attended it. There is no doubt that this is a central part of the Methodist confession, forming a key link in that rising crescendo of the "optimism of grace" which marks Wesley's treatment of the order of salvation. That note of joy which the Evanston Assembly found to be lacking in the statement of the Christian hope, here finds one of its essential sources, and one which has been strangely neglected or avoided in most of the major traditions.[86]

Here we face a peculiar difficulty. Believing that this doctrine was one of the secrets of the Methodist reformation, believing that God has given it to the people called Methodists to recall the Church to the expectation of the promise; must the Methodists insist that the doctrine be accepted by others as a precondition of union?

It seems clear that Wesley's answer was "no." Important as he believed this doctrine to be, he believed that unity in mission must not wait for agreement on this level. What is important is that those who have received this truth, make their confession in the "great congregation."

[85] *Sermons*, II, 343-44.
[86] See A. S. Yates, op. cit., p. ix.

8 THE ORDER OF SALVATION: REPENTANCE IN BELIEVERS

⏺ Luther constantly emphasized that the Christian is *simul justus et peccator*—at the same time justified but still a sinner—and that therefore his life must be marked by continual repentance and a daily return to Christ as his "alien righteousness"; that is, to a reliance on the righteousness of Christ which never becomes his possession but is his only by the unmerited gift of forgiveness.

In his sermon on "Whosoever is born of God cannot sin," Wesley at first sight seems to suggest that we must abandon this Reformation view of the Christian life.

Now one who is so born of God, as hath been above described, who continually receives into his soul the breath of life from God, the gracious influence of His Spirit, and continually renders it back; one who thus believes and loves, who by faith perceives the continual actings of God upon his spirit, and, by a kind of spiritual reaction returns the grace he receives, in unceasing love, and praise, and prayer; not only doth not commit sin, while he thus keepeth himself, but so long as this "seed remaineth in him, he cannot sin, because he is born of God." [1]

There are, however, two important limitations to this. First, Wesley is here describing sin in terms of "an actual voluntary transgression of the law; of the revealed, written law of God; of

[1] *Sermons*, I, 304.

any commandment of God, acknowledged to be as such at the time it is transgressed."[2] This is only one of two definitions.[3] In terms of the second, deeper definition, in which sin is judged by the perfect will of God, even the "perfect" Christian is a sinner and subject to continual repentance. In that sense he is simul justus et peccator.

Second, even in terms of this first, narrower definition Wesley acknowledges a difficulty.

It is plain, in fact, that those whom we cannot deny to have been truly born of God (the Spirit of God having given us in His Word this infallible testimony concerning them), nevertheless, not only could, but did, commit sin, even gross, outward sin. They did transgress the plain, known laws of God, speaking or acting what they knew He had forbidden.[4]

This is true, not only of those under the Old Covenant (such as David), but even of the Apostles themselves after Pentecost (such as Peter). Yet how can this be, if those who are born of God cannot sin? The answer is that it is possible for believers to fall from faith and therefore from the life of the new birth. Wesley traces how this fall from grace to sin occurs.

(1) The divine seed of loving, conquering faith, remains in him that is born of God. "He keepeth himself," by the grace of God, and "cannot commit sin." (2) A temptation arises; whether from the world, the flesh, or the devil, it matters not. (3) The Spirit of God gives him warning that sin is near, and bids him more abundantly watch unto prayer. (4) He gives way, in some degree, to the temptation, which now begins to grow pleasing to him. (5) The Holy Spirit is grieved; his faith is weakened; and his love of God grows cold. (6) The Spirit reproves him more sharply, and saith, "This is the way; walk thou in it." (7) He turns away from the painful voice of God, and listens to the pleasing voice of the tempter. (8) Evil desire begins and spreads in his soul, till faith and love vanish away: he is then capable of committing outward sin, the power of the Lord being departed from him.[5]

[2] Ibid.
[3] For a discussion of these definitions, see Chapter X.
[4] Sermons, I, 305.
[5] Ibid., 309.

Wesley acknowledges that this falling from faith in some degree marks the life of all who are justified, but he is convinced that in this life all believers may eventually receive the gift of perfection by which they will be kept from falling out of the faith relationship. To keep the faith however, requires continual watchfulness, and constant attendance upon the means of grace. He acknowledges further that there is a "mystery of iniquity" at work in the Church [6] so that "wherever Christianity has spread, the apostasy has spread also." [7] But it will not always be so. At the last "God will arise and maintain his own cause; and the whole creation shall then be delivered both from moral and natural corruption." [8] Meanwhile, if Christians learn to exercise due watchfulness, they may receive the promised gifts of the Spirit and be delivered from the enemy. [9]

Wesley is far from asserting that unless the Christian is sinless, he is condemned. Of the deeper "inward sin" the Christian longs to be free but is aware that his trust is in Christ, not in his own merits.

Fret not thyself because of ungodliness, though it still remain in thy heart. Repine not, because thou still comest short of the glorious image of God; nor yet because pride, self-will, or unbelief, cleave to all thy words and works. And be not afraid to know all this evil of thy heart, to know thyself as also thou art known. Yea, desire of God, that thou mayest not think of thyself more highly than thou oughtest to think. . . . See thyself nothing, less than nothing, and vanity. But still "let not thy heart be troubled, neither let it be afraid." Still hold fast, "I, even I, have an Advocate with the Father, Jesus Christ the righteous." [10]

Even the outward sin occasioned by a falling from faith is no barrier to a renewal of faith.

Wilt thou say, "But I have again committed sin, since I had redemption through His blood? And therefore it is, that 'I abhor myself, and repent in dust and ashes.'" It is meet thou should abhor thyself;

[6] Works, VI, 263.
[7] Ibid., 263.
[8] Ibid., 267.
[9] Ibid., 266.
[10] Sermons, I, 175-76.

and it is God who hath wrought thee to this self-same thing. But, dost thou now believe? Hath He again enabled thee to say, "I know that my redeemer liveth"; "and the life which I now live, I live by faith in the Son of God"? Then that faith again cancels all that is past, and there is no condemnation to thee.[11]

The Christian knows that he is *simul justus et peccator*. But he does not rest in that awareness. He seeks to open his life more and more to the Savior so that outward sins may be destroyed by the gift of an unbroken relationship with Christ, and that inward sins may be more and more laid bare by the light of Christ's presence and overcome by the strength of his grace.

Speaking of the "wilderness state" which so often follows the early exaltation of the new birth, Wesley asks: "What is the nature of this disease, into which so many fall after they have believed?" [12]

He proceeds to analyze the usual causes of this separation from God and to look for a cure.

To suppose that this is one and the same in all cases, is a great and fatal mistake; and yet extremely common, even among many who pass for experienced Christians, yea, perhaps, take upon them to be teachers in Israel, to be the guides of other souls.[13]

This tendency to try to apply one medicine to all the cases of separation from God is apparent most often in those whose only thought is to "apply the promises" to those in the wilderness—to "preach the gospel" by speaking of the comfort available in Christ. This is quackery,[14] for the Christian life is not a simple hearing but a complex doing, and the causes of separation from God are manifold.

Consequently, preaching, however primary and indispensable it may be, must be followed by a scientific care for Christians in the fellowship of believers. The pastor must seek the causes of separation from God and apply the right remedy. These causes and remedies, Wesley was convinced, can be found by making a full examination of the ordinances of God—the means that God

[11] *Ibid.*, 174.
[12] *Sermons*, II, 246.
[13] *Ibid.*, 255.
[14] *Ibid.*

has provided to keep alive his grace in our souls and to direct our lives in obedience to his will. For normally the cause will be found in the slighting of one or more of these ordinances, and the remedy will be found in obeying them.

The Means of Grace

"If a man preach like an angel," wrote Wesley, "he will do little good without exact discipline." [15] Wesley was convinced of the fact that since the Fall has turned us completely away from God so that by nature man is self-idolatrous and a slave to this world's goods,[16] only the way of discipline can wean us from our worldly attachments and free us for the service of God. In the believer this sin is still at work, and though he knows the promise of "entire renewal in the image of God," it is necessary that he should wait for the fulfillment of the promise

Not in careless indifference, or indolent inactivity; but in vigorous, universal obedience, in a zealous keeping of all the commandments, in watchfulness and painfulness, in denying ourselves, and taking up our cross daily; as well as in earnest prayer and fasting, and a close attendance on all the ordinances of God. And if any man dream of attaining it any other way (yea, or of keeping it when it is attained, when he has received it even in the largest measure,) he deceiveth his own soul. It is true, we receive it by simple faith: But God does not, will not, give that faith, unless we seek it with all diligence, in the way which he hath ordained.[17]

Wesley was convinced that fallen man, lifted up by God's grace, can remain in that grace only when he seeks to use it in obedience to God's commandments. He was further convinced that we can grow in grace only by constant attendance upon the means of grace, and that the neglect of these leads to that falling away which is the occasion of sin.

The definition of the "Means of Grace," he gives in his sermon under that title:

By "means of grace," I understand outward signs, words, or actions, ordained of God, and appointed for this end, to be the ordinary

[15] *Letters*, V, 204.
[16] *Sermons*, II, 218-22.
[17] *Works*, XI, 402-403.

130

channels whereby He might convey to men, preventing, justifying, or sanctifying grace.[18]

"Methodism, by its very name," Hildebrandt remarks, "is open to the suspicion that it gives to 'means' both an undue importance and an unorthodox content and therefore must rank with the many other forms of 'enthusiasm' which were so frequently rejected by Luther." [19] Hildebrandt quotes Wesley's admission that there was a time when

> I of means have made my boast,
> Of means an idol made.

But that was before he was introduced to the doctrine of salvation by faith alone.

Even after that, however, Wesley continued to place a central emphasis upon the necessity for close attention to these means, arguing that in the Apostolic Church there was a recognition that "Christ had ordained certain outward means, for conveying His grace into the souls of men." [20] That there has been a constant temptation to mistake means for ends and to fall into the error of seeking justification by works, he admits. Thus it is necessary to recognize the enormous folly when "they are used as a kind of commutation for the religion they were designed to subserve." [21] They have no intrinsic power in themselves, having value only when it is seen that God alone has power to forgive sins and to grant us the gifts of his Spirit. Then we are able to see that the God in whom we trust has appointed these means as channels through which he normally grants us his gifts.

We allow farther, that the use of all means whatever will never atone for one sin; that it is the blood of Christ alone, whereby any sinner can be reconciled to God; there being no other propitiation for our sins, no other fountain for sin and uncleanness. Every believer in Christ is deeply convinced that there is no merit but in Him; that there is no merit in any of his own works; not in uttering the prayer, or searching the Scripture, or hearing the Word of God, or eating of

[18] Sermons, I, 242.
[19] Hildebrandt, From Luther to Wesley, op. cit., 65.
[20] Sermons, I, 238.
[21] Ibid., 243.

that bread and drinking of that cup. So that if no more be intended by the expression some have used, "Christ is the only means of grace," than this,—that He is the only meritorious cause of it, it cannot be gainsaid by any who know the grace of God.[22]

Christ is the only source of grace, but he has appointed meeting places where we may receive his grace.

According to the decision of holy writ, all who desire the grace of God are to wait for it in the means which He hath ordained.[23]

He [the early Christian] was deeply sensible of the truth of that word, "Without Me ye can do nothing," and, consequently, of the need he had to be watered of God every moment; so he continued daily in all the ordinances of God, the stated channels of His grace to man: "in the Apostles' doctrine," or teaching, receiving that food of the soul with all readiness of heart; in "the breaking of bread," which he found to be the communion of the body of Christ; and "in the prayers" and praises offered up by the great congregation. And thus, he daily "grew in grace," increasing in strength, in the knowledge and love of God.[24]

The Instituted Means of Grace

Wesley divided the means of grace into Instituted and Prudential,[25] including under the Instituted, or means specifically instituted by Christ:

(1) Prayer. Prayer is the key to the Christian life, for the essence of that life is a living relationship with God, and prayer is the instituted means for the maintenance of that relationship.

Prayer is certainly the grand means of drawing near to God; and all others are helpful to us only so far as they are mixed with or prepare us for this.[26]

For this reason the failure to pray is the most common cause of the "wilderness" state, for "the want thereof cannot be supplied by any other ordinance whatever." [27] Nor is prayer a simple

---

[22] *Ibid.*, 243-44.
[23] *Ibid.*, 243.
[24] *Sermons*, I, 97.
[25] *Works*, VIII, 322-24.
[26] *Letters*, IV, 90.
[27] *Sermons*, II, 250.

matter, for as our relationship to God implies a total life relationship, so our prayers must express the total range of life. They must include the expression of our awareness of sin (deprecation), the longing for the fulfillment of God's promises within us (petition), requests for the needs of others (intercession), and our gratitude for all God's goodness and lovingkindness (thanksgiving). It must represent our life as individuals (private prayer), as participants in the primary social group (family prayers), [28] and as members of the great congregation (public prayer). All this needs a constant discipline so that prayer may be kept as the constant basis of the daily life.

Do you use private prayer every morning and evening? If you can, at five in the evening; and the hour before or after morning preaching? [29]

This private prayer requires an intimate connection with the reading of the Scripture, so that our prayers are truly "in the name of Jesus," so that our self-examination may be held under the searchlight of God's revealed will, and so that we may be constantly aware of how we may ask aright. Sincerity is the first requirement of prayer, for "Prayer is the lifting up of the heart to God: all words of prayer, without this, are mere hypocrisy." [30] This purity of intention requires that we should put aside "any temporal view"—any desire for praise or for temporal reward, remembering that the central purpose of prayer is to fix our eyes on God's purpose for our lives, and to gain increasingly "the sense of (our) continual dependence on Him who only is able to supply (our) wants." [31]

The aim of prayer is to learn the constant company of Christ, and its end can be to

Pray without ceasing—Which is the fruit of always rejoicing in the Lord. In everything give thanks—Which is the fruit of both the former. This is Christian perfection. Further than this we cannot go;

---

[28] Wesley published in 1744 A Collection of Prayers for Families.
[29] Works, VIII, 322-23.
[30] Sermons, I, 428.
[31] Ibid., 431.

and we need not stop short of it. Our Lord has purchased joy, as well as righteousness, for us. It is the very design of the gospel that, being saved from guilt, we should be happy in the love of Christ. Prayer may be said to be the breath of our spiritual life. He that lives cannot possibly cease breathing. So much as we really enjoy of the presence of God, so much prayer and praise do we offer up *without* ceasing; else our rejoicing is but delusion. Thanksgiving is inseparable from true prayer; it is almost essentially connected with it. He that always prays is ever giving praise, whether in ease or pain, both for prosperity and for the greatest adversity. He blesses God for all things, looks on them as coming from Him, and receives them only for His sake; not choosing nor refusing, liking nor disliking, anything, but only as it is agreeable or disagreeable to His perfect will.[32]

(2) *Searching the Scriptures.* Reading the Scriptures is not simply a matter of guidance by proof texts, it requires a knowledge of the whole revelation (he suggested the use of his *Notes*), a willingness to read with regularity ("some part every day"), and careful application to life, "immediately practising what you learn there." [33]

(3) *The Lord's Supper.* Since Christ has promised to meet us at his table, we should go "at every opportunity." [34]

(4) *Fasting.* Wesley sought to have his followers observe Friday as a fast day[35] and was concerned at the failure of so many to do so.[36] The purpose of fasting is to wean the soul from its natural attachment to earthly things and to keep before us our spiritual destiny. No extreme ascetic practices are necessary, nothing injurious to health, but a rigid self-denial which expresses the necessity for keeping our attachment to worldly things relative and our concern for our heavenly destiny absolute is a clear command of Christ.[37] When used in the right way, as a means for reminding us of our relationship to God and not as an end for seeking merit, it will be blessed.

[32] *Notes*, 762 on I Thess. 5:16-17.
[33] *Works*, VIII, 323.
[34] *Ibid.* The doctrine of the Lord's Supper is given extended treatment in the next chapter.
[35] *Ibid.*
[36] *Journal*, V, 17.
[37] *Sermons*, I, 455-57. Sugden (*ibid.*, 462) rejects Wesley's exegesis.

When you seek God with fasting added to prayer, you cannot seek His face in vain.[38]

(5) *Christian Conference.* Wesley was convinced that an indispensable emphasis in the early Church was the gathering together of believers into small groups for fellowship and nurture. He was convinced also that his church was derelict in the fulfillment of this duty.[39] So he wrote in his *Journal:*

I was more convinced than ever that the preaching like an Apostle, without joining together those that are awakened and training them up in the ways of God, is only begetting children for the murderer. How much preaching has there been for these twenty years all over Pembrokeshire! But no regular societies, no discipline, no order or connexion; and the consequence is that nine in ten of the once-awakened are now faster asleep than ever.[40]

In keeping with this conviction Wesley saw the organization of his societies as an expression of one of the essential means of grace, as a vital element for the growth of the Christian life through which believers bear one another's burdens and so fulfill the law of Christ.

The manner in which such societies are organized comes under the prudential means of grace. That is to say, the particular methods of organization can vary, but the meeting in small groups for mutual study, encouragement, and service, he believed to be an instituted necessity of the Christian life.

A second meaning of "Christian Conference" is of equal importance. Wesley believed that if one is to grow in the Christian life, he must see his conversation as a divine trust given for the purpose of witnessing to his faith.

Are you convinced how important and how difficult it is to "order your conversation right?" Is it "always in grace? seasoned with salt? meet to minister grace to the hearers?" [41]

[38] *Letters,* V, 112.
[39] This point is developed in the next chapter.
[40] *Journal,* V, 26.
[41] *Works,* VIII, 323.

The Christian is called to be a witness to his faith, and unless he so uses the grace God gives him, he may lose it.

The Prudential Means of Grace

The need to have small groups for the exercise of Christian fellowship carried with it the corollary that it was necessary to develop clear rules for the structuring of the Christian life.[42] That these could vary according to changing circumstances, Wesley knew, and for this reason he called them prudential or variable, in distinction from the instituted or invariable means of grace.

The prudential means established by Wesley in his societies must not be considered as providing a permanent detailed structure for the life of the Church, but as an illustration from the eighteenth century of the remarkably effective way Wesley provided for the essential life of Christian fellowship.

In describing the origin of the United Societies, Wesley called them:

"a company of men having the form and seeking the power of godliness, united in order to pray together, to receive the word of exhortation, and to watch over one another in love, that they may help each other to work out their salvation." [43]

The only condition for entrance into these societies was "a desire 'to flee from the wrath to come, to be saved from their sins,' " [44] but continuance in membership depended upon the acceptance of a life of discipline. This discipline was laid out in terms of the concrete situations of their daily lives, and the conditions were:

(1) "doing no harm." As examples, Wesley spoke of the need to abstain from swearing, drunkenness, smuggling, extravagant dress, useless diversions, self-indulgence, miserliness.[45]

(2) "doing good," such as caring for men's bodies, especially the poor, the sick, and the distressed; caring for men's souls by

---

[42] See the list of prudential means, ibid., 323-24.
[43] Ibid., 269.
[44] Ibid., 270.
[45] Ibid.

instruction, exhortation, and reproof, with particular responsibility for those of the household of faith.[46] (3) "attending upon all the ordinances of God." Those within the societies were expected to receive the ministrations of the great congregation by attending the liturgy and sacraments of the Church, but in view of the low ebb to which preaching had fallen in the Church, Wesley stressed the need for members to attend the ministry of the Word in the societies and to share there in prayers and mutual encouragement.

The structure of the classes[47] took into account the differences between natural groups, so that the early bands were organized in four groups for married men, married women, single men, and single women. Their purpose was to allow full freedom in speaking of their deepest concerns so that they could exercise their mutual priesthood and build each other up in their most holy faith.

Wesley insisted on the discipline of regular attendance at society meetings, at the early morning preaching services,[48] and strongly urged the reading of Christian books as well as the Scriptures.[49] He insisted upon definite moral standards, a clear discipline in regard to luxury, and a definite structuring of the use of time.[50] Yet the meaning of these prudential means is grasped only when we see their purpose. In his sermon "On Grieving the Holy Spirit," he wrote:

There is a particular frame and temper of soul, a sobriety of mind, without which the Spirit of God will not concur in the purifying of our hearts. It is in our power, through his preventing and assisting grace, to prepare this in ourselves; and he expects we should, this being the foundation of all his afterworks. Now, this consists in preserving our minds in a cool and serious disposition, in regulating and calming our affections, and calling in and checking the inordinate pursuits of our passions after the vanities and pleasures of this world; the doing of which is of such importance, that the very reason why men profit so little under the most powerful means, is, that they do

---

[46] *Ibid.*, 270-71.
[47] See Wesley's description in *Letters*, II, 292-311.
[48] *Journal*, VI, 492-93.
[49] *Letters*, VI, 201.
[50] See the Twelve Rules for his preachers. *Works*, VIII, 309-10.

not look enough within themselves,—they do not observe and watch the discords and imperfections of their own spirits, nor attend with care to the directions and remedies which the Holy Spirit is always ready to suggest. . . . There is nothing more certain than that the Holy Spirit will not purify our nature, unless we carefully attend to his motions, which are lost upon us while, in the Prophet's language, we "scatter away our time,"—while we squander away our thoughts upon unnecessary things, and leave our spiritual improvement, the one thing needful, quite unthought of and neglected.[51]

The means, then, are not our way of making ourselves fit to merit justification. They are working out our own salvation because God is at work within us; they are a response to the work of the Holy Spirit in terms of the way of life laid down in the Word and applied to the particular needs of the time. God by his Spirit gives us the freedom to respond to or to refuse his promptings, and lays out a discipline that we are enabled to follow by the strength that he provides. It is through this discipline, in which we are to exercise the gifts of his Spirit, that God produces in us the life of holiness.

Wesley was far from imagining that the use of such a discipline was in itself meritorious.

Do not some of you suppose, that gravity and composedness of behaviour are the main parts of Christianity? especially, provided you neither swear, nor take the name of God in vain. Do not others imagine, that to abstain from idle songs, and those fashionable diversions commonly used by persons of their fortune, is almost the whole of religion? To which, if they add family prayer, and a strict observation of the Sabbath, then doubtless all is well. Nay, my brethren, this is well so far as it goes; but how little a way does it go toward Christianity! All these things, you cannot but see, are merely external; whereas Christianity is an inward thing, without which the most beautiful outward form is lighter than vanity.[52]

Man cannot establish the God relationship by the use of these outward forms; it is established only by God's initiative and is received by faith alone. It is those who are already in the faith relationship and who are receiving the grace which makes obedi-

[51] Works, VII, 489.
[52] Works, VIII, 182.

138

ence possible who are guided into the way of holiness through this discipline.

The way of holiness is revealed to us by God in his Word and the refusal to allow God to lead us along this road is the main reason for falling into the "wilderness state." So Wesley's great concern was to set before his people the outline of that way—the permanent framework being set forth in the instituted means of grace, and the changing details being expressed in the prudential means. The form which he gave to the prudential means was not looked upon as the only possible form. He saw his societies as voluntary groups within the great congregation and never claimed that only members of those societies were true members of the Church. Still he was convinced that an ordered life of fellowship was necessary to growth in grace and that in the lack of such order could be found the reason why so many Christians were failing to make progress along the road of salvation.

In his treatment of the proper use by the Christian of the "means of grace" we see a creative working out of the doctrine of justification by faith. In his clear exposition of the way in which the Christian life involves "working out our own salvation," because it is God at work in us, Wesley removes all suspicion that the Classical Protestant doctrine of justification necessarily involves an antinomian tendency, and at the same time he satisfies the Free Church emphasis on the free response of the believer to the Spirit. He also places this Protestant emphasis into creative relation with the Catholic emphasis on the given forms of grace, and brings into the foreground the necessity for the mutual life of Christian fellowship in voluntary groups which seek to express the meaning of life under the Word in terms of the changing circumstances of our daily life.

Contemporary Significance

Wesley saw clearly that while the instituted means of grace provide the essential continuing framework for the Christian life, obedience to Christ in the changing circumstances requires forms of fellowship which enable us to translate the meaning of our life together under the Word into the structure of our contemporary existence. Wesley's societies enabled his people to build each other up in their faith, to relate their faith to the problems of their personal life, and to apply it to the structure of their existence in society.

Their rules for "attending upon all the ordinances of God" enabled them to supplement the worship of the great congregation in such a way as to enable them to become priests to each other by mutual counsel and encouragement in the fellowship of the Spirit, and by their rules for "doing no harm" and "doing good" they sought to relate their common life of obedience to Christ to their contemporary social situation.

Today there is a growing ecumenical recognition of the need to seek for new forms of group life in the Church which will allow the Word to set up its dialogue with the questions and problems of our contemporary existence. This is seen in the important experiments with "evangelical academies," "house churches," and various forms of "para churches." Within congregations, too, it is gradually becoming recognized that smaller groups are essential to translate faith into forms of discipline, in order to relate the faith to the common concerns of daily life and to provide for the mutual growth of the members.

Here, of course Methodism has no monopoly, but from its heritage it may itself be taught the importance of these voluntary groups and recognize the necessity for joining in the search for the relevant forms they must take today. From her tradition Methodism can witness to the revivifying power that can flow from such groups and can speak of the way these ecclesiolae with their prudential means can be related to the ecclesia with its instituted and unchanging means of grace.

It is to the relation of ecclesiolae to ecclesia in the original Methodist tradition that we now turn.

—— 9 THE DOCTRINE OF THE CHURCH

⊃ In the ecumenical encounter the doctrine of the Church has become the focus of our deepest difference and so far we have been unable to reconcile our divergent views. We turn now to Wesley to discover what was the original Methodist tradition and to see whether this doctrine throws any light on the attitude Methodists should now adopt.

In the revision of the "XXXIX Articles of the Church of England" for the Methodists in America Wesley kept unchanged the article on the Church, Article XIX becoming Article XIII.

The visible Church is a congregation of faithful men in which the pure Word of God is preached and the sacraments be duly administered according to Christ's ordinance in all those things that of necessity are requisite to the same.

This Article, in itself, is in the Reformation or Classical Protestant tradition so that, for example, the ministry is not included in the definition of the Church,[1] but clearly the Article is patient

---

[1] Compare Roger Mehl, *The Ecumenical Review* (April, 1957), IX, No. 3, pp. 247-48: "It is a remarkable fact that, while declaring that the ministry is instituted by God and that no Church could exist without a ministry, the confessions of faith of the Reformation did not make the ministry into a mark of the Church. The reason for this apparent contradiction is simple: the ministry exists only for the Church's mission. It is not a form essentially bound up with the substance; it is the indispensable instrument of a Church whose *nature* is identical with its *mission*."

of various emphases. Wesley singles out the three things that the article says are

essential to a visible Church. First: Living faith; without which, indeed, there can be no Church at all, neither visible or invisible. Secondly: Preaching, and consequently hearing, the pure word of God, else that faith would languish and die. And, Thirdly, a due administration of the sacraments,—the ordinary means whereby God increaseth faith.[2]

Historically the problem lies at the point of the priority of emphasis. It can be said that the Catholic stress falls on the third, with the due administration of the sacraments being further defined in terms of the unbroken succession of the apostolic ministry; that the Classical Protestant concentration is on the second, with living faith and due administration of the sacraments being made dependent on the preaching and hearing of the pure Word of God; that the Free Church emphasis centers on living faith. Yet it is a matter of priority of emphasis, not of exclusive interests, and the Article itself allows for strongly divergent viewpoints.

There is, for example, a further Anglican tradition concerning the ministry which, while not receiving any uniform doctrinal interpretation in the confession, places a strong stress on the importance of the historic episcopate as a symbol of continuity and upon the sacramental and liturgical life as the locus of the continuous and unbroken presence of Christ in his Church.

When we ask where Wesley stood in relation to these emphases, we soon see a strong concern for the Classical Protestant objective vertical emphasis on the pure Word. In his *Journal* he makes the claim that he is faithful in his preaching to "the fundamental doctrines of the Church, clearly laid down, both in her Prayers, Articles and Homilies," while many of the clergy are unfaithful to the Word.[3] He further claims, in expounding the article on the Church, that many of the clergy are the "worst Dissenters" from the Church, being "unholy men of all

[2] *Works*, VIII, 31. From "An Earnest Appeal."
[3] *Journal*, II, 274-76.

kinds," "men unsound in the faith," and "those who unduly administer the sacraments." [4]

It is clear that Wesley placed great emphasis upon the Classical Protestant view with its stress on the necessity for the Church to be continually formed by the "event" in which faith is aroused by the true preaching of the Word. It would seem further that Wesley diverged from the Catholic horizontal view in the way that he defined the succession of the ministry. In a letter to the *London Chronicle* in 1761 he wrote, concerning the ministry of the Reformed churches:

This Church has "a perpetual succession of pastors and teachers divinely appointed and divinely assisted." And there has never been wanting in the Reformed Churches such a succession of pastors and teachers, men both divinely appointed and divinely assisted; for they convert sinners to God—a work none can do unless God Himself appoint them thereto and assist them therein; therefore every part of this character is applicable to them. Their teachers are the proper successors of those who have delivered down through all generations the faith once delivered to the saints; and their members have true spiritual communion with the "one holy" society of true believers. Consequently, although they are not the whole "people of God," yet they are an undeniable part of His people.[5]

Here succession is defined in terms of the Word, and it would seem that Wesley stands firmly in the Classical Protestant tradition, but there are complicating factors. First, he places an important limitation on the dominance of the Classical Protestant emphasis for Wesley envisaged within the Church considerable freedom in relation to doctrine.[6] In discussing the Article definition of the Church, he comments:

[4] *Ibid.*, 335-36.
[5] *Letters*, IV, 137-38.
[6] We are speaking here in comparative terms—the standard of comparison being the usual requirement in the Classical Protestant tradition of a detailed confession of faith as essential to the being of the Church. Compare Luther's statement in his *Commentary on the Epistle to the Galatians* (James Clarke & Co., London, 1953), 472.

"The Sacramentarians, which deny the corporal presence of Christ in the Supper, object against us. . . . [They say] that we are contentious, obstinate, and intractable in defending our doctrine, seeing that for the single difference

143

I will not undertake to defend the accuracy of this definition. I dare not exclude from the Church catholic all those congregations in which any unscriptural doctrines, which cannot be affirmed to be "the pure word of God," are sometimes, yea, frequently preached; neither all those congregations in which the sacraments are not "duly administered." Certainly if these things are so, the Church of Rome is not so much as a part of the catholic Church; seeing therein neither is "the pure word of God" preached, nor the sacraments "duly administered." Whoever they are that have "one Spirit, one hope, one Lord, one faith, one God and Father of all," I can easily bear with their holding wrong opinions, yea, and superstitious modes of worship: Nor would I, on these accounts, scruple still to include them within the pale of the catholic Church; neither would I have any objection to receive them, if they desired it, as members of the Church of England.[7]

Here we see Wesley's consciousness of the importance of the first point of the Article, with its stress on living faith, and his recognition that the sovereignty and freedom of Christ are such

concerning the sacrament we do break Christian charity and rend the concord of the churches. . . .

"In philosophy, a small fault in the beginning is a great (and a foul) fault in the end. So in divinity, one little error overthroweth the whole doctrine. . . . In this matter we cannot yield even a hair's breadth. For the doctrine is like a mathematical point, which cannot be divided; that is, it can suffer neither addition nor subtraction."

In relation to this Wesley envisaged considerable freedom of doctrine, but there seems no doubt that he would have considered the present Methodist freedom in relation to doctrine as "speculative latitudinarianism." I have discussed this in Chapter I above.

For an indication of the attitude of contemporary Lutheranism to the Confession, it is well worth turning to *The Unity of the Church*, a Symposium of papers presented to the Lutheran World Federation. (Augustana Book Concern, Rock Island, 1957.) The discussions on the meaning of Article VII of the Augsburg Confession, and particularly the phrase "And to the true unity of the Church it is enough to agree concerning the doctrine of the Gospel and the administration of the Sacraments," indicate an openness not expressed in the above quotation from Luther. So Bishop Nygren comments: "Nothing at all is said here about a confession; only the gospel is being discussed." (81.) "What is decisive is that the gospel be purely preached. Here the churches should help one another to drive always deeper into the gospel. Often that cannot take place except through serious struggle. But there will be struggles carried on *within* the church. Abrogation of the church fellowship is no appropriate means." See also Peter Brunner, 99-100 and Ernst Kinder, 106.

[7] *Works*, VI, 397, in the sermon "Of The Church."

that we dare not limit this to the place where the pure Word of God is preached. As we observed in the previous chapter, this emphasis on the sovereignty of Christ enables us to make sense of our present ecumenical dilemma, where we have recognized Christ in each other, while still being forced to claim that we do not recognize in each other the pure Word of God. But just as this emphasis did not lead Wesley to suggest that God's freedom to move beyond the instituted means of grace implies their unimportance in the life of the Church, so here God's freedom to move beyond the boundaries of the pure preaching of the Word does not lead Wesley to that doctrinal indifference which sometimes characterizes the Free Church tradition.

Here then in Wesley we see an emphasis on the first part of the article—living faith—which prevents the second point—pure Word—from gaining complete dominance. However, we must note, second, that there is in Wesley as well, a strong emphasis on horizontal continuity and upon the unbroken presence of Christ in his Church through the sacraments, despite the unfaithfulness of the priests.

> Did the Jewish Sacraments convey no saving grace to the hearers, because they were administered by unholy men? If so, none of the Israelites were saved from the time of Eli to the coming of Christ. For their priests were not a whit better than ours. . . . If then no grace is conveyed by the ministry of wicked men, in what a case is the Christian world! . . . Rather say with our own Church, . . . the unworthiness of the Minister doth not hinder the efficacy of God's ordinance. The reason is plain, because the efficacy is derived, not from him that administers, but from Him that ordains it. He does not, will not suffer his grace to be intercepted, though the messenger will not receive it himself.[8]

We see here an emphasis on the objective holiness of the Church, the fact that Christ is present to the Church through the sacraments, quite apart from the faith and life of clergy and believers. This horizontal continuity of the Church he also connected with the ministry. In his last sermon on the subject of the Church, preached in 1789, Wesley distinguishes between the

---

[8] *Works*, VII, 183-84 from the sermon "On Attending the Church Service."

prophetic and priestly roles of the ministry. His lay preachers, he said, were prophets, raised up by God to preach the true Word (here he preserves the Classical Protestant emphasis), but it was not in their power to seize the priestly authority which God has continued through the regular priesthood (the Catholic horizontal emphasis).

The tension between these two emphases was considerable.[9] Wesley struggled to an amazing degree to keep unity within the Church, because he believed that not only the true preaching of the Word, but also the unity and continuity of the Church were vital to her mission. In his sermon "On Schism" he speaks of the effects of separation from "a body of living Christians, with whom we were before united," as "a grievous breach of the law of love. It is the nature of love to unite us together," but the result of separation, "being a breach of brotherly love," is that it brings forth evil fruit, "producing uncharitable attitudes— anger, resentment, argumentativeness"—which not only cause the ruin of souls within the Church, but are "a grievous stumbling-block . . . to those who are without." [10] Consequently unity is essential to the Church's mission, and for that reason Wesley struggled ceaselessly to keep the unity of the Church in terms of its continuity through the historic ministry, sacraments, and liturgy.[11]

He knew, however, that a love of unity that surrenders truth destroys itself, and therefore he emphasized that if at last the preaching of the true Word resulted in being forced out of the Church, unwillingly this had to be accepted. The resultant breach would cause serious damage to the mission of the Church, but the failure to proclaim the Word would be fatal to it. In this tragic extremity those thrust out would be used by God as the Church, as was the case with Luther and Calvin.[12] But Wesley believed that he must do everything in his power to prevent such an extremity, and he sought to hold vertical and horizontal together by organizing his lay preachers to proclaim the true

---

[9] The evidence, for this and the conclusions following, is found in the Appendix.
[10] Works, VI, 406-408.
[11] Works, VII, 278.
[12] Ibid., 182-83.

Word, while urging his followers to continue in attendance on the ministration of the regular clergy.

Does this view imply that the visible marks of continuity are not necessary marks of the Church? In one sense yes, for in Wesley's view there was no fixed pattern of order imposed upon the Church in apostolic times.[13] Nevertheless he prized these

[13] The problem of Wesley's doctrine of the ministry is peculiarly difficult. John C. Bowmer, in *The Sacrament of the Lord's Supper in Early Methodism* (London: Dacre Press, 1951), pp. 156-63, argues cogently that while Wesley believed uninterrupted succession to be a fable in that "It is impossible to draw up a list of any see with an uninterrupted succession from the Apostles' time to the present day," he never discarded a belief in succession. "Wesley's idea of succession was still, in effect, episcopal; not it is true, in the traditional and usually accepted view of episcopal succession, but in accordance with his belief that presbyters discharging their function as episkopoi, have the right to ordain. When Wesley ordained, it was as a presbyter exercising the inherent right of a New Testament episkopos. In this respect, it was still episcopal succession; and when Dr. Coke ordained, too, he did so as a Bishop. . . . Furthermore, in the ordinal to be found in Wesley's *Sunday Service of the Methodists* the presence of the Superintendent (the counterpart of episkopos of which it is a translation) for the laying on of hands is required at the ordination of all three orders of ministers—deacons, presbyters, and superintendents."

But J. S. Simon in *Proceedings of the Wesley Historical Society*, 1914, IX, No. 5, 153-54, claims that up until the time of 1788 Wesley's ordinations had been to "deacons" and "elders" orders, but that in 1788, when with "the Rev. James Creighton and the Rev. Peard Dickenson, presbyters of the Church of England, he set apart for the sacred office, by imposition of hands and prayer, Messrs. Alexander Mather, Thomas Rankin, and Henry Moore, without sending them out of England, strongly advising them at the same time, that, according to his example, they should continue united to the Established Church, so far as the blessed work in which they were engaged would permit," he ordained them "presbyter in the Church of God." It is Simon's view, suggested by Henry Moore himself, that Wesley was providing for the inevitable break with the Church of England by providing for regular presbyteral succession. This, of course, has the advantage of regularizing subsequent British practice, and Wesley's statement that the Reformed ministries were used by God as valid must here be kept in view. Nevertheless we must be careful not to make too much of Wesley's use of presbyter here. He had often used it before as a synonym for elder (as in his ordination certificate of Coke). This is by no means a proof that Wesley had decided that a single order is the best form of the ministry.

The most recent study of the problem is *Wesley: Apostolic Man* (London: The Epworth Press, 1957), by Edgar W. Thompson. It follows the view that Wesley in his ordinations followed the precedent of the Church of Alexandria in the first three centuries, where presbyters appointed and consecrated their own bishops without intervention from other sees (31-32). He also stresses that Wesley should have acknowledged that in this act he had moved "beyond obedience to the rule of the Anglican Church, and that he had taken to himself a power of consecration that the Church did not allow." (52.) This is true, and it emphasizes Wesley's belief that God in his sovereignty is not bound by the given order of the Church, and that where mission demands it, irregularity is a necessity. Nevertheless we miss the significance of Wesley's struggle unless we take account

marks of continuity and believed that the threefold order of the ministry, being consistent with the Scripture and Apostolic practice and having such universal sway in the early centuries, was the normal order of the Church. For that reason, his struggle to stay in unity with the Church of England must be seen as an attempt to maintain the catholicity of the Church. He believed that her unity and continuity must be maintained along with the true preaching of the Word if the Church is to fulfill her mission.

His emphasis then on the unbroken presence of Christ in the sacraments, despite the unfaithfulness and unholiness of the priests, witnesses to the fact that Wesley from one side defined the Church's holiness in terms of her given form. Similarly his emphasis on the preaching of the true Word, to be received by faith alone, witnesses to his further definition of the holiness of the Church in terms of justification with Christ as our "alien righteousness" while we are still sinners. But in what seems like a sheer contradiction, he also gives expression to the subjective vertical, or Free Church tradition with its emphasis upon the response of believers as providing the necessary test of the holiness of the Church.

"The holy catholic Church?" How many wonderful reasons have been found out for giving it this appelation! One learned man informs us, "The Church is holy, because Christ, the Head of it, is holy." Another eminent author affirms, "It is so called, because all its ordinances are designed to promote holiness;" and yet another,— "because our Lord intended that all the members of the Church should be holy." Nay, the shortest and the plainest reason that can be given, and the only true one, is,—The Church is called holy, because it is holy; because every member thereof is holy, though in different degrees, as He that called them is holy. How clear is this! If the Church, as to the very essence of it, is a body of believers, no

---

of his almost painful attempt, not only to maintain continuity with the threefold order by finding the precedent in Alexandria, but also to maintain unity with the Church of England. He could allow no theory of the threefold order which sought to bind God to an uninterrupted succession through bishops by claiming that the Church could not exist where that form of succession was absent. Yet he could and did allow the normality of the threefold order, and the importance of doing all that was possible to preserve continuity and unity in this ministry.

man that is not a Christian believer can be a member of it. If the whole body be animated by one Spirit, and endued with one faith, and one hope of their calling; then he who has not that Spirit, and faith, and hope, is no member of that body.[14]

Here is a clear expression of the subjective vertical tradition, and it would seem to lead necessarily to the Free Church emphasis on the "gathered" people of God, as against the "multitudinous" view of the State Church to which Wesley belonged. But, in fact, Wesley tried to hold these apparently contradictory views together.

His view of the necessary intrinsic holiness of the Church so that the Church's *life* is as much a mark of her existence as her *form* does not exclude his emphasis on the objective holiness of the Church in the sacraments, nor does it exclude the Classical Protestant emphasis that holiness has to be understood in terms of justification by faith since the believer is *simul justus et peccator*. Wesley's claim is that unless the objective holiness, in terms of the given presence of Christ in the Word and sacraments, brings forth the subjective holiness of a living response in believers, the Church is not truly the Church. The given holiness in sacramental life and the objective holiness in the Word through preaching, should result in subjective holiness through the faith relationship that is evoked. All three of these emphases Wesley believed to be essential to the being and the mission of the Church.

Yet how is it possible to hold them together? How can the "multitudinous" and the "gathered" views be reconciled? Many will be related to the sacraments and the preaching in whom no living faith bringing forth holiness is evoked. Wesley's answer seems to lie in his use of the concept of *ecclesiolae in ecclesia*, small voluntary groups of believers living under the Word and seeking under the life of discipline to be a leaven of holiness within the "great congregation" of the baptized.[15]

[14] *Works*, VI, 400, from the sermon "Of The Church."
[15] Hildebrandt, *From Luther to Wesley*, op. cit., p. 73: "The ecclesiola in ecclesia which Luther saw on the horizon, moved with Wesley directly into the foreground."

The Communion of Saints

Simon has remarked that in his admiration of the order of the Church of England Wesley found one essential point that was insufficiently stressed.

Its formularies did not sufficiently provide for the fellowship of Christian people. They recognized communion in worship and at the sacrament of the Lord's Supper, but he saw that they were defective in provision for that spiritual personal fellowship between individual believers which was a distinguishing mark of the Church at the begnning of its history. It was enjoyed by the members of the best kind of the Religious Societies in England, but he was aware that such Societies had arisen from individual initiative rather [than] from any ecclesiastical direction or command. He could not deny that in many instances, such meetings had been opposed by persons in authority as illegal or mischievous, and that the justification of this form of Christian fellowship was to be found in the pages of the New Testament rather than in the ecclesiastical law books of the Church of England. . . . He found it impossible to realize his vision unless he enlarged the conception of the Church, which satisfied most of the members of the Church of England.[16]

It should be said that we would hardly expect to find directions for these voluntary groups within the ecclesiastical law books. Wesley saw that the particular form that such groups take must vary and so placed them under the prudential means of grace. But Simon's point is sound to the extent that Wesley insisted that there must be some form of small group fellowship. Behind this emphasis on ecclesiolae lay his belief that the ecclesia is essentially a "communion of saints," and that

it is only when we are knit together that we "have nourishment from Him, and increase with the increase of God." Neither is there any time, when the weakest member can say to the strongest, or the strongest to the weakest, "I have no need of thee." Accordingly our blessed Lord, when his disciples were in the weakest state, sent them forth, not alone, but two by two. When they were strengthened a little, not by solitude, but by abiding with him and one another, he commanded them to "wait," not separate, but "being assembled together," for "the promise of the Father." And "they were all with one accord in

[16] Simon, *John Wesley and the Religious Societies*, 157-58. Used by permission of Epworth Press.

one place," when they received the gift of the Holy Ghost. Express mention is made in the same chapter, that when "there were added unto them three thousand souls, all that believed were together, and continued steadfastly" not only "in the Apostles' doctrine," but also "in fellowship and in breaking of bread," and in praying "with one accord." Agreeable to which is the account the great Apostle gives of the manner which he had been taught of God, "for the perfecting of the saints, for the edifying of the body of Christ," even to the end of the world. And according to St. Paul, all who will ever come, in "the unity of the faith, unto a perfect man, unto the measure of the stature of the fulness of Christ," must "together grow up into Him: From whom the whole body fitly joined together and compacted" (or strengthened) "by that which every joint supplieth, according to the effectual working in the measure of every part, maketh increase of the body unto the edifying of itself in love." [17]

Wesley believed that the necessity for mutual encouragement, mutual examination, and mutual service, within the context of the means of grace, required more than the hearing of the Word, the participation in the sacraments, and the joining in the prayers of the "great congregation." Wesley's view of holiness was woven into his ecclesiology. He believed that the gathering together of believers into small voluntary societies for mutual discipline and Christian growth was essential to the Church's life. Speaking of the failure of true fellowship in the Church of England, he wrote:

Who watched over them in love? Who marked their growth in grace? Who advised and exhorted them from time to time? Who prayed with them and for them, as they had need? This, and this alone is Christian fellowship: But, alas! where is it to be found? Look east or west, north or south; name what parish you please: Is this Christian fellowship there? Rather, are not the bulk of parishioners a mere rope of sand? What Christian connexion is there between them? What intercourse in spiritual things? What watching over each other's souls? What bearing of one another's burdens? . . . We introduce fellowship where it was utterly destroyed. And the fruits of it have been peace, joy, love, and zeal for every good word and work.[18]

[17] Works, XIV, 333-334.
[18] Works, VIII, 251-52.

Wesley believed that his class meetings represented the genius of primitive Christianity and that God had given him a vision of the way in which these ecclesiolae could be the means of spreading scriptural holiness throughout the land.

Those whom God sent forth "preached the gospel to every creature." . . . But as soon as any of these were so convinced of the truth, as to forsake sin and seek the gospel salvation, they immediately joined them together, took an account of their names, advised them to watch over each other, and met these . . . "catechumens" (as they were then called,) apart from the great congregation, that they might instruct, rebuke, exhort, and pray with them, and for them, according to their several necessities.[19]

This "gathered" emphasis, he believed, was a necessary mark of the Church, but he kept it along with the "multitudinous" emphasis by speaking of groups being drawn together apart from the great congregation of the baptized in order to grow in mutual fellowship under the Word towards holiness of heart and life.

Do we not see here in Wesley a creative attempt to keep all three historic emphases together? And if the tension between them seems to rise almost to the point of contradiction, is not this tension a necessary expression of the position of the Church in history as it seeks to be obedient to Christ in the fulfillment of its mission? The Catholic emphasis is right—Christ does not abandon his Church, even when the priests are unfaithful, but is always present in unbroken continuity in the sacraments he has provided. The Classical Protestant emphasis is right—the pure witness to the faith once delivered to the saints is essential to the ever renewed "event" in which believers are called into being, and since it is sinners who are justified by faith through the Word spoken and heard, the holiness of the Church is essentially an "alien" righteousness. The Free Church emphasis is right—true believers must be gathered together for mutual growth in the life of the Spirit toward the fullness of the stature

[19] *Ibid.*, 251. See also the important statement in *Journal*, V, 26: "I was more convinced than ever that the preaching like an Apostle, without joining together those that are awakened and training them up in the ways of God, is only begetting children for the murderer."

of Christ, and this transformation of life "in Christ" is essential to the being and mission of the Church.

These emphases only become wrong when one is separated from the others. The "unity," the "mission," and the "renewal" of the Church must be constantly held together. Or to put it in another way, the mission of the Church requires her to draw all men into the unity (Catholic) of the faith (Classical Protestant) unto the measure of the stature of the fullness of Christ (Free Church Protestant).

This emphasis on ecclesiolae also speaks an essential word to Methodists, who, in their movement from being a society towards becoming a Church, have never been clear as to how they could reconcile the characteristics of strict discipline in the societies to the life of the "great congregation." Usually they have ended by dropping the discipline. Wesley, however, sought to solve the problem through small voluntary groups with their specific disciplines within the wider membership formed only on the basis of baptism and profession of faith.

The Protestant Episcopal Bishop, C. B. Brewster, addressing Methodists on the occasion of the Wesley Bicentennial in 1903, said:

I need not tell the audience that Wesley's intention was far from contemplating the great separation that ensued between the Methodists and the Church of England, nor quote the language in which he urgently advised against such separation. He seems to have conceived of great organizations within the organism of the one body of all the baptized. Greater than any organization or particular church is the whole multitude of the spiritual commonwealth.[20]

That Wesley had in mind "orders" within the Church (such as the Franciscan in the Roman Church) seems quite possible. At least that is the way he seemed to view the relation of his own Methodist societies to the Church of England. He desired Methodism to have an organized life of its own, fulfilling the need for group fellowship and discipline and concentrating on the mission of the Church, while remaining within the given framework of the Church, united with her by common doctrine, ministry, sacraments and worship.[21]

This doctrine of *ecclesiolae* has ecumenical significance in the way by which Wesley sought to overcome the apparently divisive character of the Classical Protestant insistence on the Article definition of the "pure word."

Wesley's limitation of the Classical Protestant emphasis on pure doctrine was far from an encouragement of "speculative latitudinarianism." His real concern, as his "Letter to Various Clergymen" reveals,[22] was for unity in mission. So he argues that as long as the various churchmen agree on the articles in which the faith must be presented to nonbelievers, "1. Original Sin. 2. Justification by Faith. 3. Holiness of heart and life" (and these three, we have seen, presupposed other such doctrines as the Deity of Christ, the Atonement, the Deity of the Holy Spirit), then they can witness together as one Church.

This did not mean that the doctrines of remaining disagreement, such as absolute decrees on the one hand and perfection on the other, are "nonessentials." They are important in the nurture of Christians, however, rather than in the missionary proclamation of the gospel. And, in the church, since complete unity on such matters is impossible in this period in which we see through a glass darkly, there should be societies where the nurture of Christians is carried on by those of different persuasion. So Wesley welcomed the Calvinist societies of George Whitefield as partners in the work of mission,[23] while insisting strongly

[21] Here we see one of the real problems that subsequent Methodism has faced. Wesley stressed the given holiness of the Church in relation to the great congregation—the unbroken presence of Christ in the sacramental and liturgical life of the continuous visible Church. Over against this extrinsic holiness of the Church, he stressed the intrinsic holiness in the life of the ecclesiolae. When the Methodist societies became separated from the Church, the stress on the given holiness of the Church tended to be lost, and the stress on the subjective became dominant. It may well be that the lack of this polar balance, with the resultant overemphasis on the subjective, was the cause of much of the "moralism" of Methodism and of her spawning of the riotously subjective holiness movements.

[22] *Letters*, IV, 237.

[23] See *Sermons*, II, 506 ff., in his sermon "On the Death of the Rev. George Whitefield."

in his own societies that predestination was contrary to the Word of God.[24] He believed teaching on such matters to be essential to the nurture (as distinguished from the message necessary for conversion) of believers, and that therefore in the societies the Methodists should have the right to preach their convictions and the Calvinists theirs.[25] Each, however, should accept the other as true members of the Church; there should be interchange of preachers and freedom of movement from one to the other. Above all they should witness together in the common mission of the Church to the world and display their mutual love by common worship in the great congregation.[26]

Clearly a large measure of doctrinal agreement is necessary, but Wesley believed that since full agreement in doctrine cannot be expected in this life, it is essential to maintain a "Catholic spirit" on those matters which still divide us.

It may well be that his distinction between the agreement necessary for common witness to the world, as against continuing disagreements in societies for the nurture of believers, can give us real guidance in our ecumenical dilemma. Is it not possible to unite when we have reached a level of agreement sufficient for our common witness to the world while fully recognizing that on some matters there is still deep disagreement? Could not these distinctive emphases exist together in the one Church (at least at first), even as separate societies?

In summary, it may be useful to ask what Wesley's views imply for the present relation of Methodism to churches of three traditions.

Methodist Relation to the Catholic Tradition

On the basis of John Wesley's views there is a good case for arguing that Methodists should be prepared to accept the his-

[24] *Works*, VII, 373 ff., in his sermon on "Free Grace."
[25] In *Letters*, IV, 244, to Lady Huntingdon, Wesley says that they should avoid disputing with other "children of God" in order to "unite our strength to carry on the war against the 'rulers of the darkness of this world.'" In *Journal*, II, 433, in the dispute with Cennick he advises that each should choose which society he pleases. Note that Wesley allows Predestinarians to come to his societies.
[26] *Journal* II, 507-509, gives the story of his efforts to find unity in difference with the Welsh Calvinist, Howell Harris. See also *Letters*, II, 8-9. His efforts were successful.

toric episcopate.[27] But would it not also be necessary for Methodists to insist that while they are prepared to accept this ministry as a symbol of order,—an order which is normal and expresses the continuity and unity of the Church—they must also insist that God has used their ministry as valid in the same way that he has used the Reformation ministries as valid? Must they not insist in loyalty to what God has done through them that the very existence of these ministries has been a witness to the truth that the visible forms of the Church are no guarantee of the existence of the true Church in the full sense, and that God is free to move outside the forms that he has provided in order that the mission of the Church may be fulfilled? In accepting the historic episcopate, therefore, it would seem to follow that Methodists should also insist, where necessary, on remaining in communion with those Classical Protestant and Free Church Protestant denominations in whom also we have seen Christ at work.

Methodist Relation to Classical Protestant Tradition

If it is to be true to Wesley, Methodism needs to recognize once more the importance of maintaining standards of doctrine for those called to preach the Word. Here it needs the witness of the Classical Protestant churches. Yet is not Wesley's distinction between the doctrines essential to our common witness to the world and the further doctrines important to the nurture of Christians of real importance? There is a vital necessity for seeking to come to mutual understanding in the Word, and we would agree that "full church unity must be based on a large measure of agreement in doctrine." [28] Still must there not come a time when, with some differences still unreconciled, churches feel compelled by their common mission to take the leap into unity on the basis of the agreements already established. This is not to suggest that the remaining differences would be unimportant. It is to suggest that they need not prevent common witness to the world, and that the step toward unity can be taken

---

[27] See Appendix.
[28] One of the points of ecumenical consensus listed by W. A. Visser 't Hooft in *The Ecumenical Review*, VIII, No. 1, October, 1955, 22.

156

in the faith that when they draw together, God will give them the further unity they need for the nurture of his people.

Methodist Relation to the Free Church Protestant Tradition

We have seen Wesley's strong insistence on the necessity for "intrinsic" holiness. We have seen also his emphasis on the freedom of God to move beyond given forms to bring into being a life of fellowship in which believers may grow in grace and receive the many gifts of the life of the Spirit. Here we recognize the importance of the Free Church emphasis, and perhaps it should lead even to a willingness (as in the scheme of union in Ceylon) to accept the idea of the choice between infant and believer's baptism, as the sign of the necessary tension between "extrinsic" and "intrinsic" holiness. But would not Methodism also wish to witness to the way in which the two aspects of holiness—given and realized—and the two aspects of the Church—multitudinous and gathered—can be held together by the existence of ecclesiolae in ecclesia?

When we move into the area of Church order and the Free Church insistence upon a large measure of freedom and autonomy in congregational life as against the Methodist emphasis upon organizational unity and connectional coherence, we may seem to approach a deadlock. Here we must admit that the non-theological factors[29] become very strong. The emotional power of loyalty to long familiar method, the fear of the unfamiliar, the desire to retain power, the subconscious determination to justify our own tradition at the expense of all possible modifications, are but a few of the social and psychological factors working against unity.

Here we see the relevance of Wesley's insistence that no order is absolute. Methodists would have to admit the danger that the close connectional system developed in the ecclesiolae can easily become in the ecclesia a centralized bureaucracy in which free-

---

[29] These "nontheological factors" (See Lund Report, op. cit., pp. 44-47, 62-63, 174-203) more properly should be considered under the theological category of original sin and the invasion of the Church by the motives of the world.

dom to respond to the Spirit is lost.[30] Here the witness of the Free Churches is important. Still Methodists would witness to the need for forms which express the unity of the Church in mission and worship and so would remind the Free Churches of the grave, if paradoxical danger, that their emphasis on freedom can easily become a rigid insistence upon conformity. Both need to hear a higher word of freedom: that God is free to draw his people together into new forms which retain continuity with the past, while drawing them together out of their past divisions in order to fulfill their mission in unity today.

The Lord's Supper

The rather arbitrary framework of our treatment of Wesley's theology led us to treat Wesley's doctrine of Baptism under Assurance. This forces us to treat the second Sacrament separately. That we should treat it under his doctrine of the church is natural, for the Lord's Supper was in Wesley's view and practice, central to the life of the great congregation. In line with his insistence that to grow in grace requires regular attendance on all the means of grace, Wesley placed great emphasis on this sacrament [31] and spoke of it as "the grand channel whereby the grace of His Spirit was conveyed to the souls of all the children of God." [32]

In his conflict with the advocates of "stillness" in the Fetter Lane society, who interpreted the doctrine of justification by faith alone to mean that man should do literally nothing to receive God's grace but must wait in stillness on God's approach, Wesley replied that God moves us by his grace to come to him through the instituted means, to receive the further grace that leads us along the road to salvation. In his *Journal* he records his statement to the society on June 28, 1740, giving his view of the significance of the Lord's Supper.

[30] "A rigid uniformity of governmental structure (*Lund Report*, p. 34) or a structure dominated by a centralised administrative authority (Amsterdam Report, p. 127) are to be avoided." Visser 't Hooft, op. cit., p. 22.
[31] See J. C. Bowmer, *The Sacrament of the Lord's Supper in Early Methodism*, op. cit., pp. 49-61, for an analysis of Wesley's personal practice. He communicated, on average, once every four or five days throughout his ministerial life.
[32] *Sermons*, I, 440.

I showed at large: (1.) That the Lord's Supper was ordained by God to be a means of conveying to men either preventing, or justifying, or sanctifying grace, according to their several necessities. (2.) That the persons for whom it was ordained are all those who know and feel that they want the grace of God, either to restrain them from sin, or to show their sins forgiven, or to renew their souls in the image of God. (3.) That inasmuch as we come to His table, not to give Him anything, but to receive whatsoever He sees best for us, there is no previous preparation indispensably necessary, but a desire to receive whatsoever He pleases to give. And (4.) That no fitness is required at the time of communicating, but a sense of our state, of our utter sinfulness and helplessness; everyone who knows he is fit for hell being just fit to come to Christ in this as well as all other ways of His appointment.[33]

From this it is clear that Wesley saw the Lord's Supper as a sacrament in which Christ is truly present, conveying grace to the recipient. Some degree of faith is necessary, but this faith must not be interpreted as a work by which we make ourselves worthy to receive Christ. We come, bringing only a recognition of our unworthiness and a divinely wrought conviction of the trustworthiness of his promise to be present.

How the Lord's Supper is a chief means for taking us along the road to salvation can be seen from the three aspects of the Lord's Supper that Wesley presents.

(1.) To represent the sufferings of Christ which are past, whereof it is a memorial.
(2.) To convey the first-fruits of these sufferings in present graces, whereof it is a means. And
(3.) To assure us of glory to come, whereof it is an infallible pledge.[34]

(1) A Memorial

The basis of the Lord's Supper is that it directs our faith to the merits of the death of Christ by which alone we are saved. For this reason it is not simply a reminder of something that is past, for God re-presents the Sacrifice of Christ in the Supper

---

[33] Journal, 361-62.
[34] The Poetical Works of John and Charles Wesley (ed. by G. Osborn; London: Wesleyan Methodist Conference Office, 1869), p. 186.

in order that our faith may be aroused by his present action and so that we may here receive the merits of Christ made available to us through the "full, perfect and sufficient sacrifice and satisfaction for the sins of the whole world" in "the one oblation of himself once offered" on the cross.

Bowmer shows that for Wesley, memorial means "recalled" or "brought back," so that the Supper is "the extension of an act done in the past until its effects are a present power." [35]

(2) Real Presence

Of the real presence of Christ in the Supper Wesley was in no doubt.

Is not the eating of that bread, and the drinking of that cup, the outward, visible means whereby God conveys into our souls all that spiritual grace, that righteousness, and peace, and joy in the Holy Ghost, which were purchased by the body of Christ once broken, and the blood of Christ once shed for us? Let all, therefore, who truly desire the grace of God, eat of that bread, and drink of that cup.[36]

Hildebrandt, in his earlier book on the subject, raises the question as to whether Wesley, in going beyond the Reformers in his view of the Sacrifice, even to the point of seeming "to open the prospect of common ground with the Roman and Eastern concepts of the Mass," may not lead us into the danger of turning the sacrament "from a gift of God into a work of man." [37]

[35] Bowmer, op. cit., 178-79. Quoting from Dom Grégory Dix to the effect that the New Testament word for memory (anamnesis) has "the sense of 're-calling' or 'representing' before God an event in the past, so that it becomes here and now operative by its effects." Bowmer comments: "This was exactly Wesley's position. In the first place, he took care to guard against the Roman doctrine of the repetition of the Sacrifice of Calvary in the Mass. In the second place, he specially stressed that the sacrifice, offered 'once for all,' can never be supplemented. It can be, however, and is, re-presented in the Eucharist. As he wrote in his Notes on the New Testament: 'The ancient sacrifices were in remembrance of sin: this sacrifice, once offered, is still represented in remembrance of the remission of sins.'"
[36] Sermons, I, 253.
[37] Hildebrandt, From Luther to Wesley, op. cit., 70-71.

We can sense this danger if we take on its own a passage from Wesley's adaptation of Brevint's work on the Eucharist.

This sacrifice, which by a *real oblation* was not to be offered more than once, is, by a devout and thankful commemoration, to be offered up every day. This is what the Apostle calls, *to set forth the death of the Lord:* to set it forth as well before the eyes of God His Father as before the eyes of men: and what St. Austin *explained,* when he said the holy flesh of Jesus was offered in three manners; by *prefiguring sacrifices* under the Law before His coming into the world, in a *real deed* upon His Cross, and by a *commemorative sacrament* after He ascended into heaven. All comes to this: (1.) That *the sacrifice* itself can never be repeated. (2.) That nevertheless, this Sacrament, by our remembrance, becomes a kind of sacrifice, whereby we present before God the Father, that precious oblation of His Son once offered. And thus do we every day offer unto God the meritorious offerings of our Lord, as the only ground whereon God may give, and we obtain, the blessing we pray for. . . . *To men,* the holy communion is a *sacred table,* where God's minister is ordered to represent, from God His Master, the passion of His dear Son, as still fresh, and still powerful for their eternal salvation. And to God, it is an altar, whereon men mystically present to Him, the same sacrifice, as still bleeding and suing for mercy.[38]

There is a danger of the sacrament being interpreted here as a meritorious act by which we invoke the power of the once-for-all sacrifice of Christ by our re-presentation of it, but Wesley took care to prevent any such interpretation. We are commanded to represent the sacrifice of Christ, not trusting in our own act, but in the promise of Christ that he will be present.

He will meet me there, because He has promised so to do? I do expect that He will fulfil His word, that he will meet and bless me in this way. Yet not for the sake of any works which I have done, nor for the merit of my righteousness; but merely through the merits, and sufferings, and love of His Son.[39]

The nature of the presence of Christ cannot be interpreted

[38] *The Poetical Works, op. cit.,* III, 203-204.
[39] *Sermons,* I, 254.

in terms of substance; our act of consecration does not bring about any change in the elements.

No such change of substance of the bread into the substance of Christ's body, can be inferred from the Saviour's words; "This is my body," (Matt. xxvi:26;) for it is not said "This is turned into my body," but, "This is my body;" which, if it be taken literally, would rather prove the substance of the bread to be his body.[40]

While Christ is present, we must not interpret this presence in corporal terms at all, not even by adopting the view of the ubiquity of Christ's body and so allowing for his corporal pres·ence along with the elements.

We freely own that Christ is to be adored in the Lord's Supper; but that the elements are to be adored, we deny. If Christ is not corporally present in the host, they grant their adoration to be idolatry. . . . And that he is not corporally present anywhere but in heaven, we are taught, Acts i:11, iii:21, whither he went, and where he is to continue till his second coming to judgment.[41]

Christ is present, not in any corporal way, but through the mediation of the Holy Spirit. It was for this reason that Wesley reintroduced the ancient *Epiclesis*, or prayer for the descent of the Holy Spirit, by bringing Charles Wesley's

> Come, Holy Ghost, Thine influence shed,
> And realize the sign;
> Thy life infuse into the bread,
> Thy power into the wine.

into use with the Church of England liturgy.[42]

But because he saw Christ as present through the Spirit, Wesley placed equal emphasis on the response of faith which must be given by the believer to the approach of God. The Article on the Lord's Supper (XVIII) stressed that

to such as rightly, worthily and with faith receive the same, the bread which we break is a partaking of the Body of Christ; and likewise the cup of blessing is a partaking of the blood of Christ.

[40] *Works*, X, 118.
[41] *Ibid.*, 121.
[42] Bowmer, *op. cit.*, pp. 86-90.

So Wesley emphasized the need for faith in terms of a sense of "our utter sinfulness and helpfulness." [43] This faith requires also a trust in Christ's promise to be present [44] and a willingness to allow God to bring us into obedience to his commandments.[45] Bowmer is right when he says

There is no ex opere operato efficacy in the sacraments; Wesley was quite definite on that point in his sermon on "The Means of Grace," "Settle this in your heart, that the opus operatum, the mere work done profiteth nothing." [46]

In line with his emphasis that faith is a living response to Christ leading to imitation of him, Wesley saw that communion also, is a place where we not only re-present the sacrifice of Christ but present ourselves as a sacrifice.

Too many who are called Christians, live as if under the gospel there were no sacrifice but that of Christ on the cross. And indeed there is no other that can atone for sins or satisfy the justice of God. . . . But what is not necessary to this sacrifice is absolutely necessary to our having a share in that redemption. So that though the sacrifice of ourselves cannot procure salvation, yet it is altogether needful to our receiving it. . . .

This conformity to Christ, is the grand principle of the whole Christian religion.[47]

Here again we see his rejection of "cheap grace," and his insistence that the grace of Christ empowers a faith response by which the believer can die to the world and rise to a new transformed life in conformity with Christ. Wesley saw peculiar power in the sacrament to arouse this faith response because of the active presence of the Holy Spirit bringing Christ's grace through the elements. For this reason Wesley also saw the sacrament as a "converting" as well as a "confirming" ordinance.

During the Fetter Lane controversy, Wesley wrote:

[43] *Journal*, II, 362.
[44] *Works*, VII, 151.
[45] *Ibid.*, 150.
[46] Bowmer, *op. cit.*, p. 177. Used by permission of Dacre Press: A. & C. Black Ltd.
[47] *The Poetical Works*, *op. cit.*, III, 205-206.

In the ancient Church, every one who was baptized communicated daily. So in the Acts we read, they "all continued daily in the breaking of bread and in prayer."

But in latter times many have affirmed that the Lord's Supper is not a converting but a confirming ordinance.

And among us it has been diligently taught that none but those who are converted, who have received the Holy Ghost, who are believers in the full sense, ought to communicate.

But experience shows the gross falsehood of that assertion that the Lord's Supper is not a converting ordinance. Ye are the witnesses. For many present know, the very beginning of your conversion to God (perhaps, in some, the first deep conviction) was wrought at the Lord's Supper. Now, one single instance of this kind overthrows the whole assertion.

The falsehood of the other assertion appears both from Scripture, precept, and example. Our Lord commanded those who were then unconverted, who had not yet received the Holy Ghost, who (in the full sense of the word) were not believers, to do this "in remembrance of" Him. Here the precept is clear. And to these He delivered the elements with His own hands. Here is example equally indisputable.[48]

We can understand his view of the Supper as a converting ordinance only on the basis of his belief as to the dual nature of the new birth. As we saw in his doctrine of baptism, there is a new birth—a real relation to God initiated by grace—given in baptism, but this is meant to come to fulfillment in a conscious acceptance of Christ in mature years. Here he is claiming that, according to the New Testament view (confirmed by experience), the Lord's Supper is a powerful means of grace not only in the sense of bringing sanctifying grace for the nurture of the converted, but also in bringing prevenient and justifying grace leading to this conscious acceptance of Christ. For this reason, baptism is the qualification for admission, and the Supper should not be reserved for those who have reached the mature new birth of conversion.[49]

---

[48] *Journal,* II, 360-361.
[49] In line with this, Wesley was willing to admit baptised children, provided they received instruction as to its meaning. *Journal,* V, 291, 525, 526; VII, 23.

(3) Eschatological

The third meaning of the Supper for Wesley was "to assure us of *glory to come*, whereof it is an infallible pledge." Bowmer shows that three aspects of this eschatological reality explain why the sacrament was freely administered to the dying.

First, there was the belief that the Lord's Supper is a foretaste of the heavenly banquet, "The Sacrament as a Pledge of Heaven." Second, there was the belief in the Communion of Saints, and third, that in the Lord's Supper as "Heavenly Food." [50]

Wesley saw the Lord's Supper as a main means for bringing that faith which prepares us for our final destiny. Not only does it convey that justifying and sanctifying grace which prepare us for heaven, it is also a pledge of the climactic banquet with Christ which there awaits us. For that reason the Lord's Supper is pre-eminently the place where the Church Militant and the Church Triumphant draw together.

The early Methodists lived, communicated, and died in the reality of the doctrine of the Communion of Saints. The Church militant and the Church Triumphant constitute "one family," . . . divided by "the narrow stream of death." The Lord's Supper was celebrated against the background of "angels and archangels" and with "all the company of heaven." [51]

The Ecumenical Significance

It is again Wesley's "optimism of grace" that we see shining through his doctrine of the Lord's Supper. His key emphasis is upon the way Christ, through the Spirit, uses the Supper to convey prevenient and sanctifying as well as justifying grace.

If Wesley is right in speaking of it as a converting ordinance, baptism, not confirmation, is the proper qualification for admission. Hildebrandt argues that this should lead us to accept intercommunion across the lines of our present administrations, making the further point:

If intercommunion is possible in colleges, hospitals, military services, wartime emergencies and prison camps (that is, Niemoller in

---

[50] Bowmer, *op. cit.*, 145. Used by permission of Dacre Press: A. & C. Black Ltd.
[51] *Ibid.*, 185.

165

Dachau, 1945), can any human authority prevent it under "normal" conditions? [52]

To put the problem in its fullest perspective, however, we must say that the Classical Protestant refusal is based not only on the assumption that the sacrament is a confirming rather than a converting ordinance, but also on the belief that the sacrament as the *verbum visibile* must be associated with the *verbum vocale* and therefore should be administered only to those who live under the preaching of the true Word. The Catholic refusal is based on the belief that only one ordained by a Bishop in the Apostolic succession can be the celebrant, and only one confirmed by such a bishop can be a recipient.

To the former, Wesley's view that the sacrament is a converting as well as a confirming ordinance would suggest that even where we are dissatisfied with the doctrinal standards of other bodies, we are called to see the sacrament as a place where God is calling together and offering to build up in unity those whom he has used as his Church. This applies to those whom we have recognized as his in our ecumenical commitment. For this, it must be admitted, has created an emergency situation not covered by the traditional view.

With the latter the case is more complicated. Even though Wesley rejected the qualification of confirmation for the recipient, he gave real support to the Catholic view that true ordination is necessary to right administration, especially in his 1789 sermon on "The Ministerial Office." It is on the basis of the definition of apostolic succession and of the rejection of the validity of "nonepiscopal" ministries that Methodists would question this Catholic refusal of intercommunion, again pointing to the fact that our ecumenical commitment recognizes that God has exercised his freedom in using as the Church those outside the "normal'" order. They would therefore ask whether we should not see the sacrament as a means offered by God for conveying the grace which will enable us to grow into that increasing unity which we believe that God has in store for us.

[52] Hildebrandt, *Christianity According to the Wesleys*, p. 76. Used by permission of Epworth Press.

—— 10 THE ORDER OF SALVATION: CHRISTIAN PREFECTION

There can be no doubt of the importance of the doctrine of perfection in the history of Methodism. John Wesley saw the cause for the rise of Methodism in the passion for holiness that marked his life and the life of Charles while they were still at Oxford, a passion which at last was given its true focus when they were grasped by the teaching of justification by faith alone through the teaching of Peter Bohler.

Q. 4. What was the rise of Methodism, so called?
A. In 1729, two young men, reading the Bible, saw they could not be saved without holiness, followed after it, and incited others so to do. In 1737 they saw holiness comes by faith. They saw likewise, that men are justified before they are sanctified; but still holiness was their point. God then thrust them out, utterly against their will, to raise a holy people.[1]

Wesley also believed that this emphasis was a peculiar heritage given to the Methodists in trust for the Church.

This doctrine is the grand depositum which God has lodged with the people called Methodists; and for the sake of propagating this chiefly He appeared to have raised us up.[2]

[1] *Works*, VIII, 300.
[2] *Letters*, VIII, 238. (Sept. 15, 1790) Modern Methodism sometimes has found the doctrine an embarrassment, but is still officially bound to it. In British Methodism the bond is through the authoritative sermons and the Notes on the New Testament, in American Methodism it is given official expression in the

The doctrine, however, created great difficulties for Wesley, both in seeking for adequate definitions, and in seeking to avoid misunderstandings among both followers and friends. In his doctrine Wesley desired to express the promise of the great transformation of life that opens up before the believer in the living relationship with Christ. But he knew that he must guard against the *theologia gloria*, which would so define the miracle of grace that either our creaturely limitations would be destroyed or the disorders of our nature due to the effects of original sin would be forgotten.

The Son of God does not destroy the whole work of the devil in man, as long as he remains in this life. He does not yet destroy bodily weakness, sickness, pain, and a thousand infirmities incident to flesh and blood. He does not destroy all that weakness of understanding, which is the natural consequence of the soul's dwelling in a corruptible body; so that still,

Humanum est errare et nescire:
"Both ignorance and error belong to humanity."
He entrusts us with only an exceeding small share of knowledge, in our present state; lest our knowledge should interfere with our humility, and we should again affect to be as gods. It is to remove from us all temptation to pride, and all thought of independency, (which is the very thing that men in general so earnestly covet under the name of liberty,) that he leaves us encompassed with all these infirmities, particularly weakness of understanding; till the sentence takes place, "Dust thou art, and unto dust thou shalt return!" [3]

Wesley's problem is how to define a perfection that is imperfect, how to express his conviction that by faith we can re-

---

ordination vow: "Do you expect to be made perfect in this life?" In his *Understanding the Methodist Church* Nolan B. Harmon comments: "The doctrine of Christian perfection has been the one specific contribution which Methodism has made to the Church universal . . . . In all else we have been, as we should be, glad and energetic followers in the main stream of Christian belief." I have sought to show that it is only in the context of the total expression of the Christian life represented in Wesley's theology that his doctrine of perfection can be understood, for perfection is simply the climax of the limitless faith in God's grace that shines through every part of his theology. It is here that his theology comes to focus.
[3] *Works*, VI, 275-76.

ceive the promise of unbroken personal relationship with Christ and be filled with his love without becoming involved in the eschatological heresy of "angelism." We must not lift man out of his creaturely limitations and overlook the continuing effects of his fallenness, for these will remain until Christ returns to complete the destruction of the "principalities and powers."

It was at this point that he had a difference with his brother Charles.

One word more, concerning setting perfection too high. *That perfection which I believe, I can boldy preach, because I think I see five hundred witnesses of it. Of that perfection which you preach, you do not even think you see any witness at all.* Why, then you must have more courage than me, or you could not persist in preaching it. I wonder you do not in this article fall in plumb with Mr. Whitefield. For do you not as well as he ask, "Where are the perfect ones?" I verily believe there are none upon earth, none dwelling in the body. I cordially assent to his opinion that there is *no such perfection here* as *you* describe—at least, I never met with an instant of it; and I doubt I never shall. Therefore I still think to set perfection so *high* is effectually to renounce it.[4]

⁴ *Letters*, V, 20. Hildebrandt believes that the Methodist doctrine can make its contribution only when John's statement of it is balanced by Charles! "Lest it be set too high, John Wesley speaks of God's "imitable perfections"; lest it be set too low, Charles Wesley vows:
'Wherefore to Him my feet shall run,
My eyes on His perfection gaze,
My soul shall live for God alone,
And all within me shout His praise.'
"In this turn from my to His perfection lies the most important single correction which Charles Wesley administers to his brother's statements. Where John incessantly questions himself and others about the degree of salvation up to date, Charles is silent; where John readily accepts self-evidence from those who claim attainment, Charles remains sceptical; where John insists upon a time-table which fixes the reaching of the goal "five minutes before death" at the latest, Charles maintains
'A time to Thee I will not set,
Nor charge Thee with delay;
Do with me, Lord, as seems Thee meet
But let me always pray.'
"Prayer thus takes the place of pressure and makes an end to reflection. Otherwise the doctrine must become unbearable in experience and scripturally unsound. . . . All these attempts to fix the hour, early or late, in this world or the next are but different forms of the same dogmatism which leads us from the act of prayer and faith into the realm of conjecture and reflection."

It is also at this point that we encounter one of the greatest difficulties. To define this imperfect perfection Wesley resorted to two definitions of sin: one of conscious separation from God (man can be perfect in the sense of living in unbroken conscious relationship with Christ), and the other of absolute conformity to the perfect will of God (and in this sense no man can be perfect). Thus when he spoke of the time or moment when the believer becomes perfect, he was speaking in terms of the first definition, but in light of the second he still spoke of the necessity for the perfect to confess their sins and grow in grace.

The difficulty of maintaining clarity in these definitions has been a major cause of the subsequent rents in the Methodist family.[5] One such serious split came during Wesley's lifetime—in 1763—being occasioned by the "enthusiasm" of two of his preachers. Thomas Maxfield and George Bell began to claim that men can be absolutely perfect, Bell going so far as to claim that the gift of perfection carried with it the power to read the timetable of God's future plan of salvation. The resultant split caused serious damage to the societies and considerable confusion in the minds of preachers and laity alike.

Nevertheless Wesley believed that the doctrine was the secret of the renewal God was effecting through his societies. And while there was some real change in Wesley's presentation of the doctrine over the years, there was no change in his conviction as to the importance of it. For example, in the early years after 1738 Wesley so strongly stressed the power of God to remove sin from the new born Christian that Sugden is undoubtedly right in his claim that Wesley came close to identifying new birth and sanctification, and underemphasized the continuance of sin in believers.[6] Soon this was corrected, and Wesley placed greater stress on the continuing sin in the life of the justified.

Hildebrandt, *Christianity According to the Wesleys*, 61-63. Used by permission of Epworth Press.

These are important observations, but it is still necessary that we should seek to define the nature, scope, and limitations of this perfection.

[5] See John L. Peters, *Christian Perfection and American Methodism* (Nashville, New York: Abingdon Press, 1956), for the history of these divisions.

[6] See *Sermons*, I, 36; *Sermons*, II, 443.

Yet throughout his ministry he never ceased to emphasize that by faith the believer can receive the promise of sanctification. The doctrine came into greater prominence when in 1760, in a prayer meeting after a class meeting, three who "complained of the burden they felt for the remains of indwelling sin; . . . believed God had fulfilled His word and 'cleansed them from all unrighteousness.' " [7] The next evening three more made the same confession, and quickly the movement spread. As Wesley wrote in his 1781 Concise Ecclesiastical History,

Here began that glorious work of sanctification, which had been nearly at a stand for twenty years. But from time to time it spread, first through various parts of Yorkshire, afterwards in London, then through most parts of England; next through Dublin, Limerick, and all the south and West of Ireland. And wherever the work of sanctification increased the whole work of God increased in all its branches. Many were convinced of sin, many justified, many backsliders healed.[8]

The work continued to grow so that even in the year 1763, which was marked by the split led by Maxfield and Bell, he wrote in his Journal at the year's end:

The peculiar work of this season has been what St. Paul calls "the perfecting of the saints." Many persons in London, in Bristol, in York, and in various parts, both of England and Ireland, have experienced so deep and universal a change as it had not before entered into their hearts to conceive. After a deep conviction of inbred sin, of their total fall from God, they have been so filled with faith and love (and generally in a moment) that sin vanished, and they found from that time no pride, anger, desire, or unbelief. They could rejoice evermore, pray without ceasing, and in everything give thanks. Now, whether we call this destruction or suspension of sin, it is a glorious work of God—such as work as, considering both the depth and extent of it, we never saw in these kingdoms before.[9]

Wesley also had become convinced that the spread of Methodism depended on the preaching of the doctrine.

[7] Journal, IV, 365-66.
[8] Quoted in Simon, John Wesley, The Master Builder, 70.
[9] Journal, V, 41.

Wherever this is not done, the believers grow dead and cold. Nor can this be prevented but by keeping up in them an hourly expectation of being perfected in love.[10]

It was all the more serious, then, that the split of 1763 induced a large number of preachers to cease expounding the doctrine. Wesley saw in this an attempt of the devil "to drive perfection out of the kingdom," [11] and while he was not prepared to accept defeat from those quarters, he had a great struggle on his hands. By the Conference of 1767 many of the preachers were still failing to preach it so that Wesley determined that Conference would have to decide "whether *all* our preachers or none shall continually *insist* upon Christian perfection." [12] Still the struggle was far from over as his letters to Charles reveal,[13] but he was so certain of the importance of the doctrine that from 1767 to 1777 he issued four editions of "A Plain Account of Christian Perfection."

His attitude to the doctrine for whose propagation he believed Methodism was chiefly raised up is contained in his 1790 letter to Adam Clarke.

To retain the grace of God is much more than to gain it: hardly one in three does this. And this should be strongly and explicitly urged on all who have tasted of perfect love. *If we can prove that any of our Local Preachers or Leaders, either directly or indirectly, speak against it, let him be a Local Preacher or Leader no longer.* I doubt whether he shall continue in the Society. Because he that can speak thus in our congregation cannot be an honest man.[14]

Of the importance, then, as well as the difficulty of the doctrine, there can be no doubt.

The Sources of the Doctrine

Wesley was struggling with a vital doctrine that had held a strong place in the earliest Christian tradition but had proved very difficult to define and had led to considerable confusion.

[10] *Journal,* IV, 529.
[11] *Letters,* IV, 245.
[12] *Letters,* V, 61.
[13] *Letters,* V, 88, 93.
[14] *Letters,* VIII, 249. (Italics mine.)

Peters shows the continued interest in the doctrine in the earlier history of the Church, and Wesley's wide knowledge of that interest.

Wesley brought the contributions not only of Taylor, Law and a Kempis, but also of Clement of Alexandria, Plotinus, Augustine, Tauler, the Cambridge Platonists, Molinos, Antoinette Bourignon, Madame Guyon, Macarius the Egyptian, Francois de Sales, Juan de Castanzia, Fenelon, and Pascal. From among these writers representing as they do the mystical tradition of the Church, it is obvious that Wesley was most influenced by the practical type.[15]

A review of his writings soon reveals the impressive number of times that the names of these people appear, and a glance at the Christian Library shows that he included the writings of many. One fact in particular bears stressing. Wesley had a close acquaintance with the writings of the Apostolic Fathers, and their writings formed the first volume of his Christian Library. In these writings the theme of perfection was an important issue. There we see the emerging distinction between mortal and venial sins which bears such close relation to Wesley's double definition of sin. There we see the discussion as to whether a second repentance is allowed the Christian, witnessing to their expectation of a remarkable transformation in the life of the believer, such as is described in Wesley's doctrine. These writers found it very difficult to forge a terminology adequate for defining this expectation. The difficulty was not solved by the later fathers, being scarcely overcome by Augustine's statement:

We do not think that the Apostles on this earth were exempt from the struggle of the flesh against the Spirit. But we believe that these promises can be fulfilled here just so far as they were fulfilled according to our belief in the Apostles, that is to say in the measure of human perfection in which perfection is possible in this life.[16]

Such a distinction between the perfection of the pilgrim and the perfection of the glorified is important, but until the pilgrim

---

[15] Peters, op. cit., p. 20. Notice also the influence of the English Church Societies which aimed at holiness. See Simon, John Wesley, The Master Builder, particularly p. 148. For evidence of the strong interest in the subject in the literature and sermons around 1700, see Peters, pp. 16-19.

[16] Augustine, Retractiones, 1:19.

173

perfection is given some accurate description, it is of no great use. Nor was this help forthcoming in the definitions provided in medieval theology, for while it considered perfection as a possibility, it brought it under the scheme of merit, interpreted it in the ontological framework of the ladder of ascent, and normally considered it a possibility only for those in the contemplative vocation.[17] When Wesley saw that perfection must be taken away from the ladder of merit, brought under the Reformation doctrine of salvation by grace through faith alone, and presented as a promise which is for all, he therefore had no clear theological guidance to follow. We must watch him as he seeks to forge an adequate preaching statement of the doctrine.

With reference to this central emphasis on perfection, Cell calls Wesley's theology a "necessary synthesis of the Protestant ethic of grace with the Catholic ethic of holiness." [18] Peters approves the judgment.

It would be dfficult to arrive at a more apt description than Cell gives, though it may be added that, while the Catholic tradition indicated the goal, the Protestant emphasis provided the dynamic.[19]

This judgment, however, is subject to real question. We have seen that the Catholic goal of perfection kept man tied to the order of merit and was held within the framework of the ladder of ascent, but we must also remember that the Catholic goal depended entirely upon grace. The difference of the semi-pelagianism of Rome from the Protestant view does not lie in the extent of dependence upon grace. The difference lies in the fact that the Catholic doctrine sees man as enabled by grace to rise up the ladder of merit, and at last, justified by works by virtue of the proper use of God's grace, to reach the goal of perfection. To faith, which is the means for entrance into the Christian life, must be added the works made possible by grace through which perfection is reached. Because man must merit

---

[17] For the historical changes in the doctrine, see R. Newton Flew, The Idea of Perfection (Oxford: Oxford University Press, 1934).
[18] Cell, The Rediscovery of John Wesley, op. cit., p. 361.
[19] Peters, op. cit., p. 21.

his salvation by reaching the required standard of holiness, purgatory is necessary in order to enable believers who have not reached the required standard to complete the process.

This Catholic view of holiness cannot be molded onto the Protestant view of grace. In the Protestant view grace is the free gift of God, and man can never merit his salvation. Purgatory is removed for the simple reason that man's salvation is not dependent on his reaching a required standard of ethical achievement but is the gift of God's free grace to be received by grace alone. If it is true that Wesley accepted the Catholic ethic of holiness, it must also be true that he accepted the Catholic and abandoned the Protestant view of grace.

In our examination of Wesley's doctrine of justification, however, we have seen that while he placed greater emphasis than the Reformers upon the transformation that should attend the faith relationship with Christ, he still remained within Protestant categories. The "holiness without which no man shall see the Lord," of which Wesley speaks, is not a holiness that is judged by objective moral standards, but a holiness in terms of unbroken relationship to Christ the Holy One. The perfect Christian is holy, not because he has risen to a required moral standard, but because he lives in this state of unbroken fellowship with Christ.

Wesley's view is one of sanctification by faith alone. In other words, Wesley put his doctrine within the Protestant framework of justification by faith, not within the Roman framework of justification by faith and works. He put it within the order of personal relationship to Christ, not within the order of a legal relationship to a moral standard.

Peters, in speaking of Wesley's Oxford sermon of 1733 on "The Circumcision of the Heart" in which the Christian goal is described as

that habitual disposition of the soul which, in the sacred writings, is termed holiness; and which directly implies, the being cleansed from sin, . . . and, by consequence, the being endued with those virtues which were also in Christ Jesus; the being so "renewed in the

175

spirit of our mind," as to be "perfect as our Father in heaven is perfect." [20]

remarks:

Such refinements as later developed were to be more a considera-tion of paths toward the goal than any significant alteration in the concept of the goal itself.

Although the content was adequately defined by 1733, the method of attainment was evolved only through successive periods of empiri-cally determined judgments.[21]

This implies an overly neat distinction between content and method. In 1733 Wesley looked upon perfection in terms of ethical stature, and while he saw that this was possible by grace alone, it was not until 1737, when he was convinced of the Protestant emphasis on faith alone, that he moved perfection out of the realm of unbroken ethical stature into the realm of un-broken religious relationship with Christ.

Gordon Rupp has written:

The Methodist gospel has a shape and a coherence. . . . It has sometimes been explained by saying that John Wesley combined the Protestant teaching of justification by faith with the Catholic con-cept of holiness. I do not find this an enlightening statement at all. In England it is almost always made by people slightly ashamed of their Protestantism and I do not think it bears close inspection. . . . What he had to say about holiness was bound together with what he believed about justification by faith. . . .

From beginning to end John Wesley believed and preached justi-fication by faith only. . . . Nevertheless it is true, as he put it, that holiness was his point. For him the Pauline doctrine of justification was closely linked with the Epistles of John and the doctrine of love.[22]

What Perfection Is Not

In "A Plain Account of Christian Perfection" Wesley takes care to say first what perfection is not, and we meet again his insistence on our creaturely limitations and the continuing effects of the Fall.

---

[20] Sermons, I, 267-68.
[21] Peters, op. cit., p. 21.
[22] Rupp, Principalities and Powers, op. cit., p. 82. Used by permission of Ep-worth Press.

They are not perfect in knowledge. They are not free from ignorance, no, nor from mistake. We are no more to expect any living man to be infallible, than to be omniscient. They are not free from infirmities, such as weakness or slowness of understanding, irregular quickness or heaviness of imagination. Such in another kind are impropriety of language, ungracefulness of pronunciation; to which one might add a thousand nameless defects, either in conversation or behaviour. From such infirmities as these none are perfectly freed till their spirits return to God; neither can we expect till then to be wholly freed from temptation; for "the servant is not above his master." But neither in this sense is there any absolute perfection on earth. There is no perfection of degrees, none which does not admit of continual increase.[23]

Here is Wesley's constant warning against "angelism." It was for overstepping these boundaries of our creaturely existence that Maxfield was judged an enthusiast and received a letter of rebuke from Wesley.

I dislike your supposing man may be as perfect as an angel; that he can be absolutely perfect; that he can be infallible, or above being tempted; or that the moment he is pure in heart he cannot fall from it.[24]

The perfect, in fact, are never so perfect as not to need forgiveness and never perfect in such a way as to be independent of Christ.

The way in which Wesley speaks of the perfect as free from sin, yet needing forgiveness, introduces us to one of the great difficulties of his doctrine.

(1.) Every one may mistake as long as he lives. (2.) A mistake in opinion may occasion a mistake in practice. (3.) Every such mistake is a transgression of the perfect law. Therefore, (4.) Every such mistake, were it not for the blood of atonement, would expose to eternal damnation. (5.) It follows, that the most perfect have continual need of the merits of Christ, even for their actual transgressions, and may say for themselves, as well as for their brethren, "Forgive us our trespasses." [25]

[23] *Works*, XI, 374.
[24] *Letters*, IV, 192.
[25] *Works*, XI, 395.

Here we begin to see how Wesley's definition of perfection takes it out of the order of merit and the framework of the moral law. The Christian who is perfect is free from sin, not according to the objective standards of justice, but according to the measure of personal relationship with Christ. Because this perfect relationship with Christ is necessarily marked by a spirit of love, Wesley goes on to argue that even actual transgressions are not sins, because "love is the sole principle of action." But

"If they live without sin, does not this exclude the necessity of a Mediator? At least, is it not plain that they stand no longer in need of Christ in his priestly office?
"A. Far from it. None feel their need of Christ like these; none so entirely depend upon him. For Christ does not give life to the soul separate from, but in and with, himself. Hence his words are equally true of all men, in whatsoever state of grace they are: 'As the branch cannot bear fruit of itself, except it abide in the vine; no more can ye, except ye abide in me: Without' (or separate from) 'me you can do nothing.' " [26]

Thus while Wesley places greater emphasis than Luther upon the transformation that necessarily flows from our faith relationship to Christ,[27] he is at one with him in the view that Christ is our "alien righteousness," in the sense that holiness never becomes our possession, but is a gift that we must receive daily from Christ. Even where transformation results, we can never trust in this intrinsic righteousness for we are not judged morally in terms of character achievement, but religiously in terms of our dependence on Christ.

As he put it in the Plain Account:

"The holiest of men still need Christ, as their Prophet, as 'the light of the world.' For he does not give them light, but from moment to moment: The instant he withdraws, all is darkness. They still need Christ as their King; for God does not give them a stock of holiness. But unless they receive a supply every moment, nothing but

---

[26] Ibid.
[27] Flew, op. cit., p. 246, remarks that although Luther took holiness out of the monastery and away from mysticism, planting it back in the soil of faith in terms of justification, "he acquiesced in the continuance of sin in this life with more tameness than we would have expected from such a bonny fighter."

unholiness would remain. They still need Christ as their Priest, to make atonement for their holy things. Even perfect holiness is acceptable to God only through Jesus Christ.[28]

It is clear that Wesley's view of perfection depends upon a distinction between two kinds of sin. In terms of sin in the absolute sense, as measured by the "perfect law," there is no such thing as perfection in believers. It is in terms of the sin of conscious separation from Christ that there can be perfection—a perfection of unbroken conscious dependence upon Christ.

It is clear, too, that the Christian is sanctified by faith alone through a gift of grace received moment by moment. From this state we can fall by a lapse of faith; to it we can be restored by a renewal of faith.[29]

Perfection and Social Ethics

Plainly, since perfection is a description of a relationship to Christ and not to the moral law, the distinction between the two meanings of sin is all important.

I know no persons living who are so deeply conscious of their needing Christ both as Prophet, Priest, and King as those who believe themselves, and whom I believe, to be cleansed from all sin—I mean all pride, anger, evil desire, idolatry, and unbelief. These very persons feel more than ever their own ignorance, littleness of grace, coming short of the full mind that was in Christ, and walking less accurately than they might have done after their Divine Pattern; are more convinced of the insufficiency of all they are, have, or do to bear the eye of God without a Mediator; are more penetrated with the sense of the want of Him than ever they were before. . . . "Are they not sinners?" Explain the term one way, and I say, Yes; another, and I say, No.[30]

It takes no great insight to see the dangers of defining sin in terms of "a voluntary transgression of the known law of God." [31]

---

[28] Works, XI, 417.
[29] See Letters, V, 41, where he speaks of being convinced of the error of his early belief that one who has attained cannot fall, and Works, XI, 426-27 for the possibility of being lifted again.
[30] Letters, IV, 189-90.
[31] Letters, V, 322. "Every voluntary breach of the law of love is sin; and nothing else is."

It is remarkably easy to remove oneself from the scrutiny of the perfect law of God and to be satisfied with one's conscious loyalty to the unexamined standards of the community. Speaking of the dangerous results of such an easy view of sin, Niebuhr wrote:

> It is one of the curious ironies of modern culture that in the very moment when a rationalistic type of Christianity tended to consider the possibilities of human perfection in terms of its purely conscious activity, a secular science in the form of psychology on the one hand, and of social economics on the other, revealed the labyrinthian depths of the unconscious and of the endless possibilities which were hidden there. Both Marx and Freud have, each in his own way, discovered the unconscious dishonesties which dog human actions and corrupt human ideals, even though the conscious mind is intent on virtue.[32]

Wesley, of course, hardly fits the category of "a rationalistic type of Christianity," and we have seen his awareness of the need for a daily relationship to Christ in which we become increasingly aware of the deeper layers of sin. Nevertheless, as soon as the full dialectic of his two definitions of sin was overlooked, his description of perfection in terms of the absence of the sin of conscious violation of the law of God led easily to a failure to take seriously the depth of unexamined prejudices and inward sins. This was the more serious because an implicit individualism in this definition of sin prevented the implications of the doctrine for social relations from being clearly seen. In Wesley himself this was less apparent because his tender conscience led to a wide variety of works of love, in areas ranging from personal anxieties to the massive institution of slavery, but in his followers a certain social conservatism became associated with the marked individualism of their doctrine.[33]

R. W. Dale believed that the Methodists should have worked out the implications of the doctrine of perfection into the wide areas of social ethics.

[32] Reinhold Niebuhr, *Beyond Tragedy* (New York: Charles Scribners Sons, 1937), p. 265.
[33] See Maldwyn Edwards, *John Wesley and the Eighteenth Century* (London: Epworth Press), 1933.

180

There was one doctrine of John Wesley's—the doctrine of perfect sanctification—which ought to have led to a great and original ethical development; but the doctrine has not grown, it seems to remain where John Wesley left it. There has been a want of genius or the courage to attempt the solution of the immense practical questions which the doctrine suggests. The questions have not been raised, much less solved. To have raised them effectively, indeed, would have been to originate an ethical revolution which would have had a far deeper effect on the thought and life—first in England and then of the rest of Christendom—than was produced by the Reformation of the sixteenth century.[34]

It is true that Wesley took the doctrine of sanctification out of the order of merit and so removed it from the legal order to the order of faith.

"Christ is the end of the Adamic, as well as the Mosaic, law. By his death, he hath put an end to both; he hath abolished both the one and the other, with regard to man; and the obligation to observe either one or the other is vanished away. Nor is any man living bound to observe the Adamic more than the Mosaic law.

"In the room of this, Christ hath established another, namely, the law of faith. Not every one that doeth, but every one that believeth, now receiveth righteousness, in the full sense of the word; that is, he is justified, sanctified, and glorified.[35]

But this removal of the Christian from the legal to the religious order is certainly not meant to reintroduce antinomianism! In this faith relationship the Christian is filled with love to God and neighbor and so always abounds in good works.

It is true, however, that if the doctrine is to bear its true ethical fruit, the dialectic between the two definitions of sin (involving as it does the dialectic of the law and the gospel) must be kept in clearer focus and must be carried into the tangled skein of social relationships. The stress on the promise of a new relationship with Christ, reaching the point of complete dependence so that the Christian "prays without ceasing," must be accompanied by the stress that this relationship must daily bring the Christian to a deepening understanding of the extent to which devia-

[34] Quoted by Jackson in *Wesley Bicentennial, op. cit.,* 72-73.
[35] *Works,* XI, 415.

tions from the Lordship of Christ are reflected not only in his personal life, but also in his corporate commitments in the life of the Church and the world.

A contemporary Methodist has put it:

The effort to build the responsible society has added a significant dimension to the perfectionist ethic. Twentieth century holiness requires a kind of coherent personality such as earlier centuries could not have envisaged because they had no such social hope as has been awakened in modern man. Twentieth century holiness envisages a whole person in a whole society. This person-in-community holiness requires not only justification and sanctification in the traditional sense but also, for many the disciplines of higher education, technical training and competence, and interdisciplinary group cooperation.

Such a range of disciplines will produce a configuration of virtues and character traits somewhat unlike those which are traditional in the church.[36]

What Perfection Is

To discover whether Wesley's doctrine is capable of such a development we must turn to his positive statement of the doctrine.

"But whom then do you mean by 'one that is perfect?' We mean one in whom is 'the mind which was in Christ,' and who so 'walketh as Christ also walked;' a man 'that hath clean hands and a pure heart,' or that is 'cleansed from all filthiness of flesh and spirit;' one in whom is 'no occasion of stumbling,' and who accordingly, 'does not commit sin.' . . . We understand hereby, one whom God hath 'sanctified throughout in body, soul and spirit.' . . .

"This man can now testify to all mankind, 'I am crucified with Christ: Nevertheless I live; yet not I, but Christ liveth in me.' . . . He 'loveth the Lord his God with all his heart,' and serveth him 'with all his strength.' He 'loveth his neighbour,' every man, 'as himself;' yea, 'as Christ loveth us.' . . . Indeed his soul is all love, filled with 'bowels of mercies, kindness, meekness, gentleness, longsuffering.' And his life agreeth thereto, full of 'the work of faith, the patience of hope, the labour of love.' . . .

"This it is to be a perfect man, to be 'sanctified throughout;' even

[36] Walter G. Muelder, "Ethics and the Interior Life," *The New Christian Advocate* (June, 1957), pp. 18-22.

'to have a heart so all-flaming with the love of God,' (to use Archbishop Usher's words,) 'as continually to offer up every thought, word, and work, as a spiritual sacrifice, acceptable to God through Christ.' " [37]

The Christian can enter into such fullness of faith that his heart is aflame with the constant presence of Christ and his whole consciousness is diffused by God's love. As we have seen, this does not mean that there is no deviation from the will of God. In fact, the "perfect" Christian, because of his unbroken relationship to Christ, becomes more and more aware of his moral, psychological, and intellectual imperfections. For this reason Wesley emphasizes that the perfect grow in grace as the unbroken relationship to Christ brings increasing sensitivity to God's will.[38]

Peters is right then when he argues that to speak of perfection bringing either the "eradication" or "destruction" of sin is to miss Wesley's meaning.

A term far more appropriate to Wesley's thought is the term "expulsion." "Entire sanctification," he said, . . . is neither more nor less than pure love—love expelling sin and governing both the heart and life." And this is what he preached: "It is love excluding sin; love filling the heart, taking up the whole capacity of the soul. . . . For as long as love takes up the whole heart, what room is there for sin therein? [39]

The Time Problem

The question of when the gift of perfection is received presents us with another difficult problem. It would seem that immediately following Aldersgate Street, Wesley, accepting a Moravian's assertion that a second crisis follows the first work of regeneration bringing "serene peace and steadfast tranquility of mind, with a deliverance from every fleshly desire, and from

[37] Works, XI, 384. Wesley, of course, used several terms to describe the new stage of life—Perfection, Holiness, Entire Sanctification, Perfect Love, Full Salvation. For a full list of the terms and their occurrence, see Lindstrom, op. cit., p. 127.
[38] Works, XI, 426. "Q. 29. Can those who are perfect grow in grace? Undoubtedly they can; and that not only while they are in the body, but to all eternity."
[39] Peters, op. cit., 58-59.

every outward and inward sin," expected the instantaneous gift of perfection to follow immediately.[40] In October of that year he wrote to his brother Samuel:

Some measure of this faith, which bringeth salvation or victory over sin, and which implies peace and trust in God through Christ, I now enjoy by His free mercy; though in very deed it is in me but as a grain of mustard seed: for the . . . seal of the Spirit, the love of God shed abroad in my heart, and producing joy in the Holy Ghost, "joy which no man taketh away, joy unspeakable and full of glory," —this witness of the Spirit I have not; but I patiently wait for it. I know many who have received it already.[41]

Apparently the failure to receive the gift led him to doubt the instantaneous nature of it. In December 1744 he recorded his difficulty in accepting the witness of two who claimed such a gift,[42] and in 1747 he counseled great restraint in those who claimed it, and while urging strongly that the promise is held out to us in this life, stressed the gradual work that led up to it.[43] But in 1760, after the work broke out in Otley, the instantaneous emphasis returned in greater strength. The gradual and instantaneous aspects of perfection were then brought into relation to each other.

Neither dare we affirm, as some have done, that all this salvation is given at once. There is indeed an instantaneous, as well as a gradual, work of God in his children; and there wants not, we know, a cloud of witnesses, who have received, in one moment, either a clear sense of the forgiveness of their sins, or the abiding witness of the Holy Spirit. But we do not know a single instance in any place, of a person's receiving, in one and the same moment, remission of sins, the abiding witness of the Spirit, and a new, a clean heart.[44]

The gradual work precedes and follows the instantaneous, but it is true that Wesley placed great emphasis on the latter. He defined the relation between the two aspects in his claim

---

[40] *Journal*, II, 49. It is quite probably his expectation which occasioned those early moods of depression, when he deplored the absence of joy.
[41] *Letters*, I, 263-64.
[42] *Journal*, III, 154.
[43] *Works*, VIII, 293-98.
[44] *Works*, XI, 380.

that there is a gradual work of God in the soul, or that, generally speaking, it is a long time, even many years, before sin is destroyed. . . . But we know likewise, that God may, with man's good leave, 'cut short his work,' in whatever degree he pleases, and do the usual work of many years in a moment. He does so in many instances; and yet there is a gradual work, both before and after that moment: So that one may affirm the work is gradual, another, it is instantaneous, without any manner of contradiction.[45]

The gradual work that follows as well as precedes the instantaneous gift of perfection is necessary because the instantaneous gift brings an unbroken relation to Christ and a constant desire to do his will but still leaves the Christian far short of the perfect law of God. Even the "perfect" still need an increase in grace.

If the gradual work of purification is necessary, the instantaneous gift of the constant presence of Christ is also essential. To the objection that some who are filled with love have experienced no such instantaneous change, Wesley replied that

They did not perceive the instant when it was wrought. It is often difficult to perceive the instant when a man dies; yet there is an instant in which life ceases. And if even sin ceases, there must be a last moment of its existence, and a first moment of our deliverance from it.[46]

I believe that we must admit that this talk of the moment when sin ceases is rather artificial and badly oversimplified. As we have seen, it is necessary to maintain a dialectical relation between Wesley's two definitions of sin if the doctrine of perfection is to be kept free from the tendency toward unhealthy subjectivism and ethical irrelevance. Unless it is made clear that those who receive the gift of perfect love are still far short of the perfect law and need the constant illumination of God to reveal their continuing imperfections and their involvement in the corporate sins of their society, the doctrine of perfection and the emphasis on receiving it as an instantaneous gift can easily lead to a measure of moral blindness. When Wesley speaks of

[45] *Ibid.*, 423.
[46] *Ibid.*, 442.

the instant sin ceases, he reveals the tendency to remove the definition of sin in terms of conscious awareness from its necessary tension with the deeper definition of continuing moral deviation from the perfect will of God.

Faith with Expectation

This does not mean that we should cast out his emphasis on the instantaneous work of grace and keep only the gradual. The great strength of Wesley's doctrine is in his awareness that the work of sanctification is a gift, a divine work wrought by God and to be accepted by faith. There is a gradual work of transformation issuing from the day-to-day relationship with Christ, and the need for this gradual transformation continues throughout life, but there is also the promise of the immediate gift of an unbroken relationship with Christ—a new relationship in which

Perfect love having now cast out fear, he rejoices evermore. Yea, his joy is full, and all his bones cry out, "Blessed be the God and Father of our Lord Jesus Christ, who, according to his abundant mercy, hath begotten me again unto a living hope of an inheritance incorruptible and undefiled, reserved in heaven for me."

And he, who hath this hope, thus full of immortality, in everything giveth thanks, as knowing this (whatsoever it is) is the will of God in Christ Jesus concerning him. From him therefore he cheerfully receives all, saying, "Good is the will of the Lord;" and whether he giveth or taketh away, equally blessing the name of the Lord. Whether in ease or pain, whether in sickness or health, whether in life or death, he giveth thanks from the ground of the heart to Him who orders it for good; into whose hands he hath wholly committed his body and soul, "as into the hands of a faithful Creator." He is therefore anxiously "careful for nothing," as having "cast all his care on Him that careth for him;" and "in all things" resting on him, after "making" his "request known to him with thanksgiving."

For indeed he "prays without ceasing." . . . His heart is lifted up to God at all times, and in all places. In this he is never hindered, much less interrupted, by any person or thing. In retirement or company, in leisure, business, or conversation, his heart is ever with the Lord.[47]

[47] *Ibid.*, 371.

It is this emphasis upon the gift of perfect love to be received by faith that distinguishes his doctrine of sanctification by faith alone from the Roman Catholic ladder-of-merit scheme of perfection. Because of this emphasis that sanctification is a gift open to faith, Wesley placed great emphasis upon expectation.

Q. When does inward sanctification begin?
A. In the moment a man is justified. . . . From that time a believer gradually dies to sin, and grows in grace.
Q. Is this ordinarily given till a little before death?
A. It is not, to those who expect it no sooner.
Q. But may we expect it sooner?
A. Why not? For, although we grant, (1.) That the generality of believers, whom we have hitherto known, were not so sanctified till near their death; (2.) That few of those to whom St. Paul wrote his Epistles were so at that time; nor, (3.) He himself at the time of writing his former Epistles; yet all this does not prove, that we may not be so to-day.
Q. In what manner should we preach sanctification?
A. Scarce at all to those who are not pressing forward; to those who are, always by way of promise; always drawing, rather than driving.[48]

This expectation of the fulfillment of the promises of Christ in our lives is of the essence of the doctrine of holiness. The faith that leads to sanctification is essentially a conviction "that what God hath promised He is able to perform," and that "He is able and willing to do it now." [49]

Both the spontaneous and the gradual are essential to Wesley's doctrine. There is the vertical event of faith as well as the horizontal nurture of the faithful. It should be said, however, that to relate the doctrine of assurance to the gift of perfection, as Wesley does, is unscriptural.[50] Christian assurance is related to forgiveness and adoption. It follows that to speak of perfection as a state reached with an experience of a complete, instantaneous gift is also unscriptural. Instead, the promise of our unbroken relationship to Christ must be seen as a dynamic new goal. Constantly standing over the life of the believer, calling him on to

[48] Ibid., 387.
[49] Sermons, II, 457.
[50] See below, p. 245.

an ever deeper reception of the transpiring gifts that Christ offers to those who learn the practice of his presence.

Waiting for the Gift

If the expectation of the gift is of such importance, it is also important that we understand the manner in which we must wait for the gift. For here, as well as in justification, the waiting is active.

Q. How are we to wait for this change?

A. Not in careless indifference, or indolent inactivity; but in vigorous, universal obedience, in a zealous keeping of all the commandments, in watchfulness and painfulness, in denying ourselves, and taking up our cross daily; as well as in earnest prayer and fasting, and a close attendance on all the ordinances of God. And if any man dream of attaining it in any other way, (yea, or of keeping it when it is attained, when he has received it even in the largest measure,) he deceiveth his own soul. It is true, we receive it by simple faith: But God does not, will not, give that faith, unless we seek it with all diligence, in the way which he hath ordained.[51]

Here we have again Bonhoeffer's "expensive grace" as against "cheap grace," the ethical seriousness that must flow from our faith relationship to Christ and which Wesley expresses by saying that works are "conditionally" or "remotely" necessary to salvation, while faith is "immediately" necessary.[52] Wesley keeps ever before us the truth that a living faith relationship to Christ must constantly bring forth good fruits.

This sanctification, however, is always a gift. Because most believers do not expect it earlier, it is generally received "the instant of death, the moment before the soul leaves the body." [53] In all the justified God will perform his final work of purification before they leave this house of clay. It is then, not an achievement by which we merit salvation, but a gift to those who are saved by faith.

[51] Works, XI, 402-403.
[52] Sermons, II, 456.
[53] Works, XI, 446. And see Letters, V, 39.

Toward a Restatement

If Methodism is to speak to the Church concerning the unique emphasis God has given her, I believe she must take seriously Wesley's optimism of grace, stressing the doctrine of sanctification by faith, emphasizing the promises of transformation available to the believer now (and a transformation not only in individuals but in the fellowship of the Church), while keeping more central the dialectic between the gospel and the law. We need to hold in a constant, dialectical relationship the offer of freedom from the sin of separation in our personal relationship with Christ and the continuing sin in the lives of the "perfect" when judged by the perfect law. By the very gift of the unbroken moment-by-moment relation to Christ, the believer should become increasingly aware of the need for continuing transformation of his total existence. These emphases are already contained in his doctrine but need to be brought into a clearer relationship to each other.

We need also to relate this doctrine to the wide reaches of our social life, knowing that sin is deeply woven into the fabric of our social commitments, and that there too the transforming power of our relation to Christ must be realized. Further it is not only a matter of the relation of the individual believer to the social life; the transforming significance of the community of the faithful must be taken into account.

This attempt to relate the transforming power of the gift of love to the social order is certainly not foreign to Wesley, as his constant warfare against political corruption, luxury, unemployment, slavery, and war reveal. Yet in Wesley these concerns were inadequately related to his doctrine of holiness. Further, the problem of this doctrine is now vastly more complicated and requires from Methodists a much more concentrated effort to relate it to our contemporary situation.

Wesley was firmly convinced that "the time will come when Christianity will prevail over all, and cover the earth." [54] When that happens, wars will cease, the hatreds and suspicions that divide us will disappear, injustice and poverty will be done away,

[54] *Sermons*, I, 102.

and love and mercy will rule the world.[55] It is this goal that must ever guide our efforts and be the measure of our expectation concerning the gifts that God would bestow upon us.

To summarize in the words of Gordon Rupp:

Wesley kept firmly to the two doctrines of original sin and of total depravity. . . . John Wesley accepted the doctrine of total depravity, though his doctrine of prevenient grace, and of the objective results of the atonement took some of the sting from it. But, positively, this doctrine affirms two important truths concerning the Christian view of history. First, what has gone wrong is no merely negative thing, an appalling series of accidents. . . . It is, as the Bible insists, no mere deprivatio, deprivation of God, but it is a depravatio, a depravity, positive rebellion, mutiny, hostility to God, a restless egotism, a perseverance in idolatry by which man ever and again, under manifold disguises, puts himself on the altar and worships the creature. And, second, this is an all-in affair. . . . No race, culture, century can contract out of this solidarity of judgment. . . .

But the depth of this tragedy must be attached with the heights of grace; the solidarity of mankind in Adam viewed against the solidarity of mankind in the Second Adam, Jesus Christ, of whom Charles Wesley sings, "Head of all mankind art Thou." Total depravity is set in the context of total grace, of the great salvation.[56]

At a time when our theology has recaptured the depth dimension of sin and has learned again the true "pessimism of nature" that marks this awareness, it is the more imperative that we know the heights of the "optimism of grace" that flow from the faith relationship with Christ, the Victor over sin and death.

---

[55] *Ibid.*, 102-104.
[56] G. Rupp, *op. cit.*, pp. 78-81. Used by permission of Epworth Press.

── 11 THE ORDER OF SALVATION: ESCHATOLOGY

❂   Already it is apparent that Wesley's eschatology has a great deal to do with his view of the way the Christian lives now. The goal is clear—a life of holiness in the heavenly family of God. The way in which the goal is already anticipated is also clear, as is the fact that this life is only a training ground for the one that is to come.

Now we must draw together the strands of his eschatology and present in more precise form the way this goal affects our present life, noticing particularly Wesley's view of the extent to which the final transformation can be received now.

It was significant that the main theme of the Second Assembly of the World Council of Churches, "Christ the Hope of the World," should be on the subject of eschatology. It represents the increasing awareness that the nature of our Christian life and action now is determined by our understanding of our final destiny and of the extent to which the life of the final kingdom of God can be received now by way of foretaste.

On the latter point there was no agreement at the Assembly.

We are not agreed on the relationship between the Christian's hope here and now and his ultimate hope.[1]

It was suggested, however, that in the preparatory document there was an inadequate statement of our present hope.

[1] *Evanston Report, op. cit.,* p. 70.

We find that the note of joyous affirmation and radiant expectancy which should mark a statement of the Christian hope does not sufficiently illuminate the Report. We find certain important *omissions:* including the present work of the Holy Spirit in the Church and the world.[2]

In Wesley's thought we find a pervading emphasis upon the final goal, allied with a strong insistence that the life of the final kingdom is available to us in large measure now.

The *kingdom of heaven* and the kingdom of God are but two phrases for the same thing. They mean, not barely a future happy state in heaven, but a state to be enjoyed on earth; the proper disposition for the glory of heaven, rather than the possession of it. . . . It properly signifies here, the gospel dispensation, in which subjects were to be gathered to God by His Son, and a society to be formed, which was to subsist first on earth, and afterwards with God in glory. In some places of Scripture the phrase more particularly denotes the state of it on earth; in others, it signifies only the state of glory; but it generally includes both.[3]

In view of this relation between the "now" and the "not yet" Wesley sees the Christian life as a pilgrim way, with this present time as a time of decision and preparation for the final life of the kingdom still to come. The decision can be made because the kingdom is already present to us and we are invited to enter; the preparation can be undertaken for the kingdom is still future as the goal of our hope.

It is termed, "the kingdom of God," because it is the immediate fruit of God's reigning in the soul. So soon as ever He takes unto Himself His mighty power, and sets up His throne in our hearts, they are instantly filled with this "righteousness, and peace, and joy in the Holy Ghost." It is called "the kingdom of heaven," because it is (in a degree) heaven opened in the soul. For whosoever they are that experience this, they can aver before angels and men,

Everlasting life is won,
Glory is on earth begun.[4]

---

[2] *Ibid.*
[3] *Notes,* Matt. 3:2, 22.
[4] *Sermons,* I, 154.

We see then that Wesley placed great emphasis upon the reality of the gift of the kingdom of God to us now. Nevertheless, the present gift of the kingdom is truly eschatological—a foretaste of our final inheritance—a gift which leads us on to our final destiny. In fact, our relation to God, through Christ, transforms our present relation to the world, precisely because Christ rules the present world in order to lead us to a destiny beyond it. For this reason the Christian is free from the world. Every possession here is seen as relative, none of it being his treasure, for his life is hidden with Christ in God, and he shall share in the riches of glory in the life to come.

How truly wise is this man! He knows himself: an everlasting spirit, which came forth from God, and was sent down into an house of clay, not to do his own will, but the will of Him that sent him. He knows the world: the place in which he is to pass a few days or years, not as an inhabitant, but as a stranger and sojourner, in his way to the everlasting habitations; and accordingly he uses the world as not abusing it, and as knowing the fashion of it passes away. He knows God: his Father and his Friend, the parent of all good, the centre of the spirits of all flesh, the sole happiness of all intelligent beings. He sees, clearer than the light of the noon-day sun, that this is the end of man, to glorify Him who made him for Himself, and to love and enjoy Him for ever. And with equal clearness he sees the means to that end, to the enjoyment of God in glory; even now to know, to love, to imitate God, and to believe in Jesus Christ whom He hath sent.[5]

The relativity of our relation to the material things of this world in view of the goal which lies beyond is given strong expression.

Remember! You were born for nothing else. You live for nothing else. Your life is continued to you upon earth, for no other purpose than this, that you may know, love, and serve God on earth, and enjoy him to all eternity. Consider! You were not created to please your senses, to gratify your imagination, to gain money, or the praise of men; to seek happiness in any created good, in anything under the sun. All this is "walking in a vain shadow;" it is leading a restless, miserable life, in order to a miserable eternity. On the contrary, you

⁵ *Sermons,* II, 29-30.

were created for this, and for no other purpose, by seeking and finding happiness in God on earth, to secure the glory of God in heaven. Therefore, let your heart continually say, "This one thing I do,"—having one thing in view, remembering why I was born, and why I am continued in life,—"I press on to the mark." I aim at the one end of my being, God; even at "God in Christ reconciling the world to himself." He shall be my God for ever and ever, and my guide even unto death! [6]

This does not mean that Wesley saw the life of the present kingdom as purely inward with no real relation to the culture and the social structures of this fallen world. Wesley looked forward to "this strange sight, a Christian world," foreseen by the prophets and apostles, in which personal strife would be at an end, wars will have ceased, injustice will be done away, and righteousness and peace will be established.[7] There is a real sense in which Wesley stressed realized eschatology more than any other leading western theologian. This can be seen in the whole line we have traced of the relation between his pessimism of nature and his optimism of grace, and it comes to its climax in his teaching on holiness.

Henry Carter has summarized Wesley's teaching on holiness under three headings which reveal the strength of Wesley's belief in realized eschatology.

(1) *The new way of life.* Quoting Wesley's description of "religion itself" as

no other than love; the love of God and of all mankind. . . .
This love we believe to be the medicine of life, the never-failing remedy for all the evils of a disordered world, for all the miseries and vices of men. . . .
This religion we long to see established in the world.[8]

Carter comments:

In expositions of "the religion of Jesus Christ" John Wesley held two truths in constant equipoise. Christianity, he affirmed, is "inward holiness," purity of heart; this he urged against chill Deism and formal church-going. Christianity is equally "a social religion," so much so

---

[6] *Works,* VII, 230. Sermon on "What is Man?"
[7] *Sermons,* I, 102-104.
[8] *Works,* VIII, 3. From "An Earnest Appeal."

that "to turn it into a solitary one is to destroy it"; this he declared in opposition to all forms of mysticism which were in effect a retreat from the obligations and privileges of neighbourliness and from "commerce" with one's fellows. His teaching on Perfect Love is only rightly understood when these truths are considered together.[9]

For Wesley, inward holiness must flow forth in social holiness. It is these two aspects that Carter examines in his second and third points.

(2) *Inward Religion.* This is the quest for "Full Redemption."

Noticing that Wesley taught believers to exercise an "intense longing" for the gift of perfect love, Carter rightly stresses that this gift is eschatological. Perfection is limited in this life, and the believer looks forward to the higher perfection that will be his in glory.

It is also a dynamic term, for the perfection we can receive here is given us in the midst of conflict and is subject to growth. In his sermon, "On Sin in Believers" Wesley recognizes that "there are in every person, even after he is justified, two contrary principles, nature and grace, termed by St. Paul, the *flesh* and the *spirit*." [10] Not only must the believer exercise watchfulness, but the need for repentance is, in this world, the correlate of faith and applies (as we have seen) to those who have received the gift of perfection as well as to those who have received the gift of justification.

The gift then is eschatological—a foretaste leading us on. But it is a gift of holiness that every believer can claim and which carries with it great transforming power. The eschaton does break into this old world. Therefore the gift of holiness also means that true religion is

(3) *Social Religion.* This means the life of a "true neighbor" and a citizen of the world.

Carter gives a summary of Wesley's teaching on social responsibility,[11] showing the wide variety of social services, the clear

[9] Henry Carter, The Methodist Heritage, op. cit., p. 178.
[10] Sermons, II, 377.
[11] Carter, op. cit., 184-87.

recognition of political responsibility, and the forceful attitude on social evils that marked his thought.

The question arises, however, as to the extent to which Wesley expected this Christian obedience to result in social transformation, and at first sight it would seem that he expected very little.

"Ye" (Christians, ye that are lowly, serious, and meek; ye that hunger after righteousness, that love God and man, that do good to all, and therefore suffer evil; ye) "are the salt of the earth": it is your very nature to season whatever is round about you. It is the nature of the divine savour which is in you, to spread to whatsoever you touch; to diffuse itself, on every side, to all those among whom you are. This is the great reason why the providence of God has so mingled you together with other men, that whatever grace you have received of God may through you be communicated to others; that every holy temper and word and work of yours may have an influence on them also. By this means a check will, in some measure, be given to the corruption which is in the world; and a small part, at least, saved from the general infection, and rendered holy and pure before God.[12]

The final sentence would suggest that Wesley expected little in the way of "this-worldly" transformation, and it should be said that, for Wesley, the Christian's faith does not depend upon the success of his efforts for social reform, nor should we think of social reform as building the kingdom of God, for such reforms as attend our obedience to God's will are at best but temporary victories. The forces of evil are still at loose so that victory can easily be followed by defeat. Social holiness, like holiness in the believer, must be seen as being received moment by moment, and as being preserved only by the constant renewal of obedience and by constant repentance. The life of the kingdom that is ours now is an eschatological gift which is but a foretaste of the final kingdom and is subject to the vagaries of our unceasing conflict with the evil of this present world.

Nevertheless Wesley believed that the Christian is called to work for social renewal, and he rejoiced to see the transformations which (however incomplete and temporary) flowed from

[12] *Sermons*, I, 385.

the life of his societies.[13] Time's transitoriness does not imply its worthlessness and lead to a disdain of things earthly. The Christian is called to redeem the time by showing the meaning of his redemption in his life now. John Wesley had an acute sense of the stewardship of time[14] and a strong sense of the meaning of being called by God, as that calling is related to serving the present age. This sense of stewardship and vocation he sought to inscribe into the very structure of Methodism.[15]

Wesley believed that if true religion were to spread, great ethical and social transformation would follow.[16] Nevertheless, vocation here is no end in itself. We are called to witness to our redemption in our present life in order to be prepared for our vocation in glory.

God hath joined from the beginning, pardon, holiness, heaven. And why should man put them asunder? O beware of this! Let not one link of the golden chain be broken. "God for Christ's sake hath forgiven me. He is now renewing me in His own image. Shortly he will make me meet for Himself, and take me to stand before His face. . . ." Yet a little while and I shall "come to the general assembly and church of the first-born, and to God the Judge of all, and to Jesus the Mediator of the new covenant." [17]

Wesley looked forward to the final salvation when God will give

an unmixed state of holiness and happiness, far superior to that which Adam enjoyed in Paradise. In how beautiful a manner is this described by the Apostle: "God shall wipe away all tears from their eyes; and

---

[13] See *Letters*, III, 287; *Journal*, III, 338; *Journal*, IV, 416-17, and so on. Wesley apparently believed that God appoints times (kairoi) when an attack on great social evils can succeed, but that for their success the complete obedience of his followers and the leaders he has appointed is required. So in one of his last letters he wrote to Wilberforce: "Unless God has raised you up for this very thing, you will be worn out by the opposition of men and devils. But if God be for you, who can be against you? Are all of them together stronger than God? O be not weary in well-doing! Go on, in the name of God and the power of His might, till even American slavery (the vilest that ever saw the sun) shall vanish before it." *Letters*, VIII, 265.

[14] "Leisure and I have taken leave of each other." *Letters*, I, 34.

[15] See "General Rules of Employing Time," *Journal*, I, 48; "The Twelve Rules of a Helper," *Works*, VIII, 309-10.

[16] *Sermons*, I, 98.

[17] *Sermons*, II, 202.

there shall be no more death, neither sorrow nor crying: Neither shall there be any more pain; for the former things are done away!" As there will be no more death, and no more pain or sickness preparatory thereto; as there will be no more grieving for, or parting with, friends; so there will be no more sorrow or crying. Nay, but there will be a greater deliverance than all this; for there will be no more sin. And, to crown all, there will be a deep, an intimate, an uninterrupted union with God; a constant communion with the Father and his Son Jesus Christ, through the Spirit; a continual enjoyment of the Three-One God, and of all the creatures in him! [18]

The "whole animated creation" will share in this new creation, being delivered from its present bondage to evil occasioned by the Fall, and sharing in "the glorious liberty of the children of God" [19] so that there shall be truly "a new heaven and a new earth." [20]

The Judgment

But before this shall come the judgment, following the general resurrection, at which Christ shall separate the righteous from the unrighteous, with the righteous inheriting eternal life and the unrighteous being delivered into the everlasting punishment of hell.[21] The new heaven and the new earth will not be continuous with this old world. In the day of judgment this old heaven and earth will be destroyed, and just as our life of justification and sanctification are new gifts from above, so the new heaven and new earth of which they are a foretaste will be a new creation.[22] The element of continuity lies in the fact that the foretaste of the new life of salvation, which is ours now, will be consummated in glory.[23]

[18] Works, VI, 295-96.
[19] Ibid., 248.
[20] See Sermons, II, 415.
[21] Ibid., 405-12, 474. It is worth noting that Wesley, believing that the final judgment is postponed till the general resurrection, taught that there is an intermediate state where "the souls of all good men rest from their labours and are with Christ from death to the resurrection." He sharply distinguishes it from purgatory; for the concept of purgatory has place only in a scheme of merit. The intermediate state is for the faithful and is called Paradise; this being Wesley's understanding of the New Testament use of that term.
[22] Ibid., 412.
[23] Works, VI, 430-31.

Wesley's picture of hell is a literal transcription of the New Testament language, but it is important to notice that he made small use of the threat of hell. In the Minutes of 1746 he wrote:

Q. What inconvenience is there in speaking much of the wrath of God and little of the love of God?
A. It generally hardens them that believe not, and discourages them that do.[24]

Wesley's concern was to concentrate on the promises of the gospel available to us now, while at the same time showing that the appropriation of these promises is preparatory for the life that is to come. He sought to inculcate a faith that constantly stretches forward, knowing the depth of the riches available to us now, but knowing that the life that now is is not to be compared with the glory that is to come. He strove to train his followers in the faith that relates itself to every moment and every part of life in this world, while yet being attached to no moment and no thing. He knew that through faith in Christ the eternal invades time, enabling us to take time with deadly seriousness while also freeing us from slavery to time. He knew that faith is the gift of the One who, in time and through death, conquered time and death, and who offers us, who now live in time and inevitably face death, his conquest of both in the eternal life that can be ours both here and hereafter.

His theology ends as it begins, with the optimism of grace triumphing over the pessimism of nature. "With man," because of the deadly effects of sin, "it is impossible" to be reconciled to God and to do his will. "But with God all things are possible." The life available in Christ is a life of free salvation. It is a life free for all, a life that already is at work in all by the ceaseless operation of God's prevenient grace, and a life that can come to flower in all through the one way of faith in Christ. Once that personal relationship is established, we are bidden to be

---

[24] Notice also that in the Minutes of 1745 he warns against preaching sanctification in such a way as to discourage. It is to be presented "always by way of promise; always drawing rather than driving." And in the Minutes of 1747 the same theme recurs with a warning against a harsh note that produces "slavish fear." The doctrine should be placed in the most amiable light, so that it may excite only hope, joy, and desire." Works, VIII, 286 and 297.

alive with expectation for the great transformation which Christ can work—in our lives by his Spirit, in the Church where he seeks to make us one by his Spirit, and in the world which he seeks to transform by the Spirit through the obedient love of the Church.

All this, however, is but a foretaste. He shall come again to judge both the quick and the dead, gathering believers into his perfect kingdom, and completing the great salvation by the gift of the new heaven and the new earth.

It cannot be said that the ecumenical significance of Wesley's eschatology lies in its description of the details of the judgment and the life that follows. Here, as in a good deal of his theology, he must stand the correction of biblical scholarship. Rather the significance lies in the dynamic way he relates eschatology to our present life, stressing in his optimism of grace the extent of the promises of the new life available to us now, without ever falling into the danger of forgetting that the fashion of this present world passes away, and that while we labor joyfully to see the evidences of God's power transforming this present age, nevertheless we know that all this is but a foretaste. With joy we set no arbitrary limits to the transformation God can effect now and so proclaim Christ as Lord and seek to realize his will in all things, but with greater joy we look forward to the time when he will show his Lordship openly. And thus even while we labor, we pray "Maranatha, come Lord Jesus, quickly come."

CONCLUSION

◕ It has been the aim of this work to investigate the original (and still legally binding) Methodist tradition in the light of the present ecumenical situation. Two main questions have been kept in mind:

A. The question as to whether God has given to Methodism emphases which she is in duty bound to share with those of other traditions, and

B. The question as to whether her tradition throws light on the positions she should take in relation to the crucial questions which still divide the churches.

We have seen that the original Methodist tradition, as represented by the theology of John Wesley, drew a distinction between doctrines which are essential to our common Christian witness to the world (and therefore are a minimal basis for unity) and the further doctrines which are essential to the nurture of Christians in the life of fellowship in the Church (and on which there may be differences in the various societies within the Church).

While refusing to draw up a list of "fundamentals" which would form the necessary platform from which unity in mission could proceed, Wesley clearly believed that the doctrines set forth in the creeds (here distinguishing the substance of these doctrines from the illustrative language of the particular philosophy used to define them) are the general basis for our unity in witness. There are further doctrines, however, that are vital to the nurture of Christians, and it is in his view of the relation of these to the former and in his understanding of these doctrines themselves that Wesley gives us the distinctive Methodist emphases.

In 1946 the British Methodist Conference issued an official document called "The Message and Mission of Methodism" in which they sought to set forth "the elements of permanent value" in the historic witness of Methodism.[1] They suggested:

1. *Salvation by Faith:* with salvation "at every stage a gift of God," being not only something done for us but something done in us. Methodism insists that "no man can drift into a right relationship to God" and that the varieties of Christian experience must be marked "by a conscious acceptance of the love of God brought within man's reach in Christ. It is this fundamental truth which the Methodist emphasis on conversion seeks to safeguard." [2]

We have seen in Wesley's exposition of the *ordo salutis* the wide dimensions of his doctrine of salvation by faith, stretching back to his emphasis on prevenient grace and his insistence that God's grace is free for all and in all, and reaching forward to the fulfillment of the life of salvation in glory. We have seen the distinctive way he combines his pessimism of nature with his optimism of grace and the way this comes to focus in his doctrines of the New Birth, Assurance and Perfection, in which the transforming power of grace is given vivid expression.

2. *Assurance.* We have seen that while Wesley did not consider assurance as necessary to salvation, he believed it to be a gift of God that all believers may receive. He believed also that it is a gift of great value for by the confidence it instills in the believer concerning God's power to transform, it leads the recipient to open his life to the further promises of the gospel. Normally the reason why believers do not receive this witness of the Spirit is that a deficient presentation of the gospel leaves them ignorant of the promise. For that reason Wesley placed strong emphasis on the right presentation of the doctrine.

[1] *The Message and Mission of Methodism*, Published by the Methodist Conference (London: The Epworth Press, July, 1946).
[2] *Ibid.*, pp. 19-20.

We drew attention to the need for John Wesley's doctrine to be corrected in the direction of the proper dialectical relation between the "objective" assurance conveyed by the Word and Sacraments, and the "subjective" assurance conveyed by the direct witness of the Spirit—a dialectic Wesley himself maintains in other doctrines such as Baptism and the Church. Nevertheless his emphasis on assurance is needed and is given creative expression in the whole context of the ordo salutis.

3. *Holiness.* The British Conference stated:

The Gospel offers to men the assurance of divine forgiveness. But it does something more. It awakens the passion for holiness or perfect goodness, for a life that is conformed in every part to the image of Christ. Is this goal within our reach?

To this question, historic tradition gives diverse answers. The Lutheran and Reformed Churches deny that perfection, on the moral or social level, can be attained on earth. To that end, we shall need to pray "Forgive us our trespasses." Even the man who has advanced farthest on the Christian life will find that his works are defiled by sin. Hence the only peace that is open to us is the peace that comes from sin forgiven. Methodism, supported by an honorable Catholic tradition, gives a very different answer. John Wesley taught that the goal of the Christian life on this earth is perfect love. He believed that it could be reached by all and that the well-being of the Church depended on its quest.[3]

This is unfortunately expressed. Wesley no less than the other Reformers stressed that the Christian, no matter how perfect, must always pray for forgiveness and never reaches moral or social perfection. Nevertheless his optimism of grace did come to focus in his characteristic stress that the gift of perfect love is available in this life to all believers. We have seen the need for redefining some of the terms in Wesley's doctrine, and the Conference statement draws attention to three vulnerable points.

a) The defective conception of sin, with perfection defined in terms of

freedom from conscious sin. This distinction may easily become the parent of hypocrisy. The essence of hypocrisy is not the failure to respond to the highest we know, but the unexamined assumption

[3] *Ibid.,* p. 22.

that the highest we know is the highest we are capable of knowing. Our virtues may blind us to those vast tracts of our nature which are out of harmony with the will of God and the fact that we are not conscious of any willful transgressions may only mean that sin has darkened our conscience.[4]

b) "Wesley's doctrine presupposes an assurance that sin has been taken away." This, of course, is the result of defining perfection in terms of the removal of the sin of conscious separation from God, but as the Conference statement rightly affirms,

Such a claim, if it were tested, would require a knowledge of ourselves—of our motives and dispositions—which God alone possesses. To make it would bring us perilously near to the deadly sin of pride.[5]

c) Although Wesley taught that there was no holiness but social holiness, it was not sufficiently recognized by some of his followers that the ideal of perfect love must be expressed over the whole realm of human life.[6]

These defects we have examined, seeking to show how they can be corrected. Yet with all its defects, Wesley's doctrine is an important contribution to the Church's understanding of her mission. As the Conference statement rightly affirms, the great importance of the doctrine lies in its witness to the truth that no limits can be set to the sovereign love of God and that "the life of perfect love is a divine gift God is waiting to bestow on those who seek his gifts in faith." Rupp provides us with the right perspective.

Let us give the doctrine of Christian perfection, as expounded by Wesley, all the limitations and qualification with which he hedged it around. Let us add the serious and valid criticism it has derived from modern scholars, including such loyal Methodists as Dr. Newton Flew and Dr. Sangster.

Let us be content with the statement that "given the limitations inherent in existence in a body in a fallen world, we dare set no limit to what the grace of God can do for a man here and now." . . .

In the sixteenth century Luther set men looking eagerly toward the horizons with an eschatology of faith; and in the eighteenth cen-

[4] *Ibid.*, p. 23.
[5] *Ibid.*
[6] *Ibid.*

tury Wesley gave them an eschatology of love and called men to be always seeking eagerly and expectantly, new horizons of Christian experience; those spiritual gifts which the bountiful Giver is always more ready to bestow than His children to ask. Here then, is a confident reliance on the will and power of God to work the signs and wonders of redeeming grace in this present evil age.[7]

4. *Fellowship.* We have seen how central to Wesley was the emphasis on fellowship. We have seen also how Wesley envisaged the possibility within the unity of the *ecclesia*, in which there is essential agreement on the doctrines we must preach to the world of voluntary societies or *ecclesiolae*, with differing emphases on doctrines important in Christian nurture. Here Wesley's doctrine may suggest the way to real unity even before we are able to reconcile our differing traditions. In fact, it may well be, that until we are prepared to come together in common witness to the world, God will not draw us together in our understanding of the doctrines important in Christian nurture.

Here, too, Methodists must see that they must not insist that unity must wait upon the acceptance of their distinctive emphases, as these concern the nurture of Christians rather than the initial message to be preached to the world. Nevertheless, they must seek to see that this understanding of the Christian life is kept alive in the Church. For this reason the stress on voluntary *ecclesiolae* and the importance of Christian fellowship is important. In his doctrine of the Church Wesley draws attention to the way God brings his resources to believers in the life of fellowship and through common attendance on the means of grace, and we have seen the powerful way in which he related the growth of the Christian life to the invariable means of grace which express the unchanging heart of the gospel and the variable means which relate Christian discipline to the changing circumstances of life. It is here, we suggested, that Wesley provides a creative way along which the differing traditions (Catholic and Protestant) can move toward reconciliation.

Central to his whole expression of the gospel, however, is the conviction that the Church is constituted as the pilgrim people

[7] Rupp, *Principalities and Powers, op. cit.,* p. 24. Used by permission of Epworth Press.

205

of God. The life we now live is but a preparation for the life that is to come. The "foretaste" is such that a great transformation can and should take place now, and the grace of God is so wide that none need seek his face in vain, but the essence of the Church is that it is made up of those who are moving toward the final destiny in the Kingdom of Heaven.

Meanwhile, living by faith in Christ, who now offers to all preparatory membership in the final kingdom, believers see their present existence as a time of training. Essential to the training is the preparedness to receive the gift of God's love. Essential to the life of love is a readiness to witness to the new life in Christ and to God's desire to draw all men to himself. The mission of the Church is, in this life, to draw all men into unity with Christ, and for that reason the Church must seek to express that unity to the world and must seek to draw together in unity of witness to a divided world.

There are, then, important emphases to which Methodism is able to give her witness in her relation to the other Christian traditions, but it is no less true that Methodism needs to listen to these emphases herself so that God may be able to speak through her life as well as her words. Further, by listening to her own tradition, Methodism will gain a new awareness of the need for pushing on with haste toward the unity of the Church for the sake of mission.

It is true, of course, that what is needed is not a Methodist scholasticism which turns Wesley into an orthodoxy. It is vital that the important Methodist emphases should be related to the contemporary biblical and theological dialogue, and that Methodists should be prepared to hear every word that proceedeth out of the mouth of the living God as he speaks from all the traditions in which he has made his presence manifest. It is in the midst of the ecumenical encounter that the present theological task of the Church must be performed.

Appendix

THE UNRESOLVED TENSION: TRUTH AND UNITY

Wesley's Doctrine of the Church and Ministry as Seen in the History of His Relation to the Church of England

We have noticed two related tensions in Wesley's thought. The first is the tension between holiness as a "given" mark of the Church and holiness as "realized" in the life of the members. Here Wesley refused to separate from the Church despite her actual unholiness, while yet insisting that the necessities of mission required *ecclesiolae in ecclesia* through which holiness could be spread throughout the land.

The second is the tension between the necessity for unity in the Church and the necessity for truth. Here he refused to separate from the Church despite the almost universal neglect of pure doctrine by her ministers, while yet straining the tension of union to the utmost by insisting on the right of his lay preachers to proclaim the true gospel with the people still attending the services of the Church to receive the sacraments. For both unity and truth, Wesley believed, are essential to the mission of the Church.

These tensions are revealed when we trace the history of his relationship to the Church of England and examine the history of his attitude to ordination. In this examination we will discover important facets of Wesley's doctrine of the Church which have great bearing on the ecumenical problem.

The Relation to the Church of England

1. At the first Methodist Conference, in 1744, the whole matter of the relationship to the Church of England arose, and in the decisions the Conference declared their strong desire to maintain unity and their willingness to remain obedient to the authorities of the Church unless this obedience would compromise their obedience to God in matters of faith and mission. They declared that they were "zealous for the Church," that they believed and taught her doctrines, and that they would obey the Bishops and observe the Canons wherever this was possible with a safe conscience. Finally they asked:

Q. 7. Do we separate from the Church?
A. We conceive not: We hold communion therewith for conscience' sake, by constantly attending both the word preached, and the sacraments administered therein.
Q. 8. What then do they mean, who say, "You separate from the Church"?
A. We cannot certainly tell. Perhaps they have no determinate meaning; unless by the Church they mean themselves; that is, that part of the Clergy who accuse us of preaching false doctrine. And it is sure we do herein separate from them, by maintaining that which they deny.
Q. 9. But do you not weaken the Church?
A. Do not they who ask this, by the Church, mean themselves? We do not purposely weaken any man's hands. But accidentally we may, thus far: They who come to know the truth by us, will esteem such as deny it less than they did before?

But the Church, in the proper sense, the congregation of English believers, we do not weaken at all.
Q. 10. Do you not entail a schism in the Church? that is, Is it not probable that your hearers, after your death, will be scattered into all sects and parties, or that they will form themselves into a distinct sect?
A. (1.) We are persuaded the body of our hearers will even after our death remain in the Church, unless they be thrust out.
(2.) We believe notwithstanding, either that they will be thrust out, or that they will leaven the whole Church.
(3.) We do, and will do, all we can to prevent those consequences which are supposed likely to happen after our death.

(4.) But we cannot with a good conscience neglect the present opportunity of saving souls while we live, for fear of consequences which may possibly or probably happen after we are dead.[8]

We see here Wesley's recognition that mission is the primary mark of the Church and that this mission requires pure preaching. But mission not only requires continuity of doctrine, it also is important to have unity and unbroken continuity of order. Schism, therefore, should not be made on the basis of the desire to separate into a congregation of the pure. Everything possible must be done to maintain unity, and although true believers may be thrust out because of their obedience to the Word, it is not justified to separate by choice.

2. So in 1752 the Wesleys and some of their preachers signed an agreement:

We whose names are underwritten, being clearly and fully convinced, 1. That the success of the present work of God does in great measure depend on the entire union of all the labourers employed therein; 2. That our present call is chiefly to the members of that Church wherein we have been brought up; are absolutely determined by the grace of God; 1. To abide in the closest union with each other, and never knowingly or willingly to hear, speak, do, or suffer anything which tends to weaken that union; 2. Never to leave the company of the Church of England without the consent of all whose names are subjoined:

Charles Wesley	John Jones
William Shent	John Downes
John Wesley	John Nelson[9]

We see here the importance placed on unity, not simply in terms of visible continuity, but in terms of the Catholic spirit, and it was because Wesley interpreted the "oneness" of the Church in close connection with its "holiness" that it assumed for him such importance.

[8] Works, VIII, 280-81; See Simon, John Wesley and the Methodist Societies, 210-13. It is important to remember that while the Minutes arose from Conference discussion, Wesley is their author. He welcomed the group discussion but maintained the role of the final authority and was willingly accepted as such by his preachers.
[9] Journal, IV, 11 footnote; Simon, John Wesley and the Advance of Methodism, 226. Used by permission of Epworth Press.

3. In the years that followed, the pressure to separate increased, and as a result there was open discussion of it at the Conference of 1755.

The point on which we desired all the preachers to speak their minds at large was, "Whether we ought to separate from the Church?" Whatever was advanced on one side was seriously and calmly considered; and on the third day we were all fully agreed in that general conclusion—that (whether it was lawful or not) it was in no way expedient.[10]

It is not clear from this what connotation the words "lawful" and "expedient" carry although further light is thrown on this later. What is clear is that the determination to remain in union was accepted by the Conference, but it is equally clear that Wesley did not intend that this unity should hinder them in their mission. In a letter to Charles he wrote, "If we must either dissent, or be silent, actum est! We have no time to trifle." [11]

4. The determination to stay in the Church was confirmed at the 1756 Conference which the Wesley brothers closed by "a solemn declaration of their purpose never to separate from the Church; and 'all our brethren concurred therein.' " [12]

5. In 1758 Wesley published his "Reasons Against Separation from the Church of England," [13] and here we gain further light on the use of the words "lawful" or "expedient."

Whether it be lawful or not (which itself may be disputed, being not so clear a point as some may imagine) it is by no means expedient for us to separate from the Established Church.

We wish Wesley had further defined these terms. Probably under lawful he included the question of biblical authority, and we know that Wesley considered there was no final guidance in the Scripture on matters of order. What he means by expedient is made clearer in the final three of the twelve reasons listed by Wesley for refusing to separate.

[10] Journal, IV, 115.
[11] Letters, III, 131. (June 23, 1755).
[12] Simon, John Wesley and the Advance of Methodism, 329. Used by permission of Epworth Press.
[13] Works, XIII, 225-32.

10. Because the experiment has been so frequently tried already, and the success never answered the expectation. God has since the Reformation, raised up from time to time many witnesses of pure religion. If these lived and died (like John Arndt, Robert Bolton, and many others) in the churches to which they belonged, notwithstanding the wickedness which overflowed both the teachers and people therein, they spread the leaven of true religion far and wide, till they went to Paradise. But if upon any provocation or consideration whatever, they separated, and founded distinct parties, their influence was more and more confined; they grew less and less useful to others, and generally lost the spirit of religion themselves in the spirit of controversy.

11. Because we have melancholy instances of this even now before our eyes. Many have, in memory, left the Church, and formed themselves into distinct bodies. And certainly some of them from a real persuasion that they should do God more service. But have any separated themselves and prospered? . . .

12. Because by such a separation we should not only throw away the peculiar glorying which God has given us, that we do and will suffer all for our brethren's sake, though the more we love them, the less we be loved; but should act in direct contradiction to that very end, for which we believe God has raised us up. The chief design of His providence, in sending us out is undoubtedly to quicken our brethren. And the first message of all our preachers is to the lost sheep of the Church of England. Now would it not be a flat contradiction to this design to separate from the Church? These things being considered, we cannot apprehend, whether it be lawful in itself, that it is lawful for us; were it only on this ground, that it is by no means expedient.

Expediency is clearly not merely a matter of organizational convenience. Wesley believed that historical continuity was of great importance, that normally God seeks to revive his Church from within, and that schism is only necessary when the desperate situation arises of the true witnesses being thrust out. This too is tragic, for the mission of the Church is closely associated with her spirit of unity and division destroys that spirit.[14]

It seems clear that John and Charles had different grounds for supporting the principle of unity, for Charles' continuity is

[14] See a further discussion of this below.

211

far more closely associated with "order," John's with "mission." Here we may be close to the meaning of "lawful" as against "expedient." Charles wrote:

His Twelve Reasons against our separating from the Church of England are mine also. I subscribe to them with all my heart. Only with regard to the first, I am quite clear that it is neither expedient, nor lawful for me to separate. My affection for the Church is as strong as ever, and I clearly see my calling; which is, to live and die in her communion. This, therefore, I am determined to do, the Lord being my helper.[15]

"Lawful" here would seem to mean not simply a matter of biblical authority, but of the authority of the Church, guaranteed to it by a succession of ministry. Charles believed that "the uninterrupted succession" was a reality; John believed it "a fable." Consequently while John, who prized continuity highly, was nevertheless prepared to entertain the possibility that a situation may arise in which loyalty to mission would require a breach; Charles was not prepared to entertain such a possibility. For John, separation could possibly be lawful; for Charles, never.

6. So long as it was possible, however, to preach the gospel without separating and to receive the sacraments from the Church, John was as strongly insistent as Charles on the duty of preserving unity. So at the Conference of 1763 he warned:

(1.) Let all our preachers go to Church. (2.) Let all our people go constantly. (3). Receive the sacrament at every opportunity. (4). Warn against niceness in hearing; a great and prevailing evil. (5.) Warn them likewise against despising the prayers of the Church. (6.) Against calling our Society a Church, or the Church. (7.) Against calling our preachers ministers, our houses meeting-houses. (8.) Call them plain preaching-houses.[16]

The purpose of the Methodist societies was to act as ecclesiolae in ecclesia. Here the Word could be preached and applied, but the people should preserve the unity of the Church by attending her liturgy and receiving her sacraments.

[15] Simon, John Wesley, the Master Builder, p. 42. Used by permission of Epworth Press.
[16] Ibid., p. 141; See Works, VIII, 320-21.

7. This organization of ecclesiolae was very difficult to maintain as it required deviation from the established structure of the Church and establishment of another structure without any clear grant of ecclesiastical authority. It was this issue that was faced at the Conference of 1766.

Are we not Dissenters? Answer—We are irregular: 1. By calling sinners to repentance, in all places of God's dominion. 2. By frequently using extemporary prayer. Yet we are not Dissenters in the only sense which our law acknowledges; namely, persons who believe it is sinful to attend the service of the Church; for we do attend it at all opportunities. We will not, dare not, separate from the Church, for the reasons given several years ago. We are not seceders, nor do we bear any resemblance to them. We set out upon quite opposite principles. The seceders laid the very foundation of their work, in judging others; we laid the foundation of our work in judging and condemning ourselves. They begin everywhere, with showing their hearers, how fallen the Church and ministers are; we begin everywhere, with showing our hearers, how fallen they are themselves.

As we are not Dissenters from the Church now, so we will do nothing willingly, which tends to a separation from it. Therefore, let every assistant so order his circuit, that no preacher may be hindered from attending the Church more than two Sundays in a month. Never make light of going to Church, either by word or deed.

But some may say, "Our service is public worship." Yes, in a sense, but not such as supersedes the Church service. We never designed it should. We have a hundred times professed the contrary. It presupposes public prayer, like the sermons at the university. . . . Therefore, I myself frequently use only a collect, and never enlarge in prayer, unless at intercession, or on a watchnight, or on some extraordinary occasion.

If it were designed to be instead of Church service it would be essentially defective; for it seldom has the four grand parts of public prayer; deprecation, petition, intercession, and thanksgiving. Neither is it, even on the Lord's day, concluded with the Lord's Supper.[17]

In his desire to keep the societies as ecclesiolae Wesley appealed to the distinction between the prophetic and priestly offices.[18] The former could be performed by laymen, and so long

---

[17] Tyerman, *Life and Times*, II, 575-76; See *Works*, VIII, 321.
[18] *Works*, VII, 273 ff.

as they did not usurp the priestly offices of the Church, but attended her ministrations, continuity was maintained and the mission forwarded.

8. The mission, however, required a strong preaching organization, and because of the failure of ministers of the established Church to respond to his appeal to join with him,[19] at the 1769 Conference Wesley read the following paper:

My Dear Brethren. 1. It has long been my desire, that all those ministers of our Church who believe and preach salvation by faith, might cordially agree between themselves, and not hinder but help one another. After occasionally pressing this, in private conversation, wherever I had opportunity, I wrote down my thoughts upon the head, and sent them to each in a letter. Out of fifty or sixty to whom I wrote, only three vouchsafed me an answer. So I give this up. I can do no more. They are a rope of sand, and such will they continue.

2. But it is otherwise with the *travelling* preachers in our connexion. You are at present one body. You act in concert with each other, and by united counsels. And now is the time to consider what can be done, in order to continue this union. Indeed, as long as I live, there will be no great difficulty. I am, under God, a centre of union to all our travelling preachers. They all know me and my communication. They all love me for my work's sake, and, therefore, were it only out of regard to me, they will continue connected with each other. But by what means may this connexion be preserved, when God removes me from you?

3. I take it for granted, it cannot be preserved by any means, between those who have not a single eye. Those who aim at anything but the glory of God, and the salvation of men, who desire or seek any earthly thing, whether honour, profit or ease, will not, cannot continue in the connexion; it will not answer their design. Some of them, perhaps a fourth of their whole number, will procure preferment in the church. Others will turn Independents, and get separate congregations, like John Edwards and Charles Skelton. Lay your accounts with this, and be not surprised if some you do not suspect, be of this number.

4. But what method can be taken to preserve a firm union between those who choose to remain together? Perhaps you might take some

---

[19] See 1763 Letter to the Clergy, *Letters*, IV, 235-39.

such steps as these. On notice of my death, let all the preachers, in England and in Ireland, repair to London within six weeks. Let them draw up articles of agreement, to be signed by those who choose to act in concert. Let those be dismissed, who do not choose it, in the most friendly manner possible. Let them choose by vote a committee of three, five, or seven, each of whom is to be moderator in his turn. Let the committee do what I do now; propose preachers to be tried, admitted or excluded; fix the place of each preacher for the ensuing year and the time of the next Conference.

5. Can anything be done now, in order to lay a foundation for this future union? Would it not be well, for any that are willing, to sign some articles of agreement before God calls me hence? Suppose something like these:

We, whose names are underwritten, being thoroughly convinced of the necessity of a close union between those whom God is pleased to use as instruments in this glorious work, in order to preserve this union between ourselves, are resolved, God being our helper: (1.) To devote ourselves entirely to God; denying ourselves, taking up our cross daily, steadily aiming at one thing, to save our own souls, and them that hear us. (2.) To preach the old Methodist doctrines, and no other, contained in the minutes of the conferences. (3.) To observe and enforce the whole Methodist discipline, laid down in the said minutes.[20]

Wesley, then, envisaged a type of Church of England Fransiscan Order, but he recognized that of necessity, and he hoped temporarily, it had to be without ecclesiastical portfolio. Nevertheless it should organize as such an order within the Church and do all in its power to win acceptance by the Church.

Wesley did not feel that it was necessary to salvation or to membership in the Church to belong to such a voluntary society. As he wrote to Professor Luden of Sweden in 1769, "There are many thousands of Methodists in Great Britain and Ireland which are not formed into societies." [21] He saw the role of such societies to be as leaven within the Church to revivify her inwardly and also to serve as bridges to draw those outside the Church into her life.

This original organization of Methodism as a voluntary order

[20] Tyerman, Life and Times, III, 49-50.
[21] Letters, V, 155.

—as ecclesiolae—has been of great moment for her subsequent life. In a true sense she has ever since been a *society in search of the Church,* both in the sense that she seeks the unity, in true witness, of the visible continuous body of Christians and in the sense that having since been excluded from the Church of England, she has had to struggle over such questions as:

a) How can the discipline, which Wesley established for voluntary ecclesiolae, be related to the new existence as an ecclesia?

b) What should she regard as true marks of the Church, and what should be her attitude to the doctrine, liturgy, and ministry of the Church from which she has been separated?

Rattenbury expressed the dilemma in terms of English Methodism:

The struggle of Methodism to remain a mere Society within the Church of England, when she had no longer association with a Church of which she could be called a Society, lingered on till our days. It was one hundred years before his society called itself a Church. . . . Methodism seems to be standing at the crossways. Much of her distinctive denominational life has gone, and she is feeling, perhaps subconsciously, after Catholicity.[22]

In America, as we shall see, the situation that emerged was different, and yet a similar vacuum in the doctrine of Church order has been apparent.

9. The difficulty of remaining as a society within the Church became increasingly apparent as Methodists were either excluded from the ministrations of the Church of England, or else (having been converted from the nonchurch masses, or the ranks of those with dissenting backgrounds) found it psychologically impossible to accept these Church ministrations.

In 1775 Joseph Benson, one of Wesley's preachers, suggested in a letter to Fletcher that the best qualified preachers be set apart to the ministry by fasting, prayer, and the imposition of hands by John and Charles Wesley, Fletcher, and other presbyters of the Church of England. In this way the need of those excluded from the services of the regular parishes of the Church

---

[22] Rattenbury, *Wesley's Legacy to the World,* op. cit., p. 198. Used by permission of Epworth Press.

216

of England could be met. Fletcher then wrote to Wesley with a detailed proposal as to how Methodists should be kept in union with each other but still related to the Church. In point 6 of his letter he wrote:

That this petition contain a request to the Bishops to ordain the Methodist preachers which can pass their examination according to what is *indispensably* required in the canons of the Church. . . . That if his grace, etc., does not condescend to grant this request, Messrs. Wesley will be obliged to take an irregular (not unevangelical) step, and to ordain upon a Church of England independent plan such lay preachers as appear to them qualified for holy orders.

Even this ordination was not conceived as separation from the Church of England, for Fletcher included in the suggested ordination vows:

Wilt thou consider thyself as a son of the Church of England, receding from her as little as possible; never railing against her clergy, and being ready to submit to her ordination, if any of her Bishops will confer it upon thee? [23]

Simon is probably right in his comment that "as we watch the growth of the constitution of the Methodist Church, we think we can perceive the influence of Fletcher's long lost letter."

10. Meanwhile, however, Wesley still resisted any definite step and continually urged his people to attend the Church, but in America events were moving to a crisis.

Before the conflict (the Revolution against England) began, it was the custom of the Methodists to attend the sacramental services held in the English churches that then existed in many of the towns of the country. But the war led to the destruction of a large number of these churches, and to the flight of a host of clergymen into places of safety. In spite of the fierce persecution the Methodist preachers continued their perilous work in the forsaken neighbourhoods. The result was that as the societies increased in number, their members lost the opportunity to receive the sacrament of the Lord's Supper in the towns which had been abandoned by the clergy.[24]

[23] For the whole incident see Simon, *John Wesley, the Last Phase,* 60-67. Used by permission of Epworth Press.
[24] *Ibid.,* 226-27.

Consequently the issue of providing the sacraments became a strongly debated question. Discussed at the first Conference in 1773, it led to action at the *Fluvanna Conference* of 1779. A committee of four was appointed as a Presbytery. They ordained each other and proceeded to offer ordination to such preachers as desired it. A serious division resulted, and it was only the strong action of Asbury which resulted in a declaration that the ordinations were invalid and an understanding that John Wesley be consulted in seeking a more acceptable solution.[25]

That these ordinations were considered invalid emphasizes the regard for continuity and raises the question of the doctrine of the ministry held by Wesley. To this we now turn.

The Methodist Ministry

Rigg claims that Wesley's "life was divided into two distinct, and in many respects, sharply-contrasted periods, the period preceding and the period following the spring of 1738."[26] Prior to 1738 he was a strict High Churchman, but the experience of May 24 "ended his High Church stage of life. Here began his life as an evangelist and a Church revivalist."[27] There was a transition period, but by 1745-1746 the transition not to a Low Church, but to a Broad Church position was complete.

Rattenbury, on the other hand, claims that

there is no greater mistake than to suppose that Wesley ceased to be a High Churchman after 1738. The popular argument that the Wesley before 1738 and after were two different men with different views, is a modern Methodist myth which serious investigation proves to be without foundation.[28]

To dispute over the terms High, Broad, Low, is probably unprofitable, but that there has been a strong difference of opinion over Wesley's doctrine of the Ministry and his attitude to Church Order is clear. Also that to this day there is confusion over what

[25] *Ibid.*, 227.
[26] Rigg, *The Churchmanship of John Wesley, op. cit.*, p. 18. Used by permission of Epworth Press.
[27] *Ibid.*, p. 40.
[28] Rattenbury, *Wesley's Legacy to the World*, p. 63. Used by permission of Epworth Press.

is or should be the Methodist attitude to these issues is equally clear.

1. The first real statement of Wesley's after 1738 comes in the Minutes of the Conference of 1745:

Q. 5. Is Episcopal, Presbyterian, or Independent Church government most agreeable to reason?

A. The plain origin of church government seems to be this. Christ sends forth a preacher of the Gospel. Some who hear him repent and believe the Gospel. They then desire him to watch over them, to build them up in the faith, and to guide their souls in the paths of righteousness.

Here then, is an Independent congregation subject to no pastor but their own; neither liable to be controlled in things spiritual by any other man or body of men whatsoever.

But soon after, some from other parts, who are occasionally present while he speaks in the name of Him that sent him, beseech him to come over to help them also. Knowing it to be the will of God, he consents, yet not till he has conferred with the wisest and holiest of his congregation, and, with their advice, appointed one or more who have gifts and grace to watch over the flock till his return.

If it pleases God to raise another flock in the new place, before he leaves them he does the same thing, appointing one whom God has fitted for the work to watch over these souls also. In like manner, in every place where it pleases God to gather a little flock by His Word, he appoints one in his absence to take the oversight of the rest, and to assist them of the abilities which God giveth. These are deacons, or servants of the church, and look on the first pastor as their common father. And all these congregations regard him as the Shepherd of their souls.

These congregations are not absolutely independent; they depend on one pastor, though not on each other.

As these congregations increase, and as their deacons grow in years and grace, they need other Subordinate deacons or helpers, in respect of whom they may be called presbyters as their father in the Lord may be called bishop or overseer of them all.

Q. 6. Is mutual consent absolutely necessary between the pastor and his flock?

A. No question. I cannot guide any soul unless he consent to be guided by me. Neither can any soul force me to guide him if I consent not.

Q. 7. Does the ceasing of this consent on either side dissolve this relation?

A. It must, in the very nature of things. If a man no longer consents to be guided by me, I am no longer his guide. I am free. If one will not guide me any longer, I am free to seek one who will.[29]

Rigg comments:

This remarkable extract contains implicitly the whole theory of Methodist government and discipline. . . . Wesley regarded himself as a sort of bishop, his "assistants" or chief preachers in charge as quasi-presbyters, and the junior or probationary (helpers) as a sort of deacons.[30]

But Rigg is worried by the fact that though this was written in August 1745,

On December 27 of the same year he prints in his Journal a letter to his brother-in-law, Hall—a letter well known and often quoted by Churchmen—in which he upheld the doctrine of apostolic succession.[31]

If that letter reveals Wesley's position at the time, then the interpretation of the 1745 Minutes in terms of an Independent or Congregational doctrine cannot be sustained, and in fact, Rigg has misinterpreted the passage. In Q. 5 Wesley is referring to the origin of the threefold ministry in apostolic times, and at that stage (as his letter to Hall reveals) he considered that the authority for their successors, the bishops, flowed from the Apostles. The purpose of this analysis lies in Q. 6 and Q. 7, which refer to presbyters, for here Wesley is justifying his invasion of the parishes of other presbyters on the ground that they had refused to give true guidance to their parishioners, and that therefore the parishioners were no longer obliged to submit to their guidance.

2. The big change in Wesley's doctrine of the ministry came a month after his letter to Hall and is recorded in the Journal for January 20, 1746.

[29] Rigg, op. cit., 64-65. Used by permission of Epworth Press.
[30] Ibid., pp. 65-66.
[31] Ibid., p. 66. See Letters, II, 55-56.

On the road I read over Lord King's *Account of the Primitive Church*. In spite of the vehement prejudice of my education, I was ready to believe that this was a fair and impartial draught; but, if so, it would follow that bishops and presbyters are (essentially) of one order, and that originally every Christian congregation was a church independent of all others.[32]

Here would seem to be a conversion to the congregational view of the ministry and church order, and yet the situation is not as simple as that. On the basis of this reading of King, and later of Stillingfleet's "Irenicon," [33] he became convinced that he had been wrong in believing "none but Episcopal ordination valid," [34] and that the uninterrupted succession through bishops is a fable.[35] Nevertheless this still did not mean that he rejected the episcopal form of government or the importance of visible continuity.

3. In the Minutes of 1747 Wesley makes it clear that he believed that there is no one prescribed form of government in the New Testament and that the Reformed Churches have a valid order. Nevertheless he believed that the threefold order was normal in the apostolic age.

Q. You profess to obey both the governors and rulers of the Church, yet in many instances you do not obey them; how is this consistent? Upon what principles do you act, while you sometimes obey and sometimes not?
A. It is entirely consistent. We act at all times on one plain uniform principle—"We will obey the rulers and governors of the Church, whenever we can consistently with our duty to God, whenever we cannot, we will quietly obey God rather than men."
Q. But why do you say you are thrust out of the Church? Has not every minister the right to dispose of his own church?
A. He ought to have, but in fact he has not. A minister desires I should preach in his church, but the Bishop forbids him. That Bishop then injures him, and thrusts me out of that church.
Q. Does a Church in the New Testament always mean "a single congregation"?

[32] Journal, III, 232.
[33] Letters, IV, 150; see also Letters, III, 136, 182.
[34] Letters, IV, 150.
[35] Letters, IV, 140; Letters, VII, 121.

A. We believe it does. We do not recollect any instance to the contrary.

Q. What instance of ground is there in the New Testament for a national Church?

A. We know none at all. We apprehend it to be a mere political institution.

Q. Are the three orders of Bishops, Priests, and Deacons plainly described in the New Testament?

A. We think they are, and believe they generally obtained in the churches of the apostolic age.

Q. But are you assured God designed the same plan should obtain in all churches throughout all ages?

A. We are not assured of this, because we do not know that it is asserted in Holy Writ.

Q. If this plan were essential to a Christian Church, what must become of all foreign Reformed Churches?

A. It would follow they are no parts of the Church of Christ—a consequence full of shocking absurdity.

Q. In what age was the divine right of episcopacy first asserted in England?

A. About the middle of Queen Elizabeth's reign. Till then all the Bishops and clergy in England continually allowed and joined in the ministrations of those who were not episcopally ordained.

Q. Must there not be numberless accidental variations in the government of various Churches?

A. There must be in the nature of things. As God variously dispenses His gifts of nature, providence, and grace, both the offices themselves and the officers in each ought to be varied from time to time.

Q. Why is that there is no determinate plan of Church government appointed in Scripture?

A. Without doubt, because the wisdom of God had a regard to the necessary variety.

Q. Was there any thought of uniformity in the government of all Churches until the time of Constantine?

A. It is certain there was not; and would not have been then had men consulted the word of God only.[36]

Wesley believed, then, that not only the threefold order was valid. Nevertheless, the fact that as a presbyter he had the (theo-

[36] Simon, *John Wesley and the Advance of Methodism*, 37-38. Used by permission of Epworth Press.

retical) right to ordain did not allow him to solve his problems in that way for he believed visible continuity to be of real importance. When he considered the position of Methodists, therefore, in relation to the Church of England, he had to consider not only the immediate needs of the members of his society, but the necessity for doing all in his power to maintain unity.

4. We come now, however, to a puzzling and difficult problem—the use of a Greek Orthodox Bishop Erasmus to provide ordination for some of his preachers in 1764.

By that time the pressure of the large societies to receive the sacrament in their own chapels had placed Wesley in difficulties. Refusing to allow unordained preachers to administer and having only his brother Charles to help him, Wesley sought ordination for some of his preachers. When Thomas Maxfield received ordination from an Irish Bishop, the pressure in London was relieved, as he was able to give the sacrament there in Wesley's absence, but by 1764 Maxfield had left Wesley, and the pressure was greater than ever.

At this time Wesley met Erasmus, who "told me he was a Greek bishop." [37] After satisfying himself as to the authenticity of Erasmus,[38] Wesley requested him to ordain "Mr. John Jones, a man well versed both in the languages and other parts of learning," [39] and who had been an itinerant preacher for seventeen years.

This caused great trouble. Six other of Wesley's preachers, without his knowledge, went to Erasmus for ordination, and a Conference in January 1765 agreed that they:

having acted contrary to the Word of God and the duty they owe: to their ministers and their brethren
1. Can no more be owned as clergymen,

[37] *Letters*, IV, 289.
[38] Tyerman, *Life and Times*, II, 486. Jones wrote to the patriarch of Smyrna on the subject; and received an answer, stating that Erasmus was bishop of Arcadia in Crete. To this was added the testimony of several gentlemen who met the eastern prelate in Turkey. Wesley says, "he had abundant unexceptionable credentials as to his episcopal character." (*Works*, X, 432.)
[39] *Letters*, IV, 289-90.

2. Can no more be received as preachers,
3. Nor as members of the Society.[40]

Wesley then wrote to the London Chronicle disowning them on the ground that as unqualified men they bought ordination in an unknown tongue.[41]

The whole event caused a furor, not only in the Methodist connexion where even "Jones was obliged to leave the connexion," [42] but outside it, for August Toplady in 1771 in "A Letter to the Reverend Mr. John Wesley" charged that Erasmus was "a foreign mendicant" and "imposter" and that Wesley not only asked him to ordain some of his preachers but also requested Erasmus to ordain him a bishop.[43]

A Greek orthodox priest has recently examined the whole case [44] and has concluded:

The fact is that Erasmus was not a canonical Bishop of the Greek Orthodox Church, a conclusion that is reached after consideration of certain important points. First, Erasmus shows total ignorance of the practice, custom and canon law of the Church he is supposed to represent. Secondly, the certificate he gives to the ordinands differs in content from that of the Greek Orthodox Church of that period. Thirdly, his deplorable state—"being in dire need and ready to be thrown into prison"—contradicts the kindness, honors, and hospitality accorded to visiting Greek prelates by the English ecclesiastical and civil authorities and the Greek people living in London during this and previous periods. And fourthly, his name is not found in the catalogues of Bishops of Crete.[45]

Nevertheless, Tsoumas concludes that Wesley was honestly convinced that Erasmus was genuine, that Wesley was right in his denial of the reported request that Erasmus ordain him a bishop, and that "his actions, irregular and inconsistent as they may be, can be explained by remembering that Wesley con-

[40] *Letters*, IV, 290.
[41] *Letters*, IV, 290.
[42] Tyerman, *Life and Times*, II, 487.
[43] *Ibid.*, p. 488.
[44] The Very Reverend George Tsoumas, *The Greek Orthodox Theological Review* (Christmas Issue, 1956), II, No. 2, 62-73.
[45] *Ibid.*, 62.

sidered himself providentially endowed and preserved for the mission he had in life." [46]

This final point is of great importance. In the strange case of the "ordination" of Coke for America (Coke already being an ordained Presbyter of the Church of England) Wesley included in the certificate the phrase "I John Wesley think myself to be providentially called at this time to set apart some persons for the work of the ministry in America," [47] and the actions we are examining cannot be understood unless we remember that Wesley considered himself an "extraordinarius," raised up by God within the Church for this special mission. Wesley placed great store on the continuity of the ministry as this very "ordination" by Erasmus attests. For Wesley here reveals the length to which he was prepared to go to gain episcopal ordination from a Bishop recognized as valid by the Church of England, seeing that the Bishops of the Church of England refused to ordain his qualified men.

This attempt, however, having proved a failure, Wesley was now thrown back on to even more irregular (though he believed valid) steps to provide for the needs of the people committed by God to his care.

5. We have seen how the impromptu ordinations in America had been declared invalid, and that appeal had been made to Wesley to provide for the needs of the American members now without benefit of the sacrament. On August 10, 1780 Wesley wrote to Lowth, Bishop of London, pointing out the desperate situation in America, speaking of the qualifications of some of his preachers, and asking the Bishop to ordain some of them for America, [48] but the Bishop did not consent. Still Wesley waited, and by 1784 there were eighty-three nonordained, itinerant Methodist preachers in America, caring for 14,998 members with no provision for the sacraments. [49]

Finally, therefore, in September, 1784 he ordained (for America) Thomas Coke as Superintendent, and Richard What-

[46] Ibid., 68.
[47] Journal, VII, 16.
[48] Letters, VII, 30-31.
[49] Tyerman, Life and Times, III, 427.

coat and Thomas Vasey as Elders. His ordination of Whatcoat and Vasey is comparatively simple. Ever since 1746 when he had read Lord King, he was convinced that "bishops and presbyters are (essentially) of one order," [50] and that therefore he had the power to ordain.[51] The question here is whether Wesley believed this power to ordain depended in some way on succession. It has regularly been argued that Wesley's statement that "the uninterrupted succession I know to be a fable" [52] means that he placed no importance on succession. But, if so, why did he argue so strongly that his right to ordain rested on his own ordination as presbyter?

Rattenbury concludes:

It must not be thought that Wesley believed in no apostolic succession because he rejected episcopal succession. What he disbelieved was that bishops and presbyters were of orders inherently different. He thought a presbyter had the rights that a bishop claimed. . . . There is no evidence at all that he thought "orders" could be given by any other person than bishops or presbyters. He was in this matter, not a High Church Episcopalian, but a High Church Presbyterian. Whether he taught that their was a special grace bestowed or transmitted by the laying on of hands is undemonstrable, but he obviously thought that authority to administer sacraments could only be transmitted by that method.[53]

Rattenbury, I believe, has misstated the case. When Wesley says "the uninterrupted succession I know to be a fable," he does not say "episcopal." It was not mechanical succession in which he was interested. To understand the form of succession he did believe important, let us examine his "ordination" of Coke.

Tyerman contends that Wesley did not intend to ordain Coke "who, as a Presbyter of the same church, had co-equal power to go out to America for that purpose . . . But, at Coke's request, he acquiesced." [54] All that Wesley intended by the laying of of hands was

[50] *Journal*, III, 232.
[51] *Letters*, V, 121.
[52] *Ibid.*
[53] Rattenbury, *Wesley's Legacy to the World, op. cit.*, p. 193. Used by permission of Epworth Press.
[54] Tyerman, *Life and Times*, III, 430.

a mere formality to recommend his delegate to the favour of the Methodists in America: Coke, in his ambition, wished and intended it to be considered as an ordination to the Bishopric.[55]

Cooke, an American Methodist, takes a strongly opposed viewpoint.[56] He points out that Wesley invited another presbyter, Creighton, to join with him in the ordination.

If Wesley did not intend to consecrate Dr. Coke a bishop in fact but avoiding the title, why was it necessary to invite Dr. Creighton to insist in such a service at all? [57]

Further Wesley wrote in his Diary for September 2: "4. Prayed. Ordained Dr. Coke." Cooke comments:

It is presumable that Mr. Wesley knew his own intentions, and it is likewise presumable that he knew the meaning of his own words. That Mr. Wesley intended to ordain Mr. Whatcoat and Mr. Vasey as presbyters, or elders, no one has denied, but the same proof that esetablishes that fact also establishes the other fact that he did also intend by his ordination services to ordain Doctor Coke bishop in fact. It is evident that Dr. Coke was no less a bishop because Mr. Wesley changed the title "bishop" in the English Ordinal to that of "superintendent," than Whatcoat and Vasey were not presbyters, because he changed the title "presbyter" to "elder."

Cooke's case is sustained, at least in its major thesis, by the record of a conversation of Wesley with Coke in London, February, 1784. In the conversation he outlined the position in America and

then proceeded to explain a plan he had determined to adopt. In his study of Early Church History, he had much admired the mode of ordaining bishops which the Church of Alexandria had practiced. In order to preserve its purity, that Church would never suffer the interference of a foreign bishop in any of its ordinations; the presbyters, on the death of a bishop, had exercised the right of ordaining a bishop chosen from their own number. This practice continued among them for two hundred years. At the close of the conversation

[55] *Ibid.*, 431.
[56] Richard J. Cooke, "Our Methodist Episcopacy," *Methodist Review* (March, 1931), pp. 206-14.
[57] *Ibid.*, p. 212.

he suggested that, being himself a presbyter Dr. Coke should accept ordination at his hands, and then proceed to America, and ordain other presbyters for the Societies in the United States.[58]

We are now in a position to state the significance of these ordinations.

1. While Wesley did not accept a theory of mechanical succession, he was tenacious of the organic continuity of the church. His remarkable perseverance in his attempt to maintain continuity with the Church of England is explained in a passage from his sermon "On Attending the Church Service." [59] Discussing the determination never to leave the Church of England, he argues that no one has the right of schism, even where life is at a low ebb, preaching is poor, and sacraments are administered by unholy men.

"But if all this wickedness was not a sufficient reason for separating from a corrupt Church, why did Calvin and Luther, with their followers, separate from the Church of Rome? I answer, they did not properly separate from it; but were violently thrust out of it. They were not suffered to continue therein, upon any other terms than subscribing to all the errors of that Church, and joining in all their superstition and idolatry. Therefore this separation lay at *their* [Rome's] door.[60]

In England, he argues, no such necessity exists, and he condemns England's dissenters for their separation.

No sinful terms of communion were imposed upon them; neither are at this day. Most of them separated, either because of some opinions, or some modes of worship, which they did not approve of.

2. Wesley further saw the ministry as the symbol of that continuity. In his 1789 sermon on "The Ministerial Office" [61] Wesley argues the case for staying in the Church of England and says that since the Bible separates the office of preaching from that of priest, the Methodists are able to preach the true Gospel in the corrupt Church without usurping the priestly role

[58] Simon, *John Wesley, the Last Phase,* 229. Used by permission of Epworth Press.
[59] *Works,* VII, 174-185.
[60] *Ibid.,* 182-83.
[61] *Works,* VII, 273-81.

of the regular ministry. He claims, in fact, that God has raised up the Methodist preachers as "extra-ordinary messengers" to " 'provoke to jealousy,' the ordinary messengers." [62] The regular continuous ministry is, then, a symbol of unity.

3. Wesley is interested not only in a visible continuity but also in the continuity of the Word and the mission of the Church. These are in tension and if at last the breaking point comes, it is the latter which must prevail. As we have seen already, Wesley proclaimed that Luther and Calvin, holding, as they must, to the proclamation of the gospel, were thrust out of the Church so that visible continuity was broken. Yet there was still real continuity. To the London Chronicle in 1761, Wesley wrote:

The Catholic Church . . . has "a perpetual succession of pastors and teachers divinely appointed and divinely assisted." And there has never been wanting in the Reformed Churches such a succession of pastors and teachers, men both divinely appointed and divinely assisted, for they convert sinners to God—a work none can do unless God Himself doth appoint them thereto and assist them therein, therefore every part of this character is applicable to them. Their teachers are the proper successors of those who have delivered down through all generations the faith once delivered to the saints; and their members have true spiritual communion with the "one holy" society of true believers. Consequently, although they are not the whole "people of God," yet they are an undeniable part of His people.[63]

In this true sense the Roman Catholic Church is not in apostolic succession:

All the doctrines and practices wherein she differs from us were not instituted by Christ; they are unknown to the ancient Church of Christ; they are unscriptural novel corruptions.[64]

The "vertical" continuity of the Word, then, is in tension with the "horizontal" continuity of order and ministry, and where it is impossible to hold them together, and where true believers are

[62] Ibid., 280.
[63] Letters, IV, 137-38.
[64] Ibid., 138.

"thrust out" for proclaiming the faith once delivered to the saints, continuity is maintained through the true believers.

In England, however, Wesley believed the case was different, for the Church of England was essentially right in her doctrine, and Methodists were not, in general, refused communion. Therefore the symbol of horizontal continuity must be preserved.

4. Wesley believed, in fact, that though there was no one "order" laid down in the New Testament, and that, therefore, the Reformed Church was a valid Church (but not the whole Church), nevertheless the threefold order of the ministry was normal, and that for the sake of continuity and unity it should, if possible, be maintained. We quoted above his statement from the 1747 Minutes.

Q. Are the three orders of Bishops, Priests, and Deacons plainly described in the New Testament?
A. We think they are, and believe they generally obtained in the Churches of the Apostolic Age.[65]

That Wesley continued to believe strongly in the normality of this order is indicated by the statement of one of his preachers, Pawson, concerning the American ordinations:

He was deeply prejudiced against presbyterian, and as such in favour of episcopal government. In order, therefore, to preserve all that is valuable in the Church of England among the Methodists, he ordained Mr. Mather and Dr. Coke, bishops. These he undoubtedly designed should ordain others. Mr. Mather told us so at the Manchester Conference, in 1791.[66]

The case of Mather, we have yet to consider, but the case of Coke now seems clear. Wesley determined to keep for America the threefold order that was normative though not exclusive. That Charles Wesley so understood his brother's action is clear from this letter to Chandler:

I can scarcely believe it, that, in his eighty-second year, my brother, my old, intimate friend and companion, should have assumed the episcopal character, ordained elders, consecrated a bishop, and sent him to ordain our lay preachers in America! . . .

---

[65] See above 333.
[66] Tyerman, *Life and Times*, III, 443.

Lord Mansfield told me last year, that ordination was separation. This my brother does not or will not see, or that he has renounced the principles and practice of his life. . . .

Had they patience a little longer, they would have seen a real bishop in America [67] consecrated by three Scotch bishops who have their consecration from the English bishops and are acknowledged by them as the same with themselves. . . . But what are our poor Methodists now? Only a new sect of Presbyterians.[68]

John differed from Charles on two counts:

a) He did not believe in the necessity for a succession of Bishops through unbroken episcopal succession and therefore believed that the ordination of Coke was valid. Moreover he believed that in America a new situation had arisen and that for the sake of the mission of the Church, freedom from the English hierarchy was essential. His letter to "Our Brethren in America" makes that clear:

Lord King's *Account of the Primitive Church* convinced me many years ago that bishops and presbyters are the same order, and consequently have the same right to ordain. For many years, I have been importuned from time to time to exercise this right by ordaining part of our travelling preachers. But I have still refused, not only for peace sake, but because I was determined as little as possible to violate the established order of the National Church to which I belonged.

But the case is widely different between England and North America. Here there are bishops who have a legal jurisdiction; in America there are none, neither any parish ministers. So that for some hundred miles together there is none to baptize or to administer the Lord's Supper. Here, therefore, my scruples are at an end; and I conceive myself at liberty, as I violate no order and invade no man's right by appointing and sending labourers into the harvest.

I have accordingly appointed Dr. Coke and Mr. Francis Asbury to be Joint Superintendents over our brethren in North America; as also Richard Whatcoat and Thomas Vasey to act as elders among them, by baptizing and administering the Lord's Supper. And I have prepared a Liturgy little differing from that of the Church of England (I think the best constituted National Church in the world), which

[67] Samuel Seabury, first Bishop of the Episcopal Church, after failing to receive ordination in England, was granted it in Scotland, and ordained by three Bishops on November 14, 1784.
[68] Tyerman, *Life and Times*, III, 439-40.

I advise all the travelling preachers to use on the Lord's Day in all the congregations, reading the Litany only on Wednesdays and Fridays and praying extempore on all other days. I also advise the elders to administer the Supper of the Lord on every Lord's Day. . . .

It has, indeed, been proposed to desire the English bishops to ordain part of our preachers for America. But to this I object; (1.) I desired the Bishop of London to ordain only one, but could not prevail. (2) If they consented, we know the slowness of their proceedings; but the matter admits of no delay. (3.) If they would ordain them now, they would likewise expect to govern them. And how grievously would this entangle us. (4.) As our American brethren are now totally disentangled both from the State and from the English hierarchy, we dare not entangle them again with the one or the other. They are now at full liberty simply to follow the Scriptures and the Primitive Church. And we judge it best they should stand fast in that liberty wherewith God has so strangely made them free.[69]

The situation in America had convinced Wesley that the necessity of the Mission of the Church demanded the provision of the threefold order on the model of the Church of Alexandria, and that as the "extraordinarius" placed by God over the Methodists, he was called to exercise his power of ordination.[70]

Nevertheless there was a second count on which he differed from Charles.

b) He did not believe this was separation from the Church. In the *Methodist Magazine* in 1785, he wrote:

These are the steps which, not of choice, but of necessity, I have slowly and deliberately taken. If any one is pleased to call this *separating from the Church*, he may. But the law of England does not call it so; nor can anyone properly be said so to do, unless, out of conscience, he refuses to join in the service, and partake of the sacraments administered therein.[71]

Wesley apparently believed that since America was now beyond English jurisdiction, and since her ministry was no longer available to the Methodists, he had provided for their con-

[69] *Letters*, VII, 238-39.
[70] For evidence that Jerome was right in saying that in Alexandria bishops were appointed by local presbyters without intervention from other sees, see E. W. Thompson, op. cit., pp. 31-32.
[71] Tyerman, *Life and Times*, III, 436.

tinuity with the Church in a way providentially ordained by God.[72]

One fact further needs to be considered. Wesley's letter to Asbury on September 20, 1788:

You are the elder brother of the American Methodists: I am under God the father of the whole family. . . . But in one point, my dear brother, I am a little afraid both the Doctor (Coke) and you differ from me. I study to be little: you study to be great. I creep: you strut along. I found a school: you a college! nay, and call it after your own names! O beware, do not seek to be something! Let me be nothing, and "Christ be all in all"!

One instance of this, of your greatness, has given me great concern. How can you, how dare you suffer yourself to be called Bishop? I shudder, I start at the thought! . . . Let the Presbyterians do what they please, but let the Methodists know their calling better.[73]

What was the reason for this? Either personal pique or a deeper principle. The former seems inconsistent with Wesley's whole character, the latter may well be that Wesley wished to make clear by the change of names that the Methodist Church made no claim to be the whole Church but was looking forward to the time when greater unity would be manifest in America. The action of Coke and Asbury, therefore, in using the title "Bishop" seemed to Wesley to be claiming a status for Methodism that he was unwilling for it to claim. Methodism had been raised up to provoke the dead regular clergy to jealousy, and though in America the ecclesiastical vacuum had forced Wesley to give to Methodism a clergy, Articles of Religion, and a Liturgy, still, in a manner he could not see, he hoped for a fuller manifestation of the Church.

5. One further question merits consideration. Walter Muelder writes:

The episcopacy has never in Methodism been considered a "third order," but rather the investiture of an "elder" with certain definite executive functions and powers.[74]

[72] See Coke's Ordination Certificate: Journal, VII, 16.
[73] Letters, VIII, 91.
[74] The Quest for Christian Unity (ed. by R. S. Bilheimer, New York: Association Press, 1952), p. 161.

233

From our investigation we have seen that Wesley believed the threefold order was normal, but not exclusive. That the orders of bishop and priest were originally the same, he believed, and on the basis of the Alexandrian Church practice he accepted the idea that elevation to the episcopacy could be performed by presbyters. Yet in acting on this, he nevertheless ordained Coke, thereby showing that a third order was involved. On the basis of the Alexandrian precedent this third order had no exclusive right to ordain, and there could be no thought of succession through the episcopacy. Nevertheless, a third order was involved.

This issue has arisen already in Methodist union negotiations, and it would seem that the points which must be kept in mind are:

a) On the basis of our original tradition we could accept no theory which proclaimed that apostolic succession through the episcopacy is of the *esse* of the Church.

b) We would insist that Churches without the threefold order can be owned and blessed by God as his Church, and that therefore in this true sense their ministries are valid, and a united Church should keep open the channels of communion with them.

c) We would nevertheless agree that the threefold order is the normal tradition of the Church, is a valuable symbol of unity and continuity, and can be accepted wholeheartedly, provided the above two considerations are maintained.

It would seem clear that Wesley would not have insisted on the Alexandrian method of ordination. He was happy with the Anglican tradition but insisted only that the Alexandrian system was also valid. It is, in fact, quite possible that Wesley changed the title "bishop" to "general superintendent" and "presbyter" to "elder" as a symbol that his ordinations for America were "valid but irregular." On that point, however, no certainty seems possible.

We must turn back, now, to the situation in England. And there we see that Wesley was forced to ordain first, for Scotland; then, for other mission fields; finally for England, but that always he went to great lengths to prevent a final rupture with

234

the Church of England. In his *Journal* for August 1, 1785, he records:

> Having with a few select friends, weighed the matter thoroughly, I yielded to their judgment, and set apart three of our own well-tried preachers, John Pawson, Thomas Hanby, and Joseph Taylor, to minister in Scotland.[75]

Commenting on these ordinations in the Conference Minutes of 1786, Wesley wrote that seeing the Methodists are denied the means of grace in Scotland

> I, at length, consented to take the same step with regard to Scotland, which I had done with regard to America. But this is not separation from the Church at all. Not from the Church of Scotland; for we were never connected therewith, . . . nor from the Church of England; for this is not concerned in the steps which are taken in England. Whatever therefore is done in America, or Scotland, is no separation from the Church of England. I have no thought of this; I have many objections against it.[76]

Wesley was struggling hard to keep unity, unity for the sake of the mission of the Church, for he believed that a divisive spirit was fatal to the Church's witness. Yet he knew also how increasingly difficult it was to maintain that unity when so great a part of the Church was not only spiritually dead, but even hostile to her mission. Yet struggle on he did. The ordinations continued, at first only for Scotland and the mission fields: [77]

1785: for Scotland: Robert Johnson, Joshua Keighley, and Charles Atmore. William Warrener for Antigua. William Hammett for Newfoundland. John Clarke for Nova Scotia.
1787: for Scotland: Duncan M'Allum and Alexander Suter. James Wray for Nova Scotia. J. Harper for St. Eustatius.
1788: for Scotland: John Barber, Joseph Cownley, and James Bogie. Robert Gamble, Thomas Owens, Matthew Lumb, William M'Cornock, and Benjamin Pearce for the West Indies.

Still Wesley struggled on to prevent a final breach with the Church of England. When Pawson, for example, returned to

[75] *Journal*, VII, 101.
[76] Tyerman, *Life and Times*, III, 442.
[77] See the Appendix in Carter, *The Methodist Heritage, op. cit.*

England from Scotland, Wesley refused to allow him to exercise his priestly office,[78] and the reason for this was not an inconsistent remnant of his High Church views, as writers such as Simon allege,[79] but the fact that continuity of order as well as continuity of the Word was considered to be vital to the mission of the Church. It is true that where the two could no longer be held together, the Word must have the pre-eminence, but even then Wesley considered the consequent breach as a serious blow to the mission of the Church.[80]

Finally, however, Wesley ordained Alexander Mather in 1788 as Superintendent for England, and in 1789 ordained Henry Moore and Thomas Rankin for England. The English societies clearly needed clergy, for so many members were excluded from communion, and Rankin was ordained as Superintendent apparently to provide for continuation of clergy until Methodism was accepted by the Church. Even these ordinations were not regarded by Wesley as separation, and Methodists were still urged to attend Church. In his final statement on the subject in his sermon on "The Ministerial Office" in May 1789 his concluding admonition to his preachers was:

God hath commissioned [you] to call sinners to repentance. It does by no means follow from hence, that ye are commissioned to baptize, or to administer the Lord's Supper. . . . O contain yourselves within your bounds; be content with preaching the gospel. . . . Ye were, fifty years ago, those of you that were then Methodist preachers, extraordinary messengers of God, not going in your own will, but thrust out, not to supersede, but to "provoke to jealousy," the ordinary messengers. In God's name, stop there! . . . Ye yourselves were at first called in the Church of England; and though ye have and will have a thousand temptations to leave it, . . . regard them not; be Church-of-England men still.[81]

The tension which he sought to keep between mission and unity is made quite explicit in this same sermon when he asked

[78] See Tyerman, Life and Times, III, 496-98.
[79] Simon, John Wesley and the Religious Societies, 251; see also Tyerman, Life and Times, III, 449.
[80] See e.g., Journal, III, 409 on Luther, and his "Reasons Against Separation," Works, XIII, 225-32.
[81] Works, VII, 279-280.

that we observe his two principles: the one, that he would dare not separate from the Church, that he believed it would be a sin so to do; the other, that he believed it would be a sin not to vary from it in the points above mentioned: preaching abroad where churches are closed to him; uniting followers together

to build up the flock of Christ in faith and love, . . . and of dividing them into little companies, that they may provoke one another to love and good works. . . . I say, put these two principles together, First, I will not separate from the Church; yet, Secondly, in cases of necessity, I will vary from it, (both of which I have constantly and openly avowed for upwards of fifty years,) and inconsistency vanishes away. I have been true to my profession from 1730 to this day.[82]

Wesley knew what we are only beginning to relearn, that schism "is evil in itself," and that unity is essential to the true mission of the Church. "To separate ourselves from a body of living Christians, with whom we were before united, is a grievous breach of the law of love." Separation is damaging to the Church's mission: first, because within the Church:

being a breach of brotherly love, so it brings forth evil fruit. . . . It leads directly to a whole train of evil surmisings, to severe and uncharitable judging of each other.

Consequently within the Church

a plentiful harvest of all the works of darkness may be expected to spring from this source; whereby, in the end, thousands of souls, and not a few of those who once walked in the light of God's countenance, may be turned from the way of peace, and finally drowned in everlasting perdition. . . . These have been the fruits which we have seen over and over, to be consequent upon such a separation.

But not only within the Church does disunity hinder her mission, for

what a grievous stumbling-block must these things be to those who are without, to those who are strangers to religion, who have neither the form nor the power of godliness! . . . How will they harden their hearts more and more against the truth, and bless themselves in

[82] *Ibid.*, 278-279.

their wickedness, from which, possibly, the example of the Christians might have reclaimed them, had they continued unblamable in their behaviour. Such is the complicated mischief which persons separating from a Christian Church or society do, not only to themselves, but to that whole society, and to the whole world in general.[83]

Here is the reason Wesley fought so hard to keep Methodism from separation; here is the reason he sought union in witness with all Christians. And here is the reason why his doctrine of the Church requires a readiness to seek all possible means, consistent with the Christian truth, to bring reunion to the divided Body of Christ. Moreover, Wesley was aware that Love and Truth are two poles of the Christian faith, which likewise are in constant tension with each other, and that they can be held together only when Mission is seen as the primary meaning of the Church. Love requires that we should constantly reach out in a spirit of reconciliation, and that even when we differ in opinions, we should be ready to respect the opinions of others and seek to keep the unity of the Spirit in the bond of peace. Truth requires that we should recognize that there are indispensable elements of the Christian faith which we cannot surrender. As Wesley puts it in the same sermon:

I know God has committed to me a dispensation of the gospel; yea, and my own salvation depends upon preaching it: "Woe is me if I preach not the gospel." If then I could not remain in the Church without omitting this, without desisting from preaching the gospel, I should be under a necessity of separating from it, or losing my own soul.[84]

The poles of Love and Truth are in tension, but knowing that the mission of the Church requires that both be maintained, we cannot cease to explore our differences. On some matters differences may have to be held together in the one Church, for remaining separate for their sake would do greater harm than drawing our people into a united consideration of them, believing that in all things essential God will grant us the light that we need to understand his truth.

[83] From the Sermon "On Schism," Works, VI, 408.
[84] Ibid., 408.

That Wesley failed in his immediate purpose was true. Methodism was not accepted in England as a society within the Church and was not able to win acceptance within her life. For many years Methodism hesitated in England, refusing to become a separate Church, not knowing what she should become. Speaking at the Wesley Bicentennial at Wesleyan University in 1903, George Jackson commented: [85]

It has been stated by Canon Overton (though I have not been able to verify the statement) that when the British and Foreign Bible Society was founded in 1804, and each denomination was invited to appoint a representative, the Wesleyans declined the invitation on the ground that they were already represented by the Bishops of the Mother Church; and, as late as 1821, we find Richard Watson writing, "Though Methodism stands now in a different relation to the Establishment than in the days of Mr. Wesley, dissent has never been professed by the body. To leave that Communion (the Church of England) is not in any sense a condition of membership with us." [86]

It was not until 1836 that ordinations were resumed; it was not until the end of the century that Methodism began to call herself a Church.[87]

We see, then, the reason for the hesitations among Methodist writers as they approach the problem of Church union. On what basis shall they negotiate? On the basis of Wesley's attitude, or on the actual basis of their present position? One group of writers, represented by men such as John Lawson, responding to the famous appeal of the Archbishop of Canterbury that the free churches "take episcopacy into their system," argues that because in practice

the episcopal ministry was still for him (Wesley) the token of continuity, (and because) the one statement on the question of ministerial Order in the authoritative *Standard Sermons* is: "I believe the Episcopal form of Church government to be scriptural and apostolical" (XXXIV. ii. 2), the example and words of Wesley agree together. If we today follow them—we (Methodists) will adopt episcopacy as

[85] George Jackson, "The Old Methodism and the New," *Wesley Bicentennial* (Middletown, Connecticut: Wesleyan University, 1904), pp. 65-82. Used by permission.
[86] *Ibid.*, 67.
[87] See Bowmer, op. cit., pp. 159-62.

a requisite to full communion, but not grudgingly or of necessity. Did not our founder hail this institution as "scriptural and apostolical" that is "right"? [88]

Another group, however, rejects the proposal, arguing not only that John Wesley believed no one form of the ministry to be absolute, but also that God having blessed our ministry, we cannot allow that it is in any way invalid nor accept a reordination which implicitly judges our ministry to have been defective.[89]

From the evidence we have gathered, I believe we must say that Lawson's suggestion is far too simple. Not only must we insist that Wesley explicitly rejected the doctrine of uninterrupted succession, and that therefore any thought of being bound to a view which implies a necessary unbroken communication of authority and grace through episcopal channels must be rejected, but we must also insist that the problem of the reunification of the ministry must be handled on a wider theological front. The doctrine of the ministry cannot be taken in isolation from the doctrine of the Church, and even within the doctrine of the ministry the problem of ordination cannot be treated in isolation.

It is true, as we have seen, that Wesley saw the ministry as an important symbol of visible continuity and unity and believed the threefold order to be the normal (though not exclusive) order of the ministry. Still it is also true that he insisted that for the fulfillment of her mission, the Church must proclaim the true gospel, and that the emphasis of the universal grace of God, the new birth, assurance, and holiness were central to her mission. If we are to reach out for union, it is not enough to grasp at a means for unifying the ministry, we must seek to bring unity in the Church for the sake of mission. It is also true that Methodism may have as much to relearn at this point as the churches with whom we seek union have to learn from us, but if the purpose of this union is to further the mission of the Church this makes the task of rediscovering our message and the meaning of our corporate life the more urgent still.

[88] John Lawson, *Methodism and Catholicism* (London S.P.C.K., 1954), p. 16.
[89] See F. Hildebrandt, *Christianity According to the Wesleys*, op. cit., pp. 67-71.

240

Moreover, if we are to be true to Wesley's emphasis, we must not isolate the problem of ordination from the wider doctrine of the ministry. It is true that Wesley desired unity and continuity of the ministry with that of the Church of England, but he also desired a ministry suited to the mission of the Church. In the Minutes of 1746 he wrote:

Q. How shall we try those who think they are moved by the Holy Ghost, and called of God to preach?
A. Inquire, 1. Do they know God, as a pardoning God? Have they the love of God abiding in them? Do they desire and seek nothing but God? And are they holy in all manner of conversation? 2. Have they gifts (as well as grace) for the work? Have they (in some tolerable degree) a clear, sound understanding? Have they a right judgment in the things of God? Have they a just conception of salvation by faith? And has God given them a degree of utterance? Do they speak justly, readily, clearly? 3. Have they fruits? Are any truly convinced of sin, and converted to God by their preaching? As long as these three marks concur in any, we believe he is called of God to preach. These we receive as sufficient proof that he is moved thereto by the Holy Ghost.[90]

The unification of the ministry must be seen in the wider context of the unity of the Church for the sake of mission, but given that context it is true that we will have to face the question of the unification of the ministry. If we are to remain true to John Wesley's perspective, we will be prepared to accept the threefold order, provided only that we do not accept a theory of necessary succession nor renounce the right of Communion with those who have a different order—such as the Reformed.

Here it seems to me that John Wesley's principles are maintained by the Ceylon scheme for the unification of the ministries. There the wider context is included; the acceptance of episcopal order is not made dependent upon a theory of uninterrupted succession; the relationship with other bodies is maintained; and in the service of reunification Bishops from several traditions are invited to participate as a symbol that here the Churches are committing themselves to a wider mission which God makes possible through increasing unity.

[90] Simon, John Wesley and the Advance of Methodism, 30. Used by permission of Epworth Press.

We must now face the different situation in American Methodism, where the threefold order is in some sense recognized. What should be the attitude there in reunification? As we have seen, Wesley sought to provide the symbol of continuity in this ministry, but there is at least the suspicion that while he considered it valid, he desired a wider unity with the historic Church. It would seem therefore that on this basis a service of reunification on the Ceylon pattern would be welcomed.

The major point, however, is that reunification should always be seen as a means to the furtherance of the mission of the Church.

What is the end of all ecclesiastical order? Is it not to bring souls from the power of Satan to God; and to build them up in his fear and love? Order, then is so far valuable, as it answers these ends; and if it answers them not, it is nothing worth.

We would be untrue to our tradition, then, if we allowed the question of ordination such a dominant place in schemes of union that the primary question of mission was obscured, and the importance of the gospel we proclaim and the life the Church must express were made subservient to the problem of order.

Bibliography

No attempt is made here to provide a complete list of books concerning Wesley. Instead I have listed the books that have proved of value to me. In this way it is hoped to provide some guidance to those who are unfamiliar with the field.

Primary Sources

Curnock, Nehemiah, ed. *The Journal of John Wesley*. Standard Edition, 8 vols.; London: The Epworth Press, 1938.

Jackson, Thomas, ed. *The Works of John Wesley*, A.M., 14 vols; Third Edition, London: John Mason, 1829.

Osborn, G., ed. *The Poetical Works of John and Charles Wesley*. London: Wesleyan Methodist Conference Office, 1869.

The Standard Sermons of John Wesley. Annotated by E. H. Sugden, London: The Epworth Press, 1956.

Telford, John, ed. *The Letters of John Wesley*. Standard Edition, 8 vols.; London: The Epworth Press, 1931.

Wesley, John. *Explanatory Notes upon the New Testament*. London: The Epworth Press, 1948.

For a bibliography giving a complete account of the publications of John and Charles Wesley, see Richard Green, *The Works of John and Charles Wesley*. London: C. H. Kelley, 1896.

Secondary Sources

Anderson, William K., ed. *Methodism*. Nashville: The Methodist Publishing House, 1947.

Arnett, William. *John Wesley—Man of One Book*. Ph.D. Thesis, Madison, New Jersey: Drew University, 1954.

Baker, Frank. *Methodism and the Love Feast*. London: The Epworth Press, 1957.

————. *A Charge to Keep: An Introduction to the People Called Methodists*. London: The Epworth Press.

Bebb, E. D. *Wesley, A Man with a Concern*. London: The Epworth Press, 1950.

Bett, Henry. *The Spirit of Methodism*. London: The Epworth Press, 1937.

Bowmer, J. C. *The Sacrament of the Lord's Supper in Early Methodism*. London: Dacre Press, 1951.

Brailsford, Mabel R. *A Tale of Two Brothers: John and Charles Wesley*. London: Rupert Hart-Davis, 1954.

Bready, J. Wesley. *England Before and After Wesley*. New York: Harper and Brothers, 1938.

Burridge, The Rev. A., S. J., *Methodism*, Catholic Truth Society, no date.

Cannon, W. R. *The Theology of John Wesley*. Nashville: Abingdon Press, 1946.

Carter, Henry. *The Methodist Heritage*. Nashville: Abingdon Press, 1951.

Cell, G. C. *The Rediscovery of Wesley*. New York: Henry Holt and Co., 1935.

Doughty, W. L. *John Wesley, Preacher*. London: The Epworth Press, 1955.

John Wesley, His Conferences and Preachers. London: The Epworth Press, 1944

Edwards, Maldwyn. *John Wesley and the Eighteenth Century*. London: The Epworth Press, 1933.

———. *After Wesley*. London: The Epworth Press, 1935.

———. *Methodism and England*. London: The Epworth Press, 1943.

———. *Family Circle*. London: The Epworth Press, 1949.

Flew, R. N. *The Idea of Christian Perfection*. Oxford: Oxford University Press, 1934.

Gill, F. C. *John Wesley's Prayers*. Nashville: Abingdon Press, 1951.

———. *Through the Year with Wesley*, London: The Epworth Press,

———. These, together with *The Wesley Orders of Common Prayer*, published by the Methodist Student Movement, 1957.

Goodloe, Robert W. *The Sacraments in Methodism*. Nashville: The Methodist Publishing House, 1943.

Green, J. Brazier. *John Wesley and William Law*. London: The Epworth Press, 1945.

Green, Richard. *The Mission of Methodism*. Wesleyan Methodist Book Room, 1890.

Harmon, Nolan B. *Understanding The Methodist Church*. Nashville: Abingdon Press, 1955.

Harrison, A. H. *The Separation of Methodism from the Church of England*. London: The Epworth Press, 1945.

Harrison, G. Elsie. *Son to Susanna*. New York and London: Penguin Books, 1937.

Hildebrandt, Franz. *From Luther to Wesley*. London: Lutterworth Press, 1951.

———. *Christianity According to the Wesleys*. London: The Epworth Press, 1956.

Kennedy, Gerald. *The Methodist Way of Life*. Prentice Hall, N. J.: 1958.

Hill, A. Wesley. *John Wesley Among the Physicians*. London: The Epworth Press, 1958.

Lawson, J. *Full Communion with the Church of England*. London: The Epworth Press, 1951.

———. *Methodism and Catholicism*. London: S.P.C.K., 1954.

Lawson, N. *Notes on Wesley's Forty-Four Sermons*, London: The Epworth Press, 1952.

Luccock, Hutchinson, Goodloe. *The Story of Methodism*. Nashville: Abingdon Press, 1949.

Lee, Umphrey. *John Wesley and Modern Religion*. Nashville: Cokesbury Press, 1936.

———. *The Lord's Horseman*. New York: Abingdon Press, 1944.

Lindstrom, Harald. *Wesley and Sanctification*. London: The Epworth Press, no date.

MacArthur, Kathleen W. *The Economic Ethics of John Wesley*. New York: Abingdon Press, 1936.

Norwood, Frederick A. *Church Membership in the Methodist Tradition*. Nashville: The Methodist Publishing House, 1958.

Peters, John L. *Christian Perfection and American Methodism*. Nashville: Abingdon Press, 1956.

Piette, Maximin. *John Wesley in the Evolution of Protestantism*. Sheed and Ward, 1937.

Rattenbury, J. E. *The Conversion of the Wesleys*. London: The Epworth Press.

———. *Wesley's Legacy to the World*. London: The Epworth Press, 1938.

———. *The Eucharistic Hymns of John and Charles Wesley*. London: The Epworth Press, 1948.

Rigg, James H. *The Churchmanship of John Wesley*. London: Wesleyan Methodist Book Room, 1886.

———. *The Living Wesley*. London: Wesleyan Methodist Book Room, 1891.

Rupp, Gordon. *Principalities and Powers*. London: The Epworth Press, 1952.

———. *Methodism in Relation to the Protestant Tradition*. London: The Epworth Press.

Sangster, W. E. *The Pure in Heart*. Nashville: Abingdon Press, 1954.

Schmidt, Martin. *The Young Wesley: Missionary and Theologian of Missions*. London: The Epworth Press, 1958.

Simon, John S. *John Wesley and the Religious Societies*. London: The Epworth Press, 1921.

————. *John Wesley and the Methodist Societies*. London: The Epworth Press, 1923.

————. *John Wesley and Advance of Methodism*. London: The Epworth Press, 1925.

————. *John Wesley, the Master Builder*. London: The Epworth Press, 1927.

————. *John Wesley, the Last Phase*. London: The Epworth Press, 1934.

Telford, John. *The Life of John Wesley*. London: The Epworth Press.

Thompson, Edgar W. *Wesley: Apostolic Man*. London: The Epworth Press, 1957.

Todd, John M. *John Wesley and the Catholic Church*. London: Hodder and Stoughton, 1958.

Tyerman, Luke. *The Life and Times of the Rev. John Wesley, M.A.*; 3 vols.; New York: Harper and Brothers, 1870.

Wesley Bicentennial, 1703-1903. Various authors. Middletown, Connecticut: Wesleyan University, 1904.

Workman, H. B. *The Place of Methodism in the Catholic Church*. London: The Epworth Press, 1921.

Yates, A. S. *The Doctrine of Assurance*. London: The Epworth Press, 1952.

The Message and Mission of Methodism. Published by the Methodist Conference, London: The Epworth Press July, 1946.

Index

247

Printed in the United States
26520LVS00001B/116

9 780687 205318